CU00945065

CAMBRIDGE GREEK /

GENERAL EDITORS

P. E. EASTERLING
Regius Professor of Greek, University of Cambridge

PHILIP HARDIE
Reader in Latin Literature, University of Cambridge

RICHARD HUNTER
Reader in Greek and Latin Literature, University of Cambridge

E. J. KENNEY
Emeritus Kennedy Professor of Latin, University of Cambridge

PLAUTUS

CASINA

EDITED BY

W. T. MacCARY

AND

M. M. WILLCOCK

PUBLISHED BY THE PRESS SYNDICATE OF THE UNIVERSITY OF CAMBRIDGE
The Pitt Building, Trumpington Street, Cambridge, United Kingdom

CAMBRIDGE UNIVERSITY PRESS
The Edinburgh Building, Cambridge CB2 2RU, UK   http://www.cup.cam.ac.uk
40 West 20th Street, New York, NY 10011–4211, USA   http://www.cup.org
10 Stamford Road, Oakleigh, Melbourne 3166, Australia
Ruiz de Alarcón 13, 28014 Madrid, Spain

© Cambridge University Press 1976

This book is in copyright. Subject to statutory exception
and to the provisions of relevant collective licensing agreements,
no reproduction of any part may take place without
the written permission of Cambridge University Press.

First published 1976
Reprinted 1988, 1990, 1994, 1996, 1999

ISBN 0 521 21041 0 hardback
ISBN 0 521 29022 8 paperback

Transferred to digital printing 2004

CONTENTS

[v]

PREFACE

Our association started in the relationship of tutor (M.M.W.) and pupil (W.T.M.) at Sidney Sussex College, Cambridge, in the years 1963-5, and continued when we were colleagues at the University of Minnesota in 1971. It was there that the work for this book began, in a jointly given graduate seminar. Responsibility for the finished product is divided, in that the Introduction is the work of W.T.M., the text and metre (including the Appendices) that of M.M.W., who also composed the first draft of the Commentary. All parts, however, have been continuously discussed between us, and there is little or nothing here now with which either would disagree.

We wish to thank particularly Professor Kenney and Mrs Easterling, the Cambridge editors, for most conscientious and careful reading of the typescript and countless helpful suggestions; also Mr J. C. B. Foster of the University of Liverpool, who read and commented on most of the Commentary at an early stage, and Mr R. H. Martin of Leeds, who did the same for the Introduction and Appendix 2. Professor Chauncey E. Finch of the University of St Louis kindly helped with information about manuscript readings; Professor F. H. Sandbach of Cambridge communicated a characteristically clear-sighted argument about the speaker of line 392, and Miss Susan Hines, then of the University of Minnesota, convinced us about the speaker of the second half of 814. We are indebted also, for speedy provision of microfilms or photocopies of manuscripts, to the Vatican and Ambrosian Libraries, the University Library at Leiden, and the British Museum.

April 1975   W.T.M.
                                                                 M.M.W.

NOTE. For the full titles of works cited by author's name only, see the Bibliography, pp. 236–8.

INTRODUCTION

1. GREEK NEW COMEDY

The plays of Plautus are not completely original creations, but adaptations into Latin, for the Roman stage, of Greek comedies first produced in Athens. Attic comedy is conventionally divided into three periods: Old Comedy, Middle Comedy and New Comedy. Old Comedy was the work of various poets active during the fifth century B.C.; only nine plays of Aristophanes have survived from this period, though the work of Eupolis, Cratinus and others is known to us through fragments. The beginning of Middle Comedy is set either at the end of the fifth century or in 388 at the death of Aristophanes, whose last two extant plays, *Ecclesiazusae* and *Plutus*, differ in important respects from his earlier plays and are considered to mark the transition to this second period. In addition, we have fragments of plays by Alexis, Anaxandrides, Antiphanes and others. The first production of Menander, in 321, is taken as the beginning of New Comedy, which extends to the middle of the third century, when our evidence for activity on the comic stage in Athens comes to an end. From this period we have one complete play, and five others more or less complete, of Menander, and fragments of plays by Diphilus, Philemon and others. All of Plautus' plays are thought to have been adapted from New Comedy originals.[1]

Greek New Comedy is a dramatic form which is in some respects quite foreign to modern audiences and in others essentially the same as much of the comedy which is even now being produced. We can reconstruct the plots of about fifty of these plays. Generally there are two young lovers who are separated by some kind of barrier: the girl is thought to be a slave or a foreigner and therefore unmarriageable; the boy is not acceptable to her father; there are rival lovers or previously arranged marriages. The action of the play is concen-

---

[1] For earlier dating of the originals of the *Amphitruo* and the *Menaechmi*, see Webster 67–97.

trated on removing these barriers so that the lovers can be married.
This is accomplished by recognition and reconciliation between
estranged members of the family or changes in attitude which unexpected new circumstances bring about. These 'barrier comedies'
tend to end in some form of marriage: usually the young lovers gain
their parents' approval for an actual marriage; if the plot turns on a
misunderstanding between husband and wife, there is reconciliation;
if the girl is in fact unmarriageable under Attic law, her arrangement
with the boy is nevertheless stabilized by a guarantee of financial
support from his father. We see in this achievement of the young
lovers a promise of new life and fertility, and a restatement of the
values of social life: people can and should get along with each other,
and, when they understand each other's good intentions, they do.
Menander put this succinctly: ὡς χάριέν ἐστ' ἄνθρωπος, ἂν ἄνθρωπος
ᾖ (fr. 484), 'man is a thing of grace and goodness, so long as he
follows his nature'. The barriers are perversions of human nature;
youth triumphs over age, love over money, charity and goodness over
selfishness and aggressiveness.

There are complications to this main action, and characters
subordinate to the young lovers and their parents. We find various
professional types – soldiers, courtesans, cooks, parasites, pimps,
doctors, money-lenders – in addition to household slaves and family
friends. The social conventions which make the plots work seem
strange to us: babies are abandoned and raised by strangers or stolen
by pirates and sold into slavery; free women of the upper classes are
secluded from male company and a variety of professional women
fill their place; members of wealthy families have no occupations, but
live off their lands, which are worked by slaves. We seldom find
serious social criticism in the plays, nor indeed does our appreciation
of them depend essentially on knowledge of the times in which they
were written. Nevertheless we should know that there is some relation
between their conventions and reality. So, too, we should see New
Comedy as a development – the final development – in the long
history of Greek drama; it did not spring suddenly from the context
of fourth-century society, but grew out of the combined traditions of
earlier comedy, tragedy and satyr play.

Drama was produced at Athens at the various festivals held in honour of Dionysus. There were the great mythological tragedies, represented for us by the plays of Aeschylus, Sophocles and Euripides, with their companion pieces the satyr plays, which treated the same mythological material in a ludicrous manner. In a different category altogether was the comedy of Aristophanes and his contemporaries. Aristophanes based his comedies on purely fictional, i.e. non-mythical, material. If gods and heroes appear in his plays, it is not to act out famous myths. This is an important distinction, since in New Comedy we find patterns of action similar to those, based on myth, which characterize tragedy and satyr play.

There are other differences between Aristophanes and the poets of New Comedy. Aristophanic comedy celebrates the triumph of the individual; in New Comedy, individuals are forced to meet the requirements of society. Aristophanic comedy is full of fantasy: one old Athenian flies to heaven on a dung beetle to free the personified abstraction Peace from bondage; another establishes his own kingdom in the sky; the god Dionysus descends into Hades to bring back Euripides from the dead, changes his mind and brings back Aeschylus instead. In New Comedy the essential comic element of wish-fulfilment is still there, but the scope has been reduced. There is no cosmic change, only the removal of barriers which have prevented desired marriages. The only fantasy is circumstantial: a passer-by is asked to masquerade as a young girl's father and turns out to be her father in fact; a young man who quarrels with his wife when he discovers she became pregnant before their marriage hires a prostitute, who happens to have been present when the wife was sexually assaulted and can identify the assailant as the husband himself; two young men are in love with a girl and one turns out to be her brother.

Aristophanic comedy is musical, full of complex choral sections and all sorts of metrical variation. New Comedy is written almost entirely in iambic trimeters, the standard dialogue metre of Greek drama. It is uncertain to what extent the fantastic scenes described in Aristophanes' plays were physically represented on stage by means of sets and other equipment, but contemporary vase-paintings show how elaborate his costumes were. By contrast, Menander needed only two or three house fronts for his action; his characters wore ordinary clothes. Aristophanes' language is rich and allusive; Menander's is remarkably free of imagery and artifice.

Ancient critics remarked on the influence of Euripides on Menander. This was indirect as well as direct: Menander knew Euripides from contemporary revivals of his plays as well as from written copies of them in circulation, but Euripides had already had a tremendous influence on the development of Greek drama and it is this indirect influence, through the tradition, which can be claimed for Philemon and Diphilus as well as for Menander. In his late plays Euripides experimented with the conventions of tragedy to such an extent that the genre barely survived his career. He allowed the audience such intimacy with his characters, demanded of them such close scrutiny of their condition and exposed so ruthlessly the insignificance of human action, the capriciousness of divine, that theatre was more 'absurd' at the time of his death than at any other until the present. All sorts of labels have been attached to Euripides' *Helen* and *Ion* and *Iphigenia in Tauris*: tragicomedy, romantic comedy, comedy of ideas, melodrama. The suggestion is that since Euripides presents in these plays characters who are less than heroic, situations which are outlandish and slightly ludicrous, plots which turn on coincidence and the supernatural, and happy endings, he is somehow confounding tragedy with comedy. Since there is nothing of Aristophanes and the contemporary comic stage in Euripides, one would have to credit him with complete originality if these very elements had not been the mainstay of the satyr plays produced as after-pieces with tragic trilogies by all the masters of tragedy throughout the fifth century. What Aeschylus and Sophocles had kept in its place to conclude a sequence of three serious pieces, Euripides expanded to become the whole dramatic experience. Already in the *Alcestis*, an early tragedy produced in the position normally assigned to a satyr play, we find that mixture of the ludicrous and the serious, the fantastic and the familiar, which is to characterize his later work. The basic pattern of action in the *Alcestis*, like that of the later *Helen* and *Iphigenia in Tauris*, is the woman freed from bondage: a Persephone-like figure is carried off to a foreign land by an unchosen lover and her rescue is the climax of the play. This is the pattern of all romantic comedies, from Plautus' *Rudens* to Bergman's *Smiles of a Summer Night*. In Euripides' treatments it has rich suggestions and associations: the conflict between life and death, the power of love to change life, the persistence into adult life of a child's sexual fantasies. In combining the two forms of mythological drama, tragedy and satyr play, Euripides laid the foundations for later comedy.

Most Greek drama, with the exception of Aristophanes, is domestic: the *Agamemnon* and the *Oedipus Rex*, like the plays of New Comedy, deal with family problems. This is not surprising, since the most popular of the Greek myths – those which were written about and re-interpreted most often – concern relations within the family, and Greek tragedy is based directly, New Comedy indirectly, on these myths. There is, however, a vast difference between the two types of treatment, and Euripides bridges the gap. In Euripides' late plays we see the beginnings of realistic drama. Like Chekhov and Ibsen Euripides delights in trivia: he is concerned with whether or not Electra's face is clean, with the style of her dress and the way in which her house is furnished. The introduction of these intimate details destroys any illusions one might have of her heroic nature; her thoughts and reactions confirm us in the opinion that she is a bitter, frustrated woman very much like the bitter, frustrated women we have met outside the theatre. She is a quite ordinary human being caught up in extraordinary events over which she has no control. Once Euripides had changed the point of view in drama, so that we see the characters as no better than ourselves, it only remained for Menander to change the actual events and drop the mythical names. We do not find in New Comedy a man marrying his mother, but a man who is suspected by his adoptive father of being seduced by his father's mistress; a wife does not murder her husband upon his return from war, but a soldier's mistress does desert her lover in his absence and seek refuge in a temple. The patterns of sexual attraction and antagonism are the same, but they have been given a more mundane, realistic treatment. Gone is the rich fantasy life captured by Euripides, and instead of the fabulous Helen we are presented with Pamphile or Glykera or some other unremarkable young girl.

(*b*) ITS RELATION TO REALITY

The quality of the realism in New Comedy is a major problem. Some of the plots seem so outlandish that we have difficulty believing they

had any relation to reality. The major institution with which they are
concerned is marriage, but citizenship, inheritance and other related
social circumstances are involved. Athenian laws and customs of
marriage are known mainly from the orators in their speeches on
private as opposed to political cases, but comedy itself offers corrobora-
tion of that evidence. A woman's legal activity was entirely regulated
by a guardian (κύριος); this would be her father or someone
appointed by him to assume this function on his death, or, with
limitations, her husband. The premise on which this protective
custody seems to have been based is that a woman, like a slave, was
not a person. She was a citizen in so far as she could produce children
who were citizens, but she had no legal standing. Since she could not
initiate contracts or court cases or in any other way proceed before the
law, someone must do these things for her. Marriage being a legal
contract, she could not enter into it on her own, but must be committed to it by her father. She then moved physically out of her
father's house and into her husband's and legally under her husband's
guardianship. She took with her a dowry consisting of money, goods
or land, and this was inalienable from her. If the marriage was
dissolved she returned with the dowry to her father.

Life in her husband's house would have been very much the same
as in her father's. She was restricted to a set of rooms which only
women, and occasionally her husband and the male members of her
family, entered. Here she spun wool, wove cloth and made clothes;
she managed the education of her male children to the age of six and
of her female children until marriage. She took no part in the social,
economic and political life of the city, rarely leaving her husband's
house, never conversing with men outside her family.

It was possible for a slave woman to move more freely in the world
than her free-born mistress. A slave woman might be forced into a
union with a man of her master's choosing, though legal marriage was
not possible for slaves, just as a free-born woman would have her
husband chosen for her by her father, but the slave woman might be
able to buy her freedom and achieve some degree of independence.
One gets the impression from New Comedy that it was these un-
attached women, freed slaves or immigrants from abroad, who
dominated Athenian society, and this was probably true. Pericles'
famous aphorism on women – that their greatest glory is to have

nothing said of them, whether good or bad[1] – was endorsed by his contemporaries and later generations; we simply do not hear of the sequestered ladies who bore children and made clothing, except on those rare occasions when they were released to perform religious functions. We do hear occasionally of women like Pericles' mistress Aspasia, a foreign-born, well-educated woman who played an active part in Athens' political and social life.

While women's lives were rigorously regulated, the lives of newborn children were sometimes simply extinguished. It was entirely at the discretion of the father as to whether a child would be raised or exposed to die.[2] We cannot tell how often fathers decided on the negative alternative but it is clear that daughters were more frequently exposed than sons. Thus the romantic possibilities for recognition which play such an important part in New Comedy had their grisly origin in reality.

(c) ITS RELATION TO UNIVERSAL PATTERNS OF COMEDY

This brief social background for New Comedy is meant only to illustrate the basis for its conventions;[3] the appeal of its patterns is quite another problem. The comic poets could construct their plots around the repression of women and the exposure of babies because these were familiar and even socially acceptable; the same situations, however, continue to be exploited even when audiences cannot recognize their own social circumstances in them. Oscar Wilde reveals at the end of *The importance of being earnest* that the character we know as Jack Worthing is in fact named Ernest Moncrieff and as an infant was left in a black leather hand-bag by an absent-minded nurse in the cloakroom of Victoria Station. At the end of Joe Orton's play *What the butler saw* we realize that the secretary whom the doctor has attempted to rape and the bellhop who has attempted to rape the doctor's wife are, in fact, the lost children of the doctor and his wife. No doubt one could find reports of such things actually happening in London during the past century, but that is hardly the point. What one must appreciate about the patterns of New Comedy is that they recur because they have a certain appeal.

---

[1] Thucydides 2.45.   [2] See Commentary at line 41.
[3] For more evidence see Harrison *passim*, Gomme and Sandbach 28–35.

This appeal is obvious in the late plays of Euripides; in *Ion*, *Iphigenia in Tauris*, and *Helen* we find the combination of two dramatic actions: the release of a woman from bondage and the recognition of a lost relative. The setting for these plays is exotic; supernatural agencies are at work; the plots are full of twists and turns; the endings are happy – these are the features of romantic comedy and they are evident to varying degrees in the plays of New Comedy. Menander frequently exploits the theme of the woman freed from bondage by recognition: in several plays we see a young girl flee her soldier-lover in search of the father who can recognize her as a free-born Athenian who should be a wife rather than a concubine. Our delight in her success is manifold: she is a good and noble person assuming her rightful place in the world; her sexual union with the soldier is blessed by the father, so she need no longer feel that she was taken from him without his consent; her marriage is symbolic of a whole new life beginning for all those around her.

Philemon's treatment of the pattern is known only from adaptations of two of his plays by Plautus. In the *Trinummus* a young man has wasted his father's fortune on a mistress, but insists on providing a dowry for his sister so that she will be considered the true wife rather than the concubine of her intended husband; in the *Mercator* father and son try to gain possession of the same slave girl, and the son, who truly loves her, is successful. In each play Philemon develops the intrigue (slaves and friends of the young man complicate the situation for his benefit) and moral implications (young men should not waste money; old men should not fall in love) rather than concentrate on the plight of the young girl. Diphilus, in two plays which are also known from adaptations by Plautus, offers further variations. In the *Rudens* a young girl is rescued from the pimp who owns her by four agents: the god Arcturus, who wrecks the ship in which she is being carried from Cyrene to a life of prostitution in Sicily; a priestess of Venus, who gives her shelter; her young lover, who attempts to prosecute the pimp for breaking his contract to sell her; and her father, who happens to live at the site of the shipwreck and recognizes her as his free-born, and therefore marriageable, daughter. Here are the exotic setting, supernatural intervention, complicated plot and happy ending in combination with the woman-in-bondage pattern. Diphilus seems even closer to Euripides than Menander does.

The other play by Diphilus of which we can speak with any
certainty is *Kleroumenoi*, on which Plautus based his *Casina*. The
situation is like that of his *Mercator*, based on Philemon's *Emporos*.
A father lusts after the slave girl his son loves; each proposes a slave
husband for her; the mother takes the son's side, but they are defeated
by the father; a male slave is dressed up like the girl for her wedding
and beats the old man when he tries to have intercourse with 'her';
the girl is finally recognized as the neighbour's daughter and marries
the son. The pattern is overwhelmingly attractive; not only is the girl
rescued from the bonds of slavery but also from the sexual threat
posed by the old man, and all the women enjoy his discomfiture; she
is finally able to choose her lover, after being recognized by her
father. We have, then, a reversal of traditional roles on three levels:
the young triumph over the old, the slaves triumph over their masters
and the women triumph over the men. In addition, Diphilus seems
to be in touch with the patterns of earlier Greek drama, the patterns
of myth, perhaps by way of more recent comedy: each of the spectacular scenes in the *Casina* and *Rudens* can be traced back through
numerous treatments on the Greek stage to early tragedy and satyr
play.[1] Though the *Casina* is more purely a play of intrigue, more of
a farce and less of a romantic comedy than the *Rudens*, nevertheless
both plays are richer in texture, more allusive and exotic than the
plays we know of Menander and Philemon.

2. ROMAN COMEDY

The principal period of comedy at Rome extended from 240 B.C.,
when a Greek play was first presented in a Latin adaptation by Livius
Andronicus, to 159 B.C., the death of Terence. It was a time when
Rome was particularly receptive to Greek art and literature, beginning
with a series of wars which brought the Roman people into contact
with many Greek cities and ending only shortly after Rome was
acknowledged master of all Greece. Whereas the political power of
Athens had been eclipsed before the period of New Comedy, Roman
comedy flourished in a period of brash expansionism. Prior to this
time a kind of native Italian popular comedy flourished in towns
where Oscan was spoken, not far from primarily Greek-speaking

[1] See below, Section 4 (*d*), and MacCary, 'Comic tradition'.

Italian cities where Greek comedies were being performed in Greek. The native Italian drama is known as Atellan Farce, because its centre was the Campanian town Atella; it was improvisational and depended upon a cast of stereotyped characters: Pappus, the old man; Maccus, the clown; Bucco, the braggart; and Dossenus, the trickster. The origins of these characters and their kind of comedy are obscure; most of our information about it comes from a later period, at the end of the Republic when it was still flourishing. Some of the titles suggest the sort of situations that are found in all comic traditions: *Maccus the virgin*, *The twin Macci*, *The bride of Pappus*. The parallels with Commedia dell'Arte tempt us to reconstruct a drama which was musical and involved a lot of stage business, but this is based on conjecture rather than evidence.

Livius Andronicus introduced literary drama to Rome in 240 B.C. He was Greek, a native of Tarentum, a Greek city in the extreme south of Italy. Since Greek comedy is known to have been produced there throughout the third century B.C., one should probably not presume that Livius was much influenced by native Italian popular comedy. Even if one doubts that his comedies were straight translations from the sophisticated plays of the Greek New Comedy, and even if one is convinced that the titles which survive of his plays – *Gladiolus*, *Ludius*, *Virgo* or *Verpus*, etc. – suggest low and obscene comedy, nevertheless Greek sources should be expected for such features: perhaps the *phlyax* plays, burlesques of mythology and everyday life popular in Tarentum and other Greek cities in Italy. These plays were full of lively and obscene stage action; the actors wore padded costumes and grotesque masks; there were scripts, but improvised jokes must have been part of the fun.

Livius' successor, or younger contemporary, in Roman comedy, Gnaeus Naevius, can more readily be aligned with native Italian popular comedy. His home was in Campania, so presumably he spoke Oscan before learning Latin – just as Livius would have spoken Greek before Latin – and Oscan was the original language of the Atellan Farce. Only thirty titles of his plays survive and some fragments of dialogue. He relied on Greek originals, probably of the New Comedy period, but seems to have interpolated into his texts references to Roman politics and other original elements. He has even been credited with introducing into Roman comedy some of the

elaborate systems of imagery which characterize Plautus' plays.
Terence links Naevius with Plautus and Ennius as poets who did not
translate literally. On indirect evidence, then, a case can be made for
considering Naevius to have been close to the tradition of native
Italian popular comedy and free in his adaptation of Greek comedies.
He was thus an important predecessor to Plautus (actually an older
contemporary since he produced his first play in 235[1] and it is generally
held that Plautus began producing his plays about 215) whom
Plautus knew, probably respected and may have imitated.

Titus Maccius Plautus seems to have derived his middle name as
well as much of his comic art from Atellan Farce: ancient authorities
suggest a long and varied career in the theatre and Maccius appears to
be a Romanization of the Atellan clown's name. Two of his plays are
securely dated on ancient evidence: the *Stichus* was produced in 200
and the *Pseudolus* in 191 B.C. Two other plays are dated by what
appear to be references to known events: mention of the imprisonment of Naevius at *Miles* 211ff. has convinced most scholars that its
first production was in 205; mention of the suppression of Baccha-
nalia at *Casina* 979ff. suggests that the play was produced after the
senatus consultum de Bacchanalibus of 186 B.C., and since Plautus died in
184 B.C.,[2] the play must have been written in 185 B.C. Attempts have
been made to construct a relative chronology of the twenty extant
plays upon these fixed points. The criteria used include general
impressions of his artistic development: he is thought to have in-
creased the lyric content of his later plays, i.e., there is no song in the
Miles, but about one-third of the *Casina* is song;[3] he handles intrigue
better and enlarges the parts of clever slaves;[4] his use of such dramatic
devices as soliloquies and overheard conversations is more adroit;[5]
his imagery becomes richer and more complex.[6] In general he seems

---

[1] Gellius 17.21.45.   [2] Cicero, *Brutus* 15.60.

[3] W. B. Sedgwick, *C.R.* 39 (1925) 55–8; *C.Q.* 24 (1930) 102–5; *A.J.Ph.* 70
(1949) 376–83; K. H. E. Schutter, *Quibus annis comoediae Plautinae primum
actae sint quaeritur* (1952); A. de Lorenzi, *Cronologia ed evoluzione Plautina* (1952).

[4] J. N. Hough, *A.J.Ph.* 60 (1939) 422–35; Fraenkel, *EP* 223–41.

[5] J. N. Hough, *C.Ph.* 30 (1935) 43–57; *T.A.Ph.A.* 70 (1939) 231–41.

[6] W. T. MacCary, *Servus gloriosus: a study of military imagery in Plautus*
(diss. Stanford, 1969); J. T. Svensen, *Goats and monkeys: a study of animal
imagery in Plautus* (diss. Minnesota, 1971); S. L. Hines, *The metaphorical use of
mythological and historical allusions in Plautus* (diss. Minnesota, 1973).

to have got further away from his Greek originals in his later plays. Dating on stylistic grounds is dangerous, but it focuses attention on the really important issue, Plautus' originality.

It is tempting to look upon the comedies of Caecilius Statius as a bridge between the comedies of Plautus and those of Terence, which are totally different from each other. He was a younger contemporary of Plautus who lived almost to the year of Terence's first production; the titles of most of his plays are transliterations of Greek titles, a practice followed by Terence, which might suggest that, like Terence, his rendering of the Greek originals was fairly close; he was praised for seriousness of purpose and excellence of plot-construction, two Terentian virtues, but extant fragments of his plays show the intoxication with words and the delight in low humour we associate with Plautus.[1]

Publius Terentius Afer produced six plays between 166 and 160 B.C.; he is said to have died in 159 while returning from Greece with more Greek plays to translate. All of his plays have survived; four are based on originals by Menander, two on originals by Menander's close imitator Apollodorus of Carystus. They are all quite Menandrean in structure and tone: there tends to be a central ethical problem in each and this is worked out by means of complicated intrigues and confusions. All of Terence's characters tend to be noble and true, causing others pain only out of ignorance or misconception; they all, even the slaves, tend to speak the same smooth, elevated diction. This homogeneity of characterization contrasts strongly with Menander's variety of types and is probably the cause of Caesar's unenthusiastic praise of Terence; he apostrophized him as *dimidiate Menander* and noted his lack of *vis comica*.[2] Terence's plays seem not to have met with enthusiastic reception on the stage, but they were almost immediately adopted as school books and models of polished diction. There could not be a greater disparity within the same genre than that between the robust, popular comedy of Plautus and the elegant, literary comedy of Terence; they represent two

[1] The major fragment is a speech from his *Plocion*, found with the original speech from Menander's *Plokion* in Gellius 2.23.

[2] Suetonius, *Vita Terenti* 5: *tu quoque, tu in summis, o dimidiate Menander, | poneris, et merito, puri sermonis amator. | lenibus atque utinam scriptis adiuncta foret uis | comica, ut aequato uirtus polleret honore | cum Graecis neue hac despectus parte iaceres! | unum hoc maceror ac doleo tibi desse, Terenti.*

separate strands of the comic tradition, though both derive from the
same source, Greek New Comedy.

3. PLAUTUS

The relation of Plautus to his originals has been the central concern of
scholars and critics who have studied his plays during the present
century. Because we now have more examples of Menander's comedy,
we can speak with more assurance of Plautus' originality. We must
not, however, simplify a very complex problem. All poets of the Greek
New Comedy were not imitators of Menander. Diphilus and Philemon
were original artists who wrote in their own distinctive styles. If we
are to trace the Plautine elements in the *Casina* we must establish
Plautus' relation to Diphilus. If we can determine what is Plautine in
his adaptations of Menandrean originals, we can perhaps recognize
these same elements in his adaptations of Diphilean originals.

(a) COMPARED TO MENANDER

The only complete play of Menander which survives is the *Dyskolos*;
it is quite similar in many respects to Plautus' *Aulularia*, which is
known to be based on an original by Menander. In both plays a
difficult old man stands in the way of his daughter's happy marriage,
so a god intervenes to unite the daughter and her lover. Beyond the
main character of the old man the plays share a cast consisting of the
old slave woman whom he constantly mistreats, cooks and slaves who
trick and abuse him and a rather weak and ineffective young lover.
There is a major difference, however, in the characterization of the
old man and, consequently, in the over-all movement of the two plays.
In the *Dyskolos* Knemon's character is carefully established and we are
given background information to explain his idiosyncrasies; in the
Aulularia Plautus has suppressed much of this kind of material, and
simply used Euclio as a butt for jokes. One can see this most readily in
the handling of two types of conventional scenes: when the old man
scolds his slave woman and when cooks and slaves ridicule the old
man. Euclio's abusive leave-taking of Staphyla at the beginning of the
Aulularia is similar to the scene in the *Dyskolos* where Knemon
threatens to punish Simike for dropping a jug and a hoe down the
well. In both cases we have the surly old man using the only slave he

has as a whipping post; she serves as a foil to bring out the worst
in him.

> KNEMON...Where is that wall-burrowing robber?
> SIMIKE. But listen master, I didn't mean to; it dropped.
> KNEMON Get inside.
> > SIMIKE. But what will you do to me?
> I beg you.
> > KNEMON. What will I do? Why, tie you
> To a rope and send you down after it.
> SIMIKE. Not that, oh wretched me!
>
> I'll call Daos from next door to help.
> KNEMON. Call Daos? You stupid old woman.
> What a thing to say! Now haven't I told you?
> Get inside.   (588-96)

In the *Aulularia* Plautus takes over sixty lines to develop the same sort
of material. He opens his play with Euclio calling Staphyla a robber –
and many, more extravagant epithets – then has Euclio go back
inside to check on his gold and repeats the whole sequence again.
The first exchange begins –

> EVCLIO. Exi, inquam, age exi: exeundum hercle tibi hinc est
>   foras,
> circumspectatrix cum oculis emissiciis.
> STAPHYLA. nam cur me miseram uerberas? EVCLIO. ut misera
>   sis
> atque ut te dignam mala malam aetatem exigas.
> STAPHYLA. nam qua me nunc causa extrusisti ex aedibus?
> EVCLIO. tibi ego rationem reddam, stimulorum seges?
> illuc regredere ab ostio. illuc sis uide,
> ut incedit. at scin quo modo tibi res se habet?
> si hercle hodie fustem cepero aut stimulum in manum,
> testudineum istum tibi ego grandibo gradum.   (40-9)

> EUCLIO. Get out here, I say, now! Get out here
> You swivel-headed old hag with the spy-eyes.
> STAPHYLA. But why do you beat me, wretched as I am?
> EUCLIO. For that very reason, so you'll be wretched

And lead the miserable life you deserve.
STAPHYLA. But why have you thrust me out of doors like this?
EUCLIO. Since when do I have to give you reasons,
You harvest of goads you? Now get out of the doorway.
Just look at her, the way she creeps.
Do you know what's in store for you?
If I get hold of a club or a stick
I'll quicken that tortoise-gait of yours.

Plautus delights in imaginative abuse, in assonance, alliteration and word play. The excessiveness of Euclio's attack makes him less believable as a character, more of a fantasy figure, a personification of suspicion and violence.

The same process takes place in Plautus' adaptation of a cook scene. In the *Dyskolos* there are two scenes where cooks confront Knemon, and a couple of short asides by cooks on Knemon's character in scenes where they are witnesses to his suffering. The scene Plautus has written in the *Aulularia* to allow the cooks and the slave of a neighbour to comment on Euclio's character is probably an expansion of such a brief reference. There is a sequence of jokes (296–320) which are developed through questions and answers and become increasingly absurd. This is Plautine expansion. In the entire sequence we find qualities which we do not find in Menander: repetition, a particular type of exaggeration, obscenity and absurdity. This dialogue in Plautus tends to make a caricature of the old man, while we credit Menander with subtle characterization.

Great comic characters have a tragic dimension, like Shylock: he is the barrier between his daughter Jessica and her lover, but his removal is painful for us. This is true to some extent of Knemon, but not of Euclio. Plautus has made it impossible for us to sympathize with his old miser; his comedy does not have that 'serious' dimension. As well as adding obscenity, absurdity, exaggeration and abuse, Plautus has set the whole thing to music; there are elaborate lyric scenes alternating with straight dialogue scenes. We associate all these features with Aristophanes rather than with Menander. Presumably we should put this down to the influence of native Italian popular comedy, for there is no certain evidence that Plautus had access to Aristophanes' plays. We have seen how the change in

Euclio has taken place and how this has changed the play; it is probable that Plautus has assimilated Menander's character to the conventional roles for difficult old men in Atellan Farce. The emphasis on farcical elements, the lack of subtlety in characterization, the highly figurative language with its jingling sound effects, all point towards popular comedy. Plautus has also introduced fantasy into a domestic situation; in Euclio we find those qualities of the comic hero – though he is wrong, he is irresistible – which make Aristophanes' old men so attractive.[1]

(b) COMPARED TO DIPHILUS

These same Plautine features are evident in the *Rudens*, adapted from a play by Diphilus. It is a musical comedy, full of fantasy, extravagant language and characters who tend toward caricature. There are two barrier figures in the play, characters who stand between the young girl and her lover: Labrax the pimp would force her into a life of prostitution and Gripus the slave would deny her the tokens necessary for her recognition as a free-born Athenian. Both, like Euclio in the *Aulularia*, are developed in scenes of comic exaggeration and fantastic invention. We first meet Labrax when he is washed ashore after his ship has been wrecked; with him is his friend in crime Charmides, whom he blames for his predicament. They exchange abuse in a series of jokes which centre on the storm and the sea and the gods Neptune and Venus (485–558). We recognize in this passage the reduplication which was the basis of the cook scene in the *Aulularia*. Several of the jokes are based on Latin puns and therefore cannot exactly duplicate the original. The extravagance of the final series, from Neptune as bathmaster to Labrax as carnival freak, is almost certainly Plautine. The total effect is to introduce us to two characters who, though the villains of the piece, can hardly be taken seriously. It is quite possible that this undercutting of melodramatic potential was part of Diphilus' original conception of the action, but more likely that it was brought about by Plautine expansion and exaggeration.

Another example of Plautine expansion working a major change in the play is found in the song Gripus sings as he drags ashore the trunk belonging to Labrax (906–37). He fantasizes on the gold inside,

[1] See C. H. Whitman, *Aristophanes and the comic hero* (1964).

sufficient to buy his freedom. Plautus has turned what was probably straight dialogue in the original into a lively musical number. The words are full of assonance and alliteration; the phrasing changes halfway through, coinciding with a change in the metre, which would have marked a change in musical accompaniment; this is Gripus' entrance song and we know him well when it is over. He is Plautus' creation, a slave obsessed with a fantasy of wealth and power. In this he resembles the slaves we meet in other Plautine plays who trick their old masters to get money for their young masters' mistresses, thus turning the tables on Roman dignity and morality. Here he is a minor character, but one whom Plautus has brought to life with a dream and a song.

Plautus' relation to his originals can thus be stated in general and, sometimes, in fairly specific terms. Into Menander's comedy of character, with its implied solutions to ethical problems, Plautus infuses low comedy and the comedy of stock types; there is exaggeration to the point of absurdity with farcical repetition and duplication. Diphilus' comedy was more romantic than Menander's, closer to its source in satyr play and Euripidean tragedy; it probably also had some obscenity and ironic treatment of characters. Plautus has added music and song, which heightens the atmosphere of dream and fantasy; he has caricatured both major and minor characters to produce a play that is almost masque-like in its effects; in expanding scenes of low comedy and scenes with potential for musical development, he has probably cut out or shortened scenes of exposition. The Plautine results of adapting both Menander and Diphilus are to some extent the same; music, fantasy, extravagant language, overblown characters, reversal of traditional roles – these are the elements of Aristophanic comedy. In adapting Greek New Comedy for the Roman stage Plautus changed its nature; a comedy of social convention and artifice becomes a comedy of individual wish-fulfilment.

(c) COMPARED TO REALITY

The relation between Plautus' plays and reality can be determined only to the extent that we can distinguish the Roman poet from his Greek sources and Roman institutions from Greek. Though the evidence is too fragmentary to make such comparisons quantitatively convincing, certain social phenomena seem to·be more prevalent in

Plautus than in Menander: slaves are cleverer and play larger parts; women are more prominent, often threatening or vindictive; the philandering husband replaces the young lover as sexual protagonist. To what extent are these differences due to Plautus, to Roman society or to chance?

Plautus chose Greek comedies for adaptation which he thought his Roman audience would appreciate. He knew his audience well and knew that they would respond to the familiar or the fantasized reversal of the familiar. Choosing a Greek play which involved social situations his Roman audience could recognize, Plautus emphasized some aspects, added new material and, in general, Romanized the whole.

Why would a Roman audience sympathize more with a clever slave character than would a Greek audience? The answer lies partly in the composition of the two audiences – the Greek audience was middle and upper class, while the Roman was made up of all elements, including slaves; partly the answer is in the very type of comedy Plautus wrote, a musical comedy where characters are boldly drawn; finally one might point to the Roman institution of the Saturnalia, a holiday which is paradigmatic of the whole comic pattern of the little man's triumph.

'Many peoples have been used to observe an annual period of license, when the customary restraints of law and morality are thrown aside, when the whole population give themselves up to extravagant mirth and jollity, and when the darker passions find a vent which would never be allowed them in the more staid and sober course of ordinary life...of all these periods of license the one which is best known and which in modern languages has given its name to the rest, is the Saturnalia...no feature of the festival is more remarkable, nothing in it seems to have struck the ancients themselves more than the license granted to slaves at this time. The distinction between the free and the servile classes was temporarily abolished. The slave might rail at his master, intoxicate himself like his betters, sit down at table with them, and not even a word of reproof would be administered to him for conduct which at any other season might have been punished with stripes, imprisonment, or death. Nay, more, masters actually changed places with their

slaves and waited on them at table; and not till the serf had done
eating and drinking was the board cleared and dinner set for his
master.'[1]

A holiday spirit is noticeable even in plays where slaves are not
triumphant. In the *Menaechmi*, for instance, we have a very strong
feeling that the day of the play is a special day, spent in a strange place,
where all sorts of unexpected things happen. In fact all that happens
is the reunion of two twins long separated, and if the atmosphere of
strangeness were not so strong we could not suspend our disbelief for
the length of time it takes them to recognize each other.[2] We shall see
later how important the festive atmosphere of the *Casina* is to its
effectiveness as comedy.

Women were, under the law, not so much better off in Plautus'
Rome than they were in Menander's Athens. A similar system of
guardianship (*tutela*) prevailed, and the elaborate restrictions on
marriage and inheritance make it clear that women were considered
more as conveyors of property than as human beings. There is,
however, a very important difference and this lies in the conflict
between laws and customs; Roman women were *de facto* much freer
to move about in the male world than they would appear to have been
de iure. In Plautus' time there were laws passed to restrict the dress
(*Lex Oppia*, 214 B.C.) and religious activities (*senatus consultum de
Bacchanalibus*, 186 B.C.) of women, but these were anachronistic; their
very stringency and their victims' outspoken resistance to them prove
the degree to which women had gained their independence. The most
pervasive of all Roman instincts is clear here: to preserve the *mos
maiorum*. This respect for the past is the cause of the conflict between
the legal and the actual status of women.[3] In the plays of Plautus
married women are portrayed as threatening figures who control
domestic finances and enforce domestic morality. They question
every move their husbands make, taunt them with inadequacy and
ridicule their pretensions; they are the first in comedy's long line of
emasculating females and Plautus seems to have given his invention
brilliant visual expression in the *Menaechmi* by sending on stage a man

[1] J. G. Frazer, *The golden bough*[3] (1914) IX 306–8.

[2] E. Segal, *Y.Cl.S.* 21 (1969) 75–93.

[3] C. Herrmann, *Le rôle judiciaire et politique des femmes sous la République
romaine* = Collection Latomus 67 (1964).

dressed in his wife's clothes.[1] The extent of the caricature is a measure of the fear which Plautus' male contemporaries felt at the prospect of women actually making some small social advances: anxiety is a sure source of laughter.

The old man as lover, if not a Plautine invention, is certainly a situation which the Roman adapter assiduously sought out in the hundreds of Greek comedies available to him. We find this character most prominent in *Bacchides, Casina, Menaechmi* and *Mercator*, but he rears his hoary head in *Asinaria, Aulularia, Cistellaria, Rudens, Stichus* and *Vidularia* as well. The object of his affection is always a young girl, often his son's mistress, and the situation is invariably treated as ludicrous and degrading: love is for the young and the young always win in comedy. Like the triumph of the clever slave over his stupid master, the victory of the son over his father seems to owe its appeal for the Roman audience to Roman exaltation of the *pater familias*. For this there was extraordinary legal support:

> 'This was the most fundamental and most peculiarly Roman part of family law. Children born to parents validly married at civil law came under the power (*patriapotestas*) of the father, or under that of the father's father if he were still alive. The *patriapotestas* continued so long as the father was alive. Even if the son reached the highest offices of state, he still remained under the power of his *pater*. The father had complete power of life and death over his children – though if he used his power arbitrarily he might be punished by the censors. He could sell them into slavery, his consent to their marriage was needed, and he could bring about their divorce if he wished. The children could own no property – though customarily they were given a fund (*peculium*) which they administered as if it belonged to them; anything they acquired belonged to the father.'

We can thus see a basis in Roman institutions for the persistent patterns of Roman comedy. Slaves, women and male children were all repressed social groups and their overthrow of the *pater familias* (master, husband, father) has essentially a Saturnalian attraction.

---

[1] Menaechmus models the stolen *palla*, and asks his parasite Peniculus for approval: MENAECHMVS. *age me aspice.* | *ecquid adsimulo similiter?* PENI-CVLVS. *qui istic est ornatus tuos?* | MENAECHMVS. *dic hominem lepidissumum esse me* (145–7).

[2] A. Watson, *The law of the ancient Romans* (1970) 37–8.

Like all comic patterns, however, these survive changes in social institutions. This can be explained by the fact that such changes are only of degree, that the groups which were repressed then are still repressed, and we therefore still delight in their triumph over the powerful. A more fundamental explanation lies in the very nature of the Saturnalian response. Repression of any idea creates tension and release from this tension is a cause of pleasure.[1]

4. *CASINA*

Up to this point we have been dealing generally with the kind of comedy Plautus wrote and the audience for whom he wrote it. Now we should turn our attention to the *Casina* and try to appreciate its comic appeal, which can be as profound for us as it was for its original audience, although there are several barriers between us and the play as they saw it. Most important is the fact that we must read it and cannot, under normal circumstances, see a full stage production with music, costumes and dance. A second problem is the language itself; it is not our own language and even if we have read a great deal of Latin, the Latin of Plautus is not the same as the Latin of Virgil and Cicero and we must recognize the difference. A few remarks, then, on what little we know about the original production of Plautine plays are in order, and then an analysis of his particular kind of Latin. This will lead us directly into a discussion of the imagery and themes of the play and will duplicate in the study as closely as possible the process we follow in the theatre: we respond first to the spectacle, then to the lines as the actors speak or sing them, and finally to the whole shape and significance of the play.

(*a*) PRODUCTION

Plautus' plays were produced on holidays, as part of public celebrations in honour of gods and noble Romans. On these occasions they competed for the spectators' attention with other forms of entertainment in a sort of circus setting.[2] Produced out of doors in

---

[1] See Segal *passim* for this Saturnalian element in Plautus generally; W. T. MacCary, 'Patterns of myth, ritual and comedy in Plautus' *Casina*', *Texas Studies in Literature and Language* 15 (1974) 881-9, for the *Casina* in particular.　　　　[2] See Terence, *Hecyra* 1-5, 33-42.

broad daylight on wooden stages with minimal scenery and no special effects, the plays depended entirely upon the power of the spoken word, the enchantment of music and a great deal of physical activity, or stage business, to hold an audience.

The stage was a platform, perhaps a fairly long one, and about five feet high. There was a building upon it which the actors used as a dressing room. In the front of this building were three recessed doors; these could represent three houses if the play called for three; the *Casina* requires only two, so the central one was not used. The actors could make their exits and entrances through these doors or around the sides of the stage building. Spectators sat on the ground or stood about; there might have been wooden tiers of seats by the time of the *Casina*; there were certainly special seats for senators.

In this setting, so similar to primitive theatres in medieval Europe and modern Asia – primitive in the sense of basic, not backward – there was a great deal of intimacy between actors and audience and little pretension that what was happening on the stage was real. Verisimilitude in drama is a relatively modern development and quite alien to the principles on which early drama was based. The actors might have worn masks, though this is by no means certain. Masks were certainly worn by Greek comic actors and by Italian actors of the Atellan Farce. Masks give the practical advantage of extending the range of a small acting troupe; by changing his mask an actor can assume another role in the same play. We think of masks as a strange convention, an extreme stylization we associate with academic performances of Greek tragedy and attempts to recapture the spirit of Commedia dell'Arte in Italian comedy of the seventeenth and eighteenth centuries. Their use by the Greek and Roman comedians is probably better compared to the heavy make-up of a mime like Marcel Marceau. It makes him special – human, but fantastically human – and with his elaborate gestures gives his performance the aura of ritual. The Roman actors would have used elaborate gestures, and with music the whole spectacle would have been much more like a combination of opera and ballet than like a Noel Coward play or a television show.

All of the aspects of the *Casina*'s production, then, would have emphasized salient features of its composition. The characters were overdrawn and overacted. Song and dance captures the spirit and

absurdity of particular moments, like Lysidamus' ode to love and
Olympio's description of his wedding night. There is not much
extraneous detail on the stage or in the script: all the action and all
the language elucidate major themes.

(b) LANGUAGE

Writing for the stage is communication redoubled: characters speak
to each other but the audience must get the point. The language
Plautus uses in his *Casina* approximates to the normal Latin spoken
by normal people at the end of the third, the beginning of the second
century B.C. There is great exaggeration and stylization, but it is not
like the artificial language of later Latin literature. Because dramatic
dialogue is conversation it is to be expected that all the arts and skills
employed by the normal person in conversation will be exercised to
an even greater degree by the dramatist.

'Spoken language is distinguished primarily from writing by the
greater intimacy of contact between speaker and hearer. The give-
and-take of dialogue increases the emotional tension, which reveals
itself in interjections, exclamations, forcefulness, exaggeration,
insistence and constant interruption. The speed and spontaneity of
conversation reduces the element of reflection. Sentences are not
organized into self-consistent logical structures, but meaning is
conveyed by fits and starts with parentheses, after-thoughts, and
those changes of construction which grammarians catalogue as
anacolutha, contamination, and the like. Perhaps most important
is the fact that conversation takes place in an elaborate context of
situation which often makes detailed and explicit linguistic
reference unnecessary and tedious. Hence colloquial speech is
characterized by its allusiveness, by deictic elements, abbreviation,
ellipse, and aposiopesis.'[1]

Interjections abound in Plautus; in the first confrontation between
Lysidamus and Cleostrata we have *heia, mea Iuno* (230), *eho tu nihili*
(239), and *ohe, iam satis, uxor, est* (249). Some are taken over straight
from the Greek, such as *attatae!* (468). There are many exclamatory
sentencies in the *Casina*, ranging from the abbreviated *oh perii* (236)
through short oaths, prayers and curses such as *di te seruassint mihi*

[1] Palmer 74.

(324), to fully developed clauses such as *ut ille trepidabat, ut festinabat miser*, | *ut sussultabat postquam uicit uilicus!* (432–3). There are accusatives of exclamation, which have no syntactical relation with the rest of the sentence in which they occur: *qui, malum, homini scutigerulo dare lubet?* (262) 'Why the hell do you want to marry her to that pitiful shield-bearer?' (*malum* is the neuter accusative of the adjective *malus*). Related to this construction is the *infinitiuus indignantis*: *non mihi licere meam rem me solum, ut uolo,* | *loqui atque cogitare sine ted arbitro?* (89–90) 'And so I can't attend to my own business by myself, speak or think without you listening in?'

There is much repetition in Plautus, ranging from the use of synonyms (*auxili, praesidi, perfugi* – 623) to complex, pleonastic constructions:

> Nec pol ego Nemeae credo neque ego Olympiae
> neque usquam ludos tam festiuos fieri
> quam hic intus fiunt ludi ludificabiles.   (759–61)

> I don't think Nemea or Olympia or any other place
> Ever saw games as festive as the games played,
> The playful plans that are laid, within.

Plautus uses many vocatives, repeats pronouns and doubles his negatives, all for the sake of emphasis. He also piles up superlatives, as in *pessumarum pessuma* (793).

He chooses his words for emphasis also. He uses stronger, more colourful words, such as *fabulor* (368) for *dico*, *depereo* (470) for *amo*, and *se sufflauit uxori suae* (582) for *iratus est uxori suae*. There is also a good deal of slang, which is characterized by forcefulness of expression: *ego edepol illam mediam dirruptam uelim* (326) 'I wish she would burst in the middle'. Plautus intensifies ordinary words with prefixes and suffixes: *depugnarier* (344), *fodico* (361), *perlepide* (927). He uses a lot of diminutives, often as terms of endearment – *sine tuos ocellos deosculer* (136) 'Let me kiss your little eyes!' There are even diminutives of adjectives and adverbs: *primulo* (40), *saepicule* (703). He also uses some Greek words (728–30) and coins many words himself: *commaritus* (797) 'fellow-husband'.

Plautus' syntax, like his vocabulary, is more varied than that of classical Latin. *Parataxis*, the opposite of the subordination of clauses, is frequent: *uir aberit faxo domo* (484) 'I'll see to it that the husband is

out of the house.' Many verbs of saying and thinking do not take indirect discourse, but are simply inserted parenthetically: *in adulterio,
dum moechissat Casinam, credo perdidit* (976) 'He lost it in sin, I'll bet,
when he was assaulting Casina.' Some words lose their original
meaning and grammatical construction; thus *amabo*, in *sed quid tu es
tristis, amabo?* (173) means simply 'please', having evolved from an
abbreviated conditional statement, 'I shall love you if you will tell
me.' Thoughts are introduced in parenthesis, interrupting the flow of
the sentence, but making perfectly good sense:

> nam nouom maritum et nouam nuptam uolo
> rus prosequi; noui hominum mores maleficos;
> ne quis eam abripiat. (782–4)

> I want to accompany the bride and groom
> Home to the country, so that no one
> Will snatch her from him; I know
> The evil ways of men.

Clauses are added on after the original thought and syntactical form
it has taken are complete:

> tua ancilla, quam tu tuo uilico uis
> dare uxorem, ea intus...
> imitatur malarum malam disciplinam
> uiro quae suo interminatur... (655–8)

> Your maid, the one you want to marry to your bailiff,
> She is inside and behaving in the evil manner
> Of evil women and she's threatening her husband.

This sort of supplementation by afterthought seems more natural in
Latin because relative clauses can function as causal or coordinate
clauses; it is frequent in colloquial Latin. We also find anacoluthon
or change of construction:

> is seruos, sed abhinc annos factum est sedecim
> quom conspicatust primulo crepusculo
> puellam exponi. (39–41)

> This servant – it's been sixteen years now
> Since he saw a baby girl abandoned. It was early in the evening.

In this sentence the nominative *seruos* is just a false start; the clause for which it would have served as subject is never completed and the temporal clause contains the main statement. Asyndeton, or lack of conjunctions between clauses, is also frequent: *ego illum fame, ego illum siti,* | *maledictis, malefactis amatorem ulciscar* (153–5) 'I'll plague that lover with hunger, thirst, dirty words and dirty tricks.' Finally there are a number of syntactical peculiarities which Plautus shares with other early authors, whether in colloquial or formal speech. He construes with the accusative deponent verbs which later take the ablative: *munus uelit fungier* (951). He uses the indicative in indirect questions (654, 902). He expresses purpose with the infinitive (855–6).

Plautus' morphology, the actual form of his words, differs somewhat from later Latin. He uses forms of personal, relative and demonstrative pronouns which are not found in Virgil and Cicero; e.g., there is an old ablative singular in -*i* which survives in the relative and interrogative pronoun *qui*: *qui, malum, homini scutigerulo dare lubet* (262) 'Why the hell do you want to marry her to that pitiful shieldbearer?' There is a whole range of forms to which the suffix -*ce* is attached; see the note on *illisce*, 36. Original -*d* survives in the ablatives of personal pronouns (*sine ted arbitro* (90) 'without you listening in') and in other words (*antidhac* (88) 'before'). Plautus has *face* (353) instead of *fac* in the imperative and two whole systems of verb forms based on stems in -*s*- like *faxo* (484) and *amasso* (1001); these serve as futures and as present and perfect subjunctives (see the notes on 307 and 324). There is a perfect passive of impersonal verbs: *puditumst* (878); present passive infinitives and infinitives of deponent verbs end in -*ier*: *utier* (220), *fungier* (952). Plautus has a tendency to treat participles as adjectives, resulting in periphrastic expressions (*audiens sum*) and doubled forms (*oblitus fui*).

A number of differences in pronunciation between Plautine and classical Latin are clear from spelling and scansion. We regularly find *uo*- for *uu*- as in the nominative *seruos* (738) and *uor*- for *uer*-: *uorsis gladiis* (344). Superlatives have -*u*- instead of -*i*- (*optumest* – 738, *proxumum* – 165). -*u*- is sometimes dropped between *p* and *l* or *c* and *l* (*hercle* – 368). Certain vowels were long in Plautus but short in later Latin; see Appendix 1, p. 213. It is not possible to spell Plautine Latin as he wrote it. The convention used by most editors is to follow the best evidence of the manuscripts, on the grounds that this is preferable to making firm but arbitrary decisions about words whose spelling was not uniform in Plautus' own day or later. Such is the practice in this edition, with, perhaps, slightly more modernization than in some others. Nevertheless certain old forms are adopted, such as *quom* for *cum*, *siet* for *sit*, *ap-* and *op-* in compounds for *ab-* and *ob-*; genitive singular of the first declension in *-ai* and third declension ablatives in *-i*, even of consonant stems.

Certain stylistic devices are also related to Plautus' early place in the history of Latin literature. Our fragments of old Latin show a preponderance of alliteration, assonance and repetition. Any section of Plautine song will abound with such features.

> Nulla sum, nulla sum; tota, tota occidi,
> cor metu mortuomst, membra miserae tremunt.
> nescio unde auxili, praesidi, perfugi,
> mi aut opum copiam comparem aut expetam.
> tanta factu modo mira miris modis
> intus uidi, nouam atque integram audaciam. (621–6)

> Lost, lost, totally, totally lost.
> My heart stops for fear, my legs tremble beneath me.
> I know not whither, whence nor where
> I can find peace of mind,
> Refuge from such confusion.
> Where to run to?
> Whom to turn to?
> Such a sight have I seen inside!
> No prodigy previously produced compares.
> A brouhaha beyond belief.

Alliteration is evident throughout, often as the result of repetition. Assonance is frequent and even end-rhyme. We see Plautus' preference for tricola, three often synonymous words in asyndeton: *auxili, praesidi, perfugi*. There is a jingling quality to the whole which makes it appropriate for musical rendering.

(*c*) IMAGERY

Plautus' language is also rich in metaphor, simile and allusion. There are a number of images which add colour to individual passages. Then there are patterns of imagery which inform the action of scenes and some which run through the whole play, emphasizing major themes and contributing to the development of characters.

The language of abuse is particularly rich; in the first scene Olympio threatens Chalinus with penal servitude:

> ita te aggerunda curuom aqua faciam probe
> ut postilena possit ex te fieri.   (124–5)

> I'll make you carry so much water
> That your bent body can serve
> As the strap for a horse's rear.

The basis for comparison is the shape that Chalinus will be in after hauling water, i.e., bent, like a crupper, the leather strap buckled to the back of a saddle and passing under the horse's tail to prevent the saddle from slipping forwards. It is a particularly appropriate image for a slave in charge of a farm to use, and the suggestion is that Chalinus will actually find himself in close proximity to a horse's hindquarters, so the threat is that much more unpleasant. Similarly, later in the play, Olympio threatens Chalinus:

> Sine modo rus ueniat; ego remittam ad te uirum
> cum furca in urbem tamquam carbonarium.   (437–8)

> Just let him come to the country:
> I'll send him back with a yoke
> On his neck like a charcoal salesman.

Slaves were punished by being tied to cross-shaped implements and beaten. One of the commonest terms of abuse in Plautus is *furcifer*. Here this grisly practice is compared to the appearance, presumably familiar, of a man carrying charcoal, with a pole across his shoulders supporting baskets at either end. Neither of these images is extended, but they are what we expect of Olympio, the rustic slave, who is prone to violence, as opposed to the city slave Chalinus, who is querulous and ends up dressed as a woman.

The central confrontation of the play is between Lysidamus, with his henchman Olympio, and Cleostrata, with her henchman Chalinus. This is presented as a military engagement, complete with a conference beforehand between the two generals, words of encouragement to the troops, prayers to the gods for help, and, finally, after the conflict itself (the casting of lots for Casina), a formulaic announcement of victory. Lysidamus introduces the whole sequence in military terms:

> necessum est uorsis gladiis depugnarier. (344)
>
> . . .
>
> nunc nos conlatis signis depugnabimus. (352)
>
> . . .
>
> quid si propius attollamus signa eamusque obuiam. (357)

> We shall have to fight to the finish with other weapons.
>
> . . .
>
> Now we shall raise our standards and join battle.
>
> . . .
>
> How about us raising our standard and going to meet them?

Cleostrata announces defeat to her army and Lysidamus congratulates his; Olympio, like a Scipio or a Metellus, attributes his victory to the virtue of his ancestors:

> CLEOSTRATA. uictus es, Chaline. LYSIDAMVS. cum nos di iuuere,
> Olympio,
> gaudeo. OLYMPIO. pietate factum est mea atque maiorum meum.
> (417–18)

Relations between Lysidamus and Cleostrata are described by several characters as analogous to those between Jupiter and Juno. Lysidamus introduces this comparison when he first greets his wife:

> LYSIDAMVS. heia, mea Iuno, non decet esse te tam tristem
> tuo Ioui. (230)

Lysidamus has just been singing of his love for Casina; Jupiter is notorious for his adulterous unions with goddesses and mortal women. When Olympio tells Lysidamus that Cleostrata has tried to talk him out of his claim on Casina, he states his refusal in terms which are ironic:

> negaui enim ipsi me concessurum Ioui,
> si is mecum oraret. (323–4)
>
> I said I wouldn't yield her to Jupiter himself,
> Even if he begged me.

It is a hyperbolic commonplace to refuse something to Jupiter; here, of course, Lysidamus is Jupiter and Olympio must yield up his bride to his master on the wedding night, though later in the play he tries to get hold of her first. Lysidamus refers to himself as Jupiter only a few lines later; Olympio has complained that his master's love has turned everyone against him and Lysidamus replies:

> ...quid id refert tua?
> unus tibi hic dum propitius sit Iuppiter,
> tu istos minutos caue deos flocci feceris.   (330–2)

> What difference does it make to you?
> As long as this Jupiter here is your patron,
> Don't pay any attention to those lesser deities.

Olympio is unconvinced, however, and sees a time when Lysidamus will not be around to protect him from the wrath of Cleostrata and her son Euthynicus:

> nugae sunt istae magnae; quasi tu nescias
> repente ut emoriantur humani Ioues.
> sed tandem si tu Iuppiter sis mortuos,
> cum ad deos minores redierit regnum tuom,
> quis mihi subueniet tergo aut capiti aut cruribus?   (333–7)

> What a silly thing to say, as if you didn't know
> How suddenly these mortal immortals fade away.
> Just tell me, Jupiter, when you are dead,
> And your kingdom reverts to the lesser gods,
> Who will protect me and my backside then?

In the lot-casting scene this joke is continued (404–8): the slaves assault each other, each claiming that his 'Jupiter' or his 'Juno' has ordered him to do so. The whole series, early in the play, helps establish the relations among the characters – master and slave, cheating husband and jealous wife – and a certain mock-heroic tone which persists throughout: just as Jupiter's philandering and lying is a contradiction of the dignity and power of his position as father of gods and men, so Lysidamus' role of *pater familias* is undercut by the shabby tricks he resorts to in order to get hold of a slave girl. Lysidamus' comparison of himself to Jupiter has the same effect as when those Saturnalian slaves compare themselves to famous generals and kings.

Lysidamus is constantly compared to animals and this pattern of imagery reinforces our impression of him as a man degraded by his lust for Casina. His wife calls him a *cana culex* (239) at their first meeting; flies are proverbially associated with lechery and Lysidamus is white-haired. Later she refers to Lysidamus and his friend Alcesimus as 'old castrated rams' (*uetulis ueruecibus* – 535), a term of abuse Plautus also uses for the amorous old man in the *Mercator* (567). Alcesimus himself thinks Lysidamus is a 'shameless, toothless old goat' (*illius hirqui improbi, edentuli* – 550). When Lysidamus plays on the sexual significance of *dirrumpo*, Olympio responds by likening Lysidamus to a horse; Lysidamus gives this, too, a sexual significance:

> LYSIDAMVS. perii hercle ego miser; dirrumpi cantando
> > hymenaeum licet:
> illo morbo quo dirrumpi cupio non est copiae.
> OLYMPIO. edepol ne tu, si equos esses, esses indomabilis.
> LYSIDAMVS. quo argumento? OLYMPIO. nimis tenax es.
> > LYSIDAMVS. num me expertu's uspiam?
> OLYMPIO. di melius faciant! (809-13)

> LYSIDAMUS. Damn it! I'm about to pop with singing this
> > wedding hymn.
> The popping off I want to do, I can't. OLYMPIO. For God's sake,
> If you were a horse you would be unbreakable.
> > LYSIDAMUS. How so?
> OLYMPIO. You're too wild. LYSIDAMUS. You've tried me,
> > have you?
> OLYMPIO. God forbid!

Finally, Chalinus, or whoever speaks the epilogue, asks for applause; he promises whores to those who respond, and unknowing wives; for those who refuse he promises, intead of whores, he-goats anointed with bilgewater (1015-18). The association between animals and sex is thus made explicit, just as it is at the end of the *Bacchides*, another play where the fathers try to join their sons in debauchery. There the old men are spoken of consistently throughout the final scene as sheep and the epilogue points out that if they had not been worthless and degenerate, they would never have suffered the indignities which they

have (1207–11). Profligacy in old age is treated by Plautus as an
aberration and the imagery he uses is of animals, like Shakespeare's
horns for cuckolds and asses' heads for unworthy lovers.

The most persistent pattern of imagery in the *Casina* is that which
associates food and sex. Since the basic situation in the play concerns
sex and since part of its action is a festive meal, much of the reference
to food and sex is straight rather than by way of analogy or allusion.
It is the conjunction of these two areas of interest, however, which is
so important to the play, and when characters speak of sex in terms
of food and food in terms of sex, that is imagery.

Erotic language is always full of implied comparisons with food.
In the opening scene Olympio delivers a quite conventional list of
terms of endearment, one of which is *mea mellilla* (135) 'my little
honey'. Later Lysidamus tells Olympio, in language which Chalinus
understands as erotic, that he appreciates the slave's help in gaining
access to Casina:

OLYMPIO. ecquid amas nunc me?   LYSIDAMVS. immo edepol me
                                              quam te minus.
licetne amplecti te?   CHALINVS. quid, 'amplecti'?   OLYMPIO. licet.
LYSIDAMVS. ut, quia te tango, mel mihi uideor lingere.   (456–8)

OLYMPIO. *Now* do you love me?   LYSIDAMUS. Better than life itself.
Let me put my arms around you.   CHALINUS. Arms around *him*?
                                              OLYMPIO. Sure.
LYSIDAMUS. When I touch you it's like tasting honey!

The fullest expression of this analogy is given by Lysidamus in his
entering *canticum*: life is a meal and love is its spice.

Omnibus rebus ego amorem credo et nitoribus nitidis anteuenire
nec potis quicquam commemorari quod plus salis plusque leporis
                                              [hodie]
habeat; coquos equidem nimis demiror, qui utuntur condimentis,
eos eo condimento uno non utier, omnibus quod praestat.
nam ubi amor condimentum inierit, cuiuis placiturum credo;
neque salsum neque suaue esse potest quicquam, ubi amor non
                                              admiscetur:
fel quod amarumst, id mel faciet, hominem ex tristi lepidum et
                                    lenem.   (217–23)

I believe love outshines the shiniest stars,
That there is nothing spicier.
I wonder why the cooks
Who cook with condiments
Don't use this condiment alone
Which stands out on its own.
With love mixed in
It's bound to win
Applause.
Without love
There's no dish
You could wish
For.
It sweetens the bitter,
I've never felt fitter,
Even an old man
Like me.

Cleostrata has already made it quite clear to her household slaves
that she has no intention of performing her chief function as wife,
preparing her husband's meals, as long as he continues to lust after
her maid (147–60). This is a foreshadowing of the intrigue at the
climax of the action, where Olympio and Lysidamus are sent off with
the false Casina, unfed. Lysidamus has sent Olympio to market to buy
all sorts of provisions (490–503); when the slave returns his mind is
more on food than on sex (744–50) and he brings with him the cooks
who later become part of the women's plot to starve the men:

> ...digne autem coqui
> nimis lepide ei rei dant operam, ne cenet senex.
> aulas peruortunt, ignem restingunt aqua;
> illarum oratu faciunt. illae autem senem
> cupiunt extrudere incenatum ex aedibus.   (772–6)

> ...The cooks see to it
> The master won't eat today,
> Creating chaos in the kitchen,
> Pouring water on the fire;
> And this they do at the women's request,

> Who are determined to throw the old fool
> Starving from the house.

Olympio resents the fact that he is included in their plan:

LYSIDAMVS. quid agis, mea salus? OLYMPIO. esurio hercle, atque
                                     adeo hau salubriter.
LYSIDAMVS. at ego amo. OLYMPIO. at ego hercle nihili facio; tibi
                                     amor pro cibost.
mihi ieiunitate iam dudum intestina murmurant.   (801–3)

LYSIDAMUS. What are you up to, saviour of mine?
OLYMPIO. I need food to save myself.
LYSIDAMUS. Well I feed on love. OLYMPIO. Well, I don't give a damn;
For you sex is food; for my stomach there's nothing but noise.

The pattern of food and sex imagery climaxes in this explicit statement. It is recalled, however, at the end of the play, when Olympio
recounts to Pardalisca his disreputable adventure with the false bride
(911–14).

(d) STRUCTURE AND THEMES

The structure of the *Casina* is intricate and appealing. The action
moves forward in a series of scenes which are alternately sung and
spoken. The action is continuous: no acts and no pauses between
scenes.[1] If Diphilus followed the same convention as Menander, his
Kleroumenoi was written in five acts, nor would he have used lyric

---

[1] What are effectively scene divisions, and are used as such in modern
editions of Plautus, appear in all the manuscripts, in that when a character
makes an entrance there is normally a new heading giving the names of the
speakers in the following lines. On the late origin of these divisions (produced
for book texts, not for stage production), see Andrieu 87ff. and B. Bader,
Szenentitel und Szeneneinteilung bei Plautus (1970). The ideal of five acts,
endorsed by Horace (*A.P.* 189–90), was based on ancient appreciation of
Menander's plays, which had four interludes, when the action stopped and
songs unrelated to the play were sung by performers who did not appear in
the play proper. The crucial fact for Plautus is continuous action. To divide
into acts a play which was performed without interludes of any kind is to
impose a totally meaningless convention upon it and distort its own genuine
form and structure. Unfortunately, such a convention was established in
Renaissance editions of Plautus, and we follow it here for ease of reference to
such works as LS.

metres to the same extent as Plautus. Plautus, in turning a comedy of straight dialogue into a musical comedy, discarded the structural principle of act division, whereby the action progresses through discrete units, each with the introduction of new material and each with its own rise and fall in dramatic tension. Plautus replaced this with a musical structure, of which the only indication left to us is the variety and order of metres: he used *senarii* for plain dialogue (A), iambic, trochaic and anapaestic septenarii and octonarii for sections which were chanted or spoken to musical accompaniment (B), and lyric metres of all types for the songs (C). The action then develops in sections which are dominated by songs, typically in the sequence ACB.[1] (See complete metrical analyses in the Commentary.)

There are three spectacular scenes in the play: the lot-casting (353–423), Pardalisca's false report of Casina's madness (621–718), and the wedding with its aftermath (815–1018). These three episodes are not only the liveliest, the funniest and the most important to the development of the plot, but also they carry the whole weight of meaning in the play. The lost-casting scene is farcical in that it pits a lecherous old man and his slave against his wife and her slave in a contest to determine who gets the girl: Lysidamus mistakes himself, saying, 'When I marry the girl, I mean when my slave marries her.' The slaves abuse each other verbally and physically. Behind all this there is the plight of the young girl, however: she is being randomly assigned to a lover and this is potentially tragic. In fact, the lot-casting for a bride had a tragic prototype in Euripides' *Aiolos*, where a father assigned his daughters to his sons for marriage by lot, ignorant of the love which one son had for one daughter, who then committed suicide.[2] This threat, seen from the point of view of the daughter, is integrated into the total plot of the play, which is paradigmatic of New Comedy plots. Northrop Frye, without mentioning it by name, precisely describes the *Casina* as a sort of index to the genre:

'New Comedy unfolds from what may be described as a comic Oedipus situation. Its main theme is the successful effort of the young man to outwit an opponent and possess the girl of his choice.

[1] H. H. Law, *Studies in the songs of Plautine comedy* (1922).

[2] See MacCary, 'Comic tradition'. There are numerous versions of the Macareus–Canace myth, including Ovid, *Heroides* 11, but none but Euripides' centres on the lot-casting.

The opponent is usually the father (*senex*), and the psychological descent of the heroine from the mother is also sometimes hinted at. The father frequently wants the same girl, and is cheated out of her by the son, the mother thus becoming the son's ally. The girl is usually a slave or courtesan, and the plot turns on a *cognitio* or discovery of birth which makes her marriageable.'[1]

'Comic Oedipus situation' is a felicitous phrase; it reminds us that much of the appeal of comedy is the extrication of sympathetic characters from circumstances which could take a tragic turn. Incest and parricide are not at issue in the *Casina*, but they lie beneath the surface. Plautus and Diphilus insist we realize that Cleostrata has raised Casina as her own daughter and that son and mother are allied against the father.

Mock-tragedy is the source of comedy in the false report of Casina's madness, our play's second major episode. Pardalisca, on the instructions of Cleostrata, tells Lysidamus, in a song styled after tragic laments, that Casina has gone mad within and 'will kill the man who tries to lie with her tonight'. We remember the daughters of Danaus, forced into marriage with their first cousins; Aeschylus dramatized their resistance, the murder of their husbands on the wedding night and finally their trial, in a tragic trilogy of which only the first play, *The suppliant women*, survives. Even though the report is false, part of a plan to ridicule the old man, we nevertheless feel it as a strong statement of the young girl's resistance to an unchosen lover, even stronger because this resistance is generalized: the older women join her and take vengeance for the abuse which they too have suffered at the hands of men. The play ends in confrontation between men and women: Cleostrata, Myrrhina, Pardalisca and Chalinus as the bride against Lysidamus and Olympio.

The final scenes have been much discussed by scholars.[2] It is clear

---

[1] N. Frye, *English Institute Essays – 1948*, 50.

[2] Major contributions to this discussion have been made by T. Ladewig, *Rh.M.* 3 (1845) 179–205, 537–40; F. Skutsch, *Rh.M.* 55 (1900) 272–85; P. Legrand, *R.E.G.* 15 (1902) 370–9; Leo, *PF* 168f., 207f.; E. Fraenkel, *Plautinisches im Plautus* (1922) 292–313; Jachmann 105–27; Friedrich 173–82; E. Paratore, *Plauto: Casina* (1959) 5–54. Ladewig thought the scene of the false bride must have been added by Plautus, perhaps under the influence of Atellan Farce. Leo suggested the *phlyax* drama of southern Italy. Skutsch

from the prologue and epilogue that Plautus has left out the scene
with which his Greek original ended: Casina was recognized as the
daughter of the man next door, so that as a free-born Athenian citizen
she could marry the son Euthynicus. It has been argued that since
Plautus left something out, he probably added something. The
amount of obscenity and farcical action in the false-bride scenes make
these seem the most probable Plautine addition but we can never be
certain where the original is not available for comparison. It is true
that Plautus seems to have taken greater liberties with his Greek
sources in later plays than in earlier. Also, there is evidence that
transvestite marriages were popular in the tradition of Atellan Farce:
the title *Maccus virgo* survives. If we consider the false-bride scenes in
the context of the whole play, however, we realize how consistent
they are with its thematic development and how much the structure
of the *Casina*, including these scenes, resembles the structure of the
Rudens, also based on an original by Diphilus: it too develops through
a series of spectacular scenes, each derived from a different mythological prototype, but integrated into the total dramatic pattern.

The whole complex of false bride scenes has a prototype in previous
Greek drama in the many comic treatments of the marriage of
Herakles and Omphale. Herakles served Queen Omphale of Lydia
as her maid and on one occasion the Queen dressed in the hero's
lion-skin, he in her veils, and they were married in an elaborate
ceremony; withdrawing to a grotto to consummate their union they
were overseen by Pan, who, mistaking Herakles for Omphale,
assaulted him; the hero took revenge.[1] Once one admits that the

thought it a Greek theme, though taken by Plautus from a play other than
the *Kleroumenoi*. Legrand thought it was from the *Kleroumenoi* but that
Plautus had made major changes. Fraenkel, like Skutsch, argued that there
had been *contaminatio* with another play, but later accepted Jachmann's
rebuttal of this argument (*EP* 434). Jachmann thought there was a scene of
recognition and marriage in Diphilus' play, but that it was unimportant
compared with the false bride scenes, which did derive from the original.
Friedrich followed Jachmann, but Paratore then returned to Ladewig's
original speculation, that Plautus, inspired by native Italian drama, added
the false-bride scenes after having suppressed the recognition and marriage
of his original. For comment on some of Paratore's points, see MacCary,
'Comic tradition'. Other evidence is considered in the note on 815-54.

[1] This was first noted by F. Skutsch, *Rh.M.* 55 (1900) 283ff. See Commentary at 930-1.

false-bride motif is essential to Diphilus' play and characteristic of his art, and that it has a history in previous Greek comedy, one has reduced the scope of Plautine adaptation to what is known from other plays: exaggeration of characters, expansion of farcical and obscene aspects, setting to music, enrichment of the language and allusion to Roman institutions.

The major themes of the *Casina* are the Saturnalian ones discussed above; the victory of son over father, slave over master, women over men. The expression given these themes is essentially sexual: a young girl is arbitrarily assigned a lover; this slave lover is but a surrogate for his master, who will enjoy the *ius primae noctis*;[1] the girl and her women friends resent this treatment and cause the man who would assault her to fear death or mutilation; finally the sexual aggression of the assaulter is turned against a member of his own sex and he is beaten and ridiculed and finally forgiven. The comedy, then, follows a sort of ritual pattern in which sexual tensions within the family are temporarily resolved. This amounts to what could be considered a comic equivalent of tragic catharsis. We have experienced a pattern of action which makes us recognize certain elements in our own lives for what they are. Having laughed at them we are free, for a while, from their influence.

[1] Also known as the *droit de seigneur*. There is little evidence that this 'right' has ever had even quasi-legal status, but it is implicit in the master–slave relationship and has been perennially popular on the stage. For a discussion of its psychological significance, see MacCary, 'Plautus and Beaumarchais'.

SIGLA

A = Ambrosianus (G.82 sup.) palimpsestus, saec. iv–v
B = Palatinus Vaticanus (1615), saec. x–xi
  B^1 = eiusdem corrector, de quo uide p. 233
V = Vossianus Leidensis (Q.30), saec. xii
E = Ambrosianus (I.257 inf.), saec. xii
J = Londinensis (Mus. Britann., Reg. 15 C xi), saec. xii
  P = consensus codicum 'Palatinorum' B V E J
  cett. = ceteri e codicibus B V E J
T = codex Turnebi (nunc deperditus)
F = Lipsiensis (Latinus 33), saec. xv
Z = editio princeps G. Merulae (Venetiis, 1472)
  Ital. = consensus F et Z
  recc. = codices aliquot recentiores

In textu constituto et adnotatione critica his notis usi sumus

⟨ ⟩ supplenda
[ ] delenda
† corrupta
* * lacunae
n.l. non legitur
⋕ personae spatium in A (uide p. 235)

T. MACCI PLAVTI

CASINA

PERSONAE

OLYMPIO uilicus

CHALINVS seruos

CLEOSTRATA mulier

PARDALISCA ancilla

MYRRHINA mulier

LYSIDAMVS senex

ALCESIMVS senex

CITRIO coquos

ARGVMENTVM

Conseruam uxorem duo conserui éxpetunt   *[handwritten: Not by Plautus / Plot summary, much later]*
Alium senex allegat, alium filius.
Senem adiuuat sors, uerum decipitur dolis.
Ita ei subicitur pro puella seruolus
Nequam, qui dominum mulcat atque uilicum.   5
Adulescens ducit ciuem Casinam cognitam.

Argumentum post prologum habent codd. (P); deest A usque ad u. 37   3 **senem**
adiuuat sors *Bothe*: sors senem adiuuat *P*   4 pro *B*: *om. VEJ*   5 **mulcat**
Pius: mulgat *P*

PROLOGVS

Saluere iubeo spectatores optumos,
fidem qui facitis maxumí – et uos Fides.
si uerum dixi, signum clarum date mihi,
ut uos mi esse aequos iam inde a principio sciam.
qui utuntur uino uetere sapientis puto   5
et qui lubenter ueteres spectant fabulas.
antiqua ópera et uerba cum uobis placent,
aequom est placere ante alias ueteres fabulas.
nam nunc nouae quae prodeunt comoediae
multo sunt nequiores quam nummi noui.   10
nos postquam populi rumore intelleximus
studiose expetere uos Plautinas fabulas,
antiquam éius edimus comoediam,
quam uos probastis qui estis in senioribus;
nam iuniorum qui sunt non norunt, scio;   15
uerum ut cognoscant dabimus operam sedulo.
haec cum primum acta est, uicit omnis fabulas.

2 **Fidem** *F. Skutsch*   **et ego uos** *F. Skutsch*   4 **esse** *B²*: *om. cett.*   7 anti-
cua *Camerarius*   **uerba et opera** *Acidalius*   8 **alias** *Ritschl*: *om. P*   11 rumore *Angelius*: rumorem *P*   13 anticuam *Camerarius* (*cf.* 7)

[43]

ea témpestate flos poetarum fuit,
qui nunc abierunt hinc in communem locum.
sed tamen absentes prosunt pro praesentibus.   20
uos omnis opere magno esse oratos uolo
benigne ut operam detis ad nostrum gregem.
eicite ex animo curam átque alienum aés.
ne quis formidet flagitatorem suom;
ludi sunt, ludus datus est argentariis,   25
tranquillum est, Alcedonia sunt circum forum.
ratione utuntur, ludis poscunt neminem,
secundum ludos reddunt autem nemini.
aures uociuae si sunt, animum aduortite:
comoediai nomen dare uobis uolo.   30
Clerumenoe uocatur haec comoedia
graece, latine Sortientes. Diphilus
hanc graece scripsit, postid rursum denuo
latine Plautus cum latranti nomine.
senex híc maritus habitat; ei est filius;   35
is una cum patre in illisce habitat aedibus.
est ei quidam seruos qui in morbo cubat,
immo hercle uero in lecto, ne quid mentiar;
is seruos, sed abhinc annos factum est sedecim
quom conspicatust primulo crepusculo   40
puellam exponi. ádit extemplo ad mulierem
quae illam exponebat; orat ut eam det sibi.
exorat, aufert, detulit recta domum;
dat erae suae, orat ut eam curet, educet.
era fecit, educauit magna industria,   45
quasi si esset ex se nata, non multo secus.

20 pro *Seyffert praeeunte Bosio*: *om. P*   23 aës *Camerarius*: aes foras *Foster*
27 poscunt neminem *Camerarius*: neminem poscunt *P*   30 comoediai
Pareus: comedia *BVE*: comediae *JZ*   31 Clerumenoe *L. Valla*:
Clerumoene *BV, E* (Clerri-): Clarumoenoe *J*   32 Diphilus *VEJ*:
Deiphilus *B*   38–188 *praesto est A*   40 conspicatust primulo *A* (*cf.
Amph. 737*): conspicatus est primo *P, Seruius* (*ad Aen. 10.615*)   45 fecit
A: facit *P*   46 quasi si *P*: quasi *A*

postquam ea adoleuit ad eam aetatem út uiris
placere posset, eam puellam híc senex
amat efflictim, ét item contra filius.
nunc sibi utérque contra legiones parat,   50
paterque filiusque, clam alter alterum.
pater adlegauit uilicum qui posceret
sibi istánc uxorem; is sperat, si ei sit data,
sibi fore paratas clam uxorem excubias foris.
filius is autem armigerum adlegauit suom   55
qui sibi eam uxorem poscat; scit, si id impetret
futurum quod amat intra praesepis suas.
senis uxor sensit uirum amóri operam dare;
propterea úna consentit cum filio.
ille autem postquam filium sensit suom   60
eandem illam amare et esse impedimento sibi,
hinc adulescentem peregre ablegauit pater.
sciens ei mater dat operam absenti tamen.
is, ne exspectetis, hodie in hac comoedia
in urbem non redibit: Plautus noluit;   65
pontem interrupit, quí erat ei in itinere.
sunt hic inter se quos nunc credo dicere:
'quaeso hercle, quíd istuc est? seruiles nuptiae?
seruin uxorem ducent aut poscent sibi?
nouom attulerunt, quod fit nusquam gentium.'   70
at ego aio id fieri in Graecia et Carthagini,
et hic in nostra terra, †in Apulia;
maioreque opere íbi seruiles nuptiae

47 ea *A*: om. *P*   48 eam *A*: at eam *P*   51 paterque *A*: pater *P*
alterum *AB*: alterumque *VEJ*   53 istanc *A*: istam *P*   is *del. Bothe*
54 uxorem *BVE*: uxore *AJ*   55 is *A*: om. *P* allegauit *P*: adlegat *A*
59 propterea ea *Camerarius*   60 filium sensit *A*: sensit filium *P*   61 et *del.*
Fleckeisen   62 ablegauit *P*: ablegat *A*   63 ei mater *A*: eius mater
ei *P*   absenti *P*: adsenti *A*   65 redibit *A*: rediuit *P*   66 in *P*: om. *A*
67 inter se quos nunc credo *A*: quos credo nunc inter se *P*   71 aio *AJ*:
alio *B*: alia *VE*   id *A*: hoc *P*   72 terra in Apulia *AP*: terra, terra in
Apulia *Gruter*: terra, terra in Apula *Seyffert*: terra, in terra Apulia *Lindsay*
73 opere *A*: opera *P*

quam liberales etiam curari solent.
id ni fit, mecum pignus si quis uolt dato   75
in urnam mulsi, Poenus dum iudex siet,
uel Graecus adeo, uel mea causa Apulus.
quid nunc? nihil agitis? sentio, nemo sitit.
reuortar ád illam puellam éxpositiciam,
quam serui summa ui sibi uxorem expetunt.   80
ea inuenietur et pudica et libera,
ingenua Atheniensis, neque quicquam stupri
faciet profecto in hac quidem comoedia.
mox hercle uero, post transactam fabulam,
argentum si quis dederit, ut ego suspicor,   85
ultro ibit nuptum, non manebit auspices.
tantum est. ualete, bene rem gerite, uincite
uirtute uera, quod fecistis antidhac.

77 apulus *AE*: appulus *BVJ*   78 quid *AB²*; quod *B¹*: qui *VEJ*
79 illam puellam *AP*: puellam illam *Pylades*   84 transactam fabulam *A*:
transacta fabula *P*   87 uincite *A*: et uincite *P*   88 uera *AP*: uostra *F*

ACTVS I

OLYMPIO   I 1

Non mihi licere meam rem me solum, ut uolo,
loqui atque cogitare sine ted arbitro?   90
quid tu, malum, me sequere?

CHALINVS

              quia certum est mihi
quasi umbra, quoquo tu ibis, te semper sequi.
quin edepol etiam si in crucem uis pergere,
sequi decretumst. dehinc conicito ceterum,
possisne necne clam me sutelis tuis   95
praeripere Casinam uxorem, proinde ut postulas.
OL. quid tibi negotist mecum? CH. quid ais,
                         impudens?
quid in urbe reptas, uilice haud magni preti?
OL. lubet. CH. quin ruri es in praefectura tua?
quin potius quod legatum est tibi negotium,   100
id curas, atque urbanis rebus te apstines?
huc mihi uenisti sponsam praereptum meam.
abi rús, abi díerectus tuam in prouinciam.
OL. Chaline, non sum oblitus officium meum;
praefeci ruri recte qui curet tamen.   105
ego huc quod ueni in urbem si impetrauero,
uxorem ut istam ducam quam tu deperis,
bellam et tenellam Casinam, conseruam tuam,
quando ego eam mecum rus uxorem abduxero,
ruri incubabo usque in praefectura mea.   110
CH. tun illam ducas? hercle me suspendio

89–98 *personarum notas in P turbatas correxit Acidalius*   92 tu ibeis (*sic*) te
semper sequi *A*   ibis tu te persequi *P*   97 negotist mecum *A*: negoti
mecum est *P*   98 haud *A*: hic *P*   102 mihi *A*: *om. P*   106 si *A*:
nisi *P*   107 istam *A*: istanc *P*   109 ego eam *P*: eam *A*   110 ruri]
rur· *A*: iure *B* (*ex* riure) *VE*¹: rure *E*²*J*   111 tun *A*: tu *P*

quam tu eius potior fias satiust mortuom.
OL. mea praedast illa; proin tu te in laqueum induas.
CH. ex sterculino effosse, túa illaec praeda sit?
OL. scies hóc ita esse. CH. uae tibi! OL. quot te
                                    modis   115
si uiuo, habebo in nuptiis miserum meis!
CH. quid tu mihi facies? OL. egone quid faciam tibi?
primum omnium huic lucebis nóuae nuptae facem;
postilla ut semper improbus nihilique sis;
postid locorum, quando ad uillam ueneris,   120
dabitur tibi amphora una et una semita,
fons unus, unum ahenum et octo dolia;
quae nisi erunt semper plena, ego te implebo flagris.
ita te aggerunda curuom aqua faciam probe
ut postilena possit ex te fieri.   125
post autem ruri nisi tu aceruom éderis,
aut quasi lumbricus terram, quod te postules
gustare quicquam, numquam edepol Ieiunium
ieiunumst aeque atque ego te ruri reddibo.
postid, quom lassus fueris et famelicus,   130
noctu ut condigne te cubes curabitur.
CH. quid facies? OL. concludere in fenestram
                                 firmiter,
unde auscultare possis quóm ego illam ausculer.
quom míhi illa dicet, 'mi animule, mi Olympio,
mea uita, mea mellilla, mea festiuitas,   135
sine tuos ocellos deosculer, uoluptas mea,

112 satius est P: satis est A   114 sit A: est P   115 totum uersum
Olympioni dat A   118 huic] hic Seyffert   119 nihilique A: nihilque P
sis] eris Leo u. del. Guyet, quem secuti sunt edd. complures   120 locorum P:
locarum A uillam A: illam P   121 semita] seria Pius   126 ruri nisi
AB: nisi ruri VEJ: erui nisi Leo aceruom] aut eruom Lambinus   128 ia-
iunium F. Skutsch   129 ieiunum est Lambinus: ieiunium est P: inunumst
uel iaiunumst A: iaiunumst F. Skutsch (Kl. Schr. 74; cf. 803)   132 concludere P: non cludere A fenestram P: festram Bothe: fenstram Fleckeisen:
fenestra A   133 ausculer A: osculer P

sine amabo ted amari, meus festus dies,
meus púllus passer, mea columba, mi lepus',
quom míhi haec dicentur dicta, tum tu, furcifer,
quasi mus, in medio parieté uorsabere.   140
nunc ne tu te mihi respondere postules,
abeo intro; taedet tui sermonis. — CH. te sequor.
hic quídem pol certo nil ages síne med arbitro. —

ACTVS II

CLEOSTRATA   II 1

Obsignate cellas, referte anulum ad me.
ego huc transeo in proxumum ad meam uicinam.   145
uir si quid uolet me, facite hinc accersatis.

PARDALISCA

prandium iusserat   sénex sibi parari.
        CL. st!
táce atque abi; neque paro   neque hodie coquetur.
quando is mi et filio áduorsatur suo   150
        animi amorisque causa sui,
        flagítium íllud hominis,
            ego illúm fame,
            ego illúm siti,
maledictis, malefactis amatorem ulciscar.   155
ego pól illum probe incommodis dictis angam;
faciam uti proinde ut est dignus uitam colat
        Acheruntis pabulum,

137 sine amabo te amari P (ted Camerarius): sine uero amari te A
140 pariete P: pariet· (e uel i) A: parieti Guyet   uersabere B²: uersauere
AB¹V (uors-) E   142 tui sermonis A: sermonis tui P   143 med AJ:
met BVE¹: me E²   145 uicinam P: uiciniam A ·   146 hinc A: hinc me
P   accersatis AEJ: arcersatis BV   148 st A (in fine u. 147): sta P (init.
u. 149)   150 aduorsatur suo P: suo aduersatur A   152-4 uno uersu A
157 ut A: om. P   dignus P: dignam A

   flagiti pérsequentem,
   stabulum nequitiae.   160
nunc huc meas fortunas   eo quéstum ád uicinam.   161-2
sed fóris concrepuit   atque éa ipsa eccam egreditur
                                      foras.
non pol per tempus   iter huc mi incepi.

MYRRHINA   II 2

Sequimíni, comites, in proxumum me húc. heus uos,
        ecquis haéc quae lóquor audit?   165-6
   ego hic éro, uir si aut quispíam quaeret.
   nam ubi domi sola sum, sópor manus caluitur.   168-9
   iussin colum ferri mihi?   CL. Myrrhina, salue.   170-1
MY. salue mecastor.   sed quid tu es tristis,
                        amabo?   172-3
CL. ita sólent omnes   quae sunt male nuptae;   174-5
domi et foris aégre quod sit   satis semper est.   176-7
   nam ego ibam ad te. MY. et pol   ego istuc ad te.
   sed quid est quod tuo nunc animo aegrest?
   nam quod tibist aégre   idem míhist diuidiae.   180-1
CL. credo ecastor, nam uicinam neminem amo merito
                   mágis quam te;
      nec qua in plura sunt   183a
      mihi quae ego uelim.   b
MY. amo te, atque istuc expeto scire quid sit.   184-5
CL. pessumis me modis despicatur domi.
  MY. hem, quid est? dic idem (nam pol hau sátis meo

161-2 huc *A*: hinc *P*   uicinam *A*: uicinas *P*   163 ea ipsa eccam *P*: ipsa
ecca *A*: eapse eccam *Bothe* foras *P*: om. *A*   164 pol *P*: om. *A* huc *A*:
om. *P*   165-6 loquor *A*: loquar *P*   168-9 manus caluitur *A*, *Nonius*:
manu scalpitur *P*   176-7 sit] siet *Schoell*   178 isto *C. F. W. Mueller*
180-1 diuidiae *A*: diuidue *P*   183a qua in] quacum *Camerarius* sunt *P*:
sint *A*   184-5 quid sit *AB*: quidem *V*: quid est *EƷ* *in fine uersus* ‡ uir *A*
186 *sic A*: uir me habet pessimis despicatam modis (= 189) *P* *post* 186 *P*
habet 190: *recto loco posuit Acidalius*   187 *uerba* quid est *Myrrhinae continuat*
P, Cleostratae attribuit A idem *A*: idem hoc *P*

corde accepi querellas tuas), opsecro.
CL. uir me habet pessumis despicatam modis,
nec mihi ius meum óptinendi optio est.   190
MY. mira sunt, uera si praedicas, nam uiri
ius suom ad mulieres optinere haud queunt.
CL. quin mihi ancillulam ingratiis postulat,
quae mea est, quae meo educta sumptu siet,
    uilico suo sé dare;   195
    séd ipsus eam amat.   MY. obsecro,
    táce.   CL. nam hic nunc licet dícere:
  nos sumus.   MY. ita est. unde ea tibi est?
nam peculi probam nihil habere addecet
clam uirum, ét quae habet, partum ei haud
                    commode est,   200
quin uiro aut subtrahat aut stupro inuenerit.
hoc uiri censeo esse omne quicquid tuom est.
CL. tu quidem aduórsum tuam amicam   omnia
                    loqueris.
  MY. tace sís, stulta, et mi ausculta.
  noli sis tu illi aduorsari;   205
sine amet, sine quod lubet íd faciat, quando tibi nil
            domi délicuom est.   206-7
CL. satin sána es? nam tuquidem aduorsus tuam istaéc
        rem loquere.   MY. insipiens,   208-9
semper tu huic uerbo uitato abs tuo uíro.   CL. cui
      uerbo?   MY. i fóras, mulier.   210-11
    CL. st!
táce.   MY. quid est?   CL. em!   MY. quis est?
      quem uides?   CL. uir eccum it.

189-534 deest A   190 huc traiecit Acidalius: post 186 P   193 ingratiis
recc.: ingratis BVE   194 educta recc.: educata BVE   196-8 sic Acidalius: uerba obsecro...sumus Myrrhinae, ita est Cleostratae dat P   197 tace]
dice Lindsay   200 commode Lipsius: commodi P   201 uiro B: uero
VEJ   208-9 istaec Bothe: ista BV: istam EJ   210-11 abs B¹: ab cett.
i] ei P   212 CL. st Gruter: est B (spatio ante uerbum relicto) VE   213 em
Mueller: hem P

intro abi, adpropera, age amabo.   MY. ímpetras; abeo.
CL. mox magis cum otium míhi et tíbi erit,   215
igitur tecum loquar. nunc uale.   MY. ualeas. —

LYSIDAMVS   II 3

Omníbus rebus ego amorem credo et nitoribus nitidis
                                        anteuenire,
nec pótis quicquam commemorari quod plus salis
                                        plúsque leporis [hodie]
habeat; coquos équidem nímis demiror, qui utuntur
                                        condimentis,
eos éo condimento uno non utier, omníbus quod
                                        praestat.   220
nam ubi amor condimentum inierit, cuiuis placiturum
                                        credo;
neque salsum neque suaue esse potest quicquam, ubi
                                        amor non admiscetur;
fel quod amarumst, id mel faciet, hominem ex tristi
                                        lepidum et lenem.
hanc ego de me coniecturam domi fácio mágis quam ex
                                        auditis;
qui quóm amo Casinam, mágis niteo, munditiis
                                        Munditiam antideo;   225
myropolas omnis sollicitó, ubicumque est lepidum
                                        unguentum, unguor,

214-16 *personarum notas in P turbatas corr. Dissaldeus*   214 age] *del. Geppert ut cretici fierent*   215 mihi et tibi erit *BVE*: et mihi erit et tibi *JF*: et mihi
et tibi erit *Weise*   217 credo ego amorem *Hermann* (= *Cist. 203*): amorem
ego credo *R. Klotz*   *et del. Bothe*   nitidis *J*: itidis *BVE*   218 hodie *del.
Guyet*   219 nimis *del. Meursius*   qui] tot qui *Guyet duce Pylade*   220 non
B (in marg.) E² Ital.: om. P   221 inierit *P*: inerit *Ital.*   placiturum *J
Ital.*: placituram *BVE*: placitura escam (*uel rem*) *R. Klotz duce Seyffert*
225 quom *Gronouius*: quam *P*   casinam *VEJ*: casiam *B*   niteo *Gulielmius*:
inicio *P* (-tio *VE*): multo *Spengel*   qui, quom amo, casiam magis inicio *Schoell*:
qui, quom amo Casinam magis, tanto *Seyffert*   mundiatiam antideo *Camerarius*:
munditianti deo *P* (-cianti *BJ*)   226 miropolas *B²J*: miro pol has *B¹VE*
est *J*: es *BVE*

ut illí placeam; et placeo, ut uideor. sed uxór me
                              excruciat, quia uiuit.
tristem astare aspicio; blande haec mihi mala res
                              appellanda est.
uxor mea meaque amoenitas, quid tú agis?   CL. ábi
                        atque abstíne manum.
LY. heia, mea Iuno, non decet ésse te tam tristem
                              tuo Ioui.   230
quo nunc abis? CL. mítte me. LY. mane. CL. non
            maneo.   LY. at pol ego te sequar.
  CL. obsecro, sanun es?   LY. sanus. quam ted amo!
  CL. nolo ames.   LY. non potes impetrare.
                            CL. enecas.
  LY. uera dicas uelim.   CL. credo ego istuc tibi.
  LY. respice, o mi lepos.   CL. nempe ita ut tu mihi es.   235
  unde hic, amabo, unguenta olent?   LY. oh perii!
manufesto míser teneor. cesso caput pállio détergere?
ut te bónus Mercurius perdat, myropola, quia haec
                            mihi dedisti.
CL. eho tu nihili, cana culex, uix teneor quin quae
                        décent te dicam.
sénecta aetate únguentatus per uias, ignaue, incedis?   240
LY. pol ego amico dédi cuidam operam, dum emit
                unguenta.   CL. ut cíto commentust!
ecquid te pudet?   LY. ómnia quae tu uis.   CL. ubi
                    ín lustra iacuisti?
LY. egone in lustra?   CL. scío plus quam tu me
             arbitrare.   LY. quid id est? quid scis?

227 placeam *J*: placeat *BVE*   228 res] mers *Brix* (*cf*. 754)   232 quam]
quom *recc.*   233 enecas *J*: enegas *BVE*   236 unguenta olent *E¹J*:
unguenta adolent *B*: unguent adolent *VE¹*   238 quia] qui *Lambinus*
239 nihili cana culex *J*: nihil hic anaculix *BVE*   240 senecta] senectan
Schoell duce Mueller   unguentatus *B¹*: unguentus *VEJ*: unguentis *B¹*
241 commentus est *Pylades*: commentatus est *J*: commendatus est *BVE*
242 quae tu uis omnia *Geppert* iacuisti *P*, *Nonius*: tu iacuisti *Ussing* (tu *e*
u. 243)   243 scis *Geppert*: tu scis *P*

CL. te sene omnium ⟨senum⟩ senem néminèm esse
                          ignauiorem.
unde is, nihili? úbi fuisti? úbi lustratu's? ubi bibisti?	245
mádes mecastor: uíde palliolum ut rugat.	LY. di me
                          et te infèlicent,
sí ego in os meum hodie uini guttam indidi.
    CL. immo age ut lubet,	bíbe, es, disperde rem.
LY. ohe, iam satis, uxor, est;	comprime te,
                    nimium tinnis.	249-50
relinque aliquantum orationis, cras quod mecum litiges.
sed quid ais? iam domuisti animum, potius ut quod uir
                            uelit
fieri, id facias, quam aduorsere contra?	CL. qua de
              re?	LY. rogas?
super ancilla Casina, ut detur nuptum nostro uilico,
seruo frugi atque úbi illi bene sit ligno, aqua calida,
                      cibo,	255
uestimentis, ubique educat pueros quos pariat * ,
potius quam illi seruo nequam des, armigero atque
                    improbo,
cuí homení hodie peculi nummus non est plumbeus.
CL. mirum ecastor te senecta aetate officium tuom
non meminisse.	LY. quid iam?	CL. quia, si facias
              recte et commode,	260
me sinas curare ancillas, quae mea est curatio.
LY. qui, malum, homini scutigerulo dare lubet?
            CL. quía enim filio

244 senum senem *uel* senum hominem *Spengel*: senem *P*: senum *Dissaldeus*
245 is *E¹J*: his *BVE¹*	lustratu's *Lambinus*: lustratus *P*	bibisti *B¹J*:
uiuisti *B¹VE* (unde es nihil ubi lustretur ibi bibatur *Nonius*)	246 mades
Schoell: adest *P*	di *B*: de *VE*: dem *J*	infelicent *Pius*: inflicent *B*: infilicem
VE: infelicem *J*	247 hodie *B²*: om. *cett.*	249-50 est del. *Leo*	tinnis
J: tinnes *BVE*	253 quam *Pylades*: potius quam *P*	256 pariat sibi
Schoell (sibi *e* nisi *u.* 257)	257 potius áel. *Bothe*, *Ussing*	atque *Came-
rarius*: nisi atque *P*: nili (*i.e. nihili*) atque *Merula*	260 recte *Ital.*: certe *P*
et *VEJ*: aut *B²*	261 me sinas curare *B*: curare me sinas *VEJ*	262-3
filio *cum* unico *permutauit Bothe*

nos oportet opitulari único. LY. at quamquam
                                          unicust,
nihilo magis unicus est ille mihi filius quam ego illí
                                              pater;
illum mi aequiust quam me illi quae uolo concedere.   265
CL. tu ecastor tibi, homo, malam rem quaeris;
                                  subolet, sentio.
LY. egone? CL. tu. nam quid friguttis? quíd istuc
                              tam cupide cupis?
LY. ut enim frugi seruo detur potius quam seruo
                                      improbo.
CL. quid si ego impetro atque exoro a uilico, causa mea
ut eam illi permittat? LY. quid si ego autem ab
                              armigero impetro   270
eam illí permittat? atque hoc credo ímpetrassere.
CL. conuenit. uis tuis Chalinum huc euocem uerbis
                                        foras?
tú eum orato, ego autem orabo uilicum. LY. sane uolo.
CL. iam hic erit. nunc experiemur nostrum uter sit
                                      blandior. —
LY. Hercules dique istam perdant, quod nunc liceat
                                      dícere.   275
ego discrucior miser amore, illa autem quasi ob
                                  industriam
mi aduorsatur. subolet hoc iam uxori quod ego
                                    machinor;
propter eam rem magis armigero dat operam de
                                    industria.
qui illum di omnes deaeque perdant.

264 ille unicust *Geppert, edd.* (*sed cf. Capt. 321*)   266 *uerba* subolet, sentio
Lysidamo dant Lambinus alii, conlato u. 277; *sed cf.* 58 (*senis uxor sensit*), *Pseud.*
421, Tri. 698, Bacch. 298   267 egone *Camerarius*: egon P   271 ut eam
Guyet   credo me *Reiz duce Camerario*   272 conuenit *Ital.*: conueni tu P
uis P (ius VE): uin *Geppert*   273 eum BVE: illum *J*   uilicum *J*: uilico
BVE   276 illa autem B¹: autem illa B¹VE   industriam E¹: industria
cett.

CHALINVS   II 4
Te uxor aiebat tua
me uocare.   LY. ego enim uocari iussi.   CH. eloquere
quid uelis.   280
LY. primum ego te porrectiore fronte uólo mecum loqui;
stultitia est ei te esse tristem cuius potestas plus potest.
próbum et frugi hominem te iam pridem esse arbitror.
CH. intellego.   283-4
quin, si ita arbitrare, emittis me manu?   LY. quin id
uolo.   285
sed nihil est me cupere factum, nisi tu factis adiuuas.
CH. quid uelis modo id uelim me scire.   LY. ausculta,
égo loquar.
Casinam ego uxorem promisi uilico nostro dare.
CH. at tua uxor filiusque promiserunt mihi.   LY. scio.
sed utrum nunc tu caelibem te ésse mauis liberum   290
an maritum seruom aetatem degere et gnatos tuos?
optio haec tua est; utram harum uis condicionem accipe.
CH. liber si sim, meo periclo uiuam; nunc uiuo tuo.
de Casina certum est concedere homini nato nemini.
LY. intro abi atque actutum uxorem huc euoca ante
aedis cito,   295
et sitellam huc tecum efferto cúm aqua et sortis.
CH. sátis placet.
LY. ego pol istam iam aliquouorsum tragulam decidero.
nam si sic nihil impetrare potero, saltem sortiar.
ibi ego te et suffragatores tuos ulciscar.   CH. attamen
mihi obtínget sors.   LY. ut quídem pol pereas cruciatu
malo.   300

279 aiebat *B¹J*: alebat *B¹VE*   280 iussi *B²J*: iussit *B¹VE*: iussi te *Z*
281 porrectiore *V¹J*: porrectiorem *BE*   fronte *VJ*: frontem *BE*   282 esse
B¹E²J: esset *B¹VE¹*   283-4 probum et frugi *Seyffert*: pro bone (bonae *B¹*)
frugi *P*: perbonae frugi *Pylades*: te bonae frugi *Lambinus*   te *J*: *om. BVE*
iam pridem *BVE*: *om. J*   287 me scire *Merula*: miscere *P*   loquar *P* (-or
J): eloquar *Mueller*   297 deiecero 'aliqui' secundum *Vallam*   298 potero
VEJ: potuero *B*

CH. míhi illa nubet; machinare quidlubet quouis modo.
LY. ábin hinc ab oculis?   CH. inuitus me uides:
                uiuam tamen. —
LY. sumne ego míser homo? satin omnes res sunt
                aduorsae mihi?
iam metuo ne Olympionem mea uxor exorauerit
ne Casinam ducat. si id factum est, ecce me nullum
                senem.   305
si non impetrauit, etiam specula in sórtitust mihi.
si sors autem decolassit, gladium faciam culcitam
eumque incumbam. sed progreditur optume eccum
                Olympio.

OLYMPIO   II 5

Vna edepol opera in furnum calidum condito
atque ibi torreto me pro pane rubido,   310
era, qua istuc opera a me impetres quod postulas.
LY. saluos sum, salua spes est, ut uerba audio.
OL. quid tu me tua, era, libertate territas?
qui si tu nolis filiusque etiam tuos,
uobis inuitis atque amborum ingratiis   315
una libella liber possum fieri.
LY. quid istúc est? quicum litigas, Olympio?
OL. cum eadem qua tu semper.   LY. cum uxori mea?
OL. quam tu mi uxorem? quasi uenator tu quidem es;
dies átque noctes cum cane aetatem exigis.   320
LY. quid agit? quid loquitur tecum?   OL. orat,
                obsecrat,
ne Casinam uxorem ducam.   LY. quid tu postea?

301 quidlubet *B²VEJ*: quod lubet *B¹ Ital.*   303 res *J*: *om. BVE*
305 Casinam *VEJ*: casiam *B*   306 in sortitust *Acidalius*: insortita sunt
P: in sortist *Guyet duce Camerario*   307 decolassit *Ital.*: decollassit *P* (-asit
VE)   311 qua *Brix*: quam *P*   istuc *Mueller*: istam *P*   opera *BV*: operam
EJ   313 tua era *Leo*: uera *BVE*: hera *J*   314 qui *uel* quin *Acidalius*:
quid *P*   318 uxori *Lindsay*: uxore *P*: uxoren *Bentley*   321 agit *B*: ait
V¹EJ

OL. negaui enim ipsi me concessurum Ioui,
si is mecum oraret. LY. di te seruassint mihi!
OL. nunc in fermento totast; ita turget mihi.   325
LY. ego edepol illam mediam dirruptam uelim.
OL. credo edepol esse, siquidem tu frugi bonae es.
uerum edepol tua mihi odiosa est amatio;
inimica est tua uxor mihi, inimicus filius,
inimici familiares. LY. quíd id refert tua?   330
unus tibi hic dum propitius sit Iuppiter,
tu istos minutos cáue deos flócci feceris.
OL. nugae sunt istae magnae; quasi tu nescias
repente ut emoriantur humani Ioues.
sed tandem si tu Iuppiter sis mortuos,   335
cum ad deos minores redierit regnum tuom,
quis mihi subueniet tergo aut capiti aut cruribus?
LY. opinione melius res tibi habet tua,
si hoc impetramus, ut ego cum Casina cubem.
OL. non hercle opinor posse; ita uxor acriter   340
tua instat ne mihi detur. LY. at ego sic agam:
coniciam sortis in sitellam et sortiar
tibi et Chalino. ita rem natam intellego;
necessum est uorsis gladiis depugnarier.
OL. quid si sors aliter quam uoles euenerit?   345
LY. benedice. dis sum fretus, deos sperabimus.
OL. non égo istud uerbum émpsim tittibilicio.
nam omnes mortales dis sunt freti, sed tamen
uidi ego dis fretos saepe multos decipi.

---

326 ego edepol *J*: edepol ego *BVE*   332 minutos *B*: munitos *VEJ*
335 mortuus *Acidalius*: emortuus *P* (*ex* emoriantur 334)   337 subueniet
Ital.: subueniens *P*   338 opinione melius *Saracenus*: opinionem eius *P*
tibi *del Pareus*: se *Koch*   habet *Camerarius*: habeat *P*   341 instat *B¹J*:
instar *B¹VE*   344 necessum est *VEJ*: necessu est *B*: necessust *Geppert*
346 sperabimus *Dousa*: sperauimus *P. Seruius*   347 istud *BE, Festus*:
istuc *VJ* empsim *Acidalius*: emissum *BE*: emisim *VJ*: empsi cum *Festus*
tittibilicio *Festus*: tittiuilicio *Fulgentius*: tit tibi stalitio *V*: tit tibi est alicio *J*:
tibi stalitio *B*: ut tibi stalitio *E¹*: ut tibi est stalino *F*   349 dis fretos *B*:
disertos *VEJ*

LY. st! táce parumper.　OL. quid uis?　LY. eccum

exit foras　　350

Chalinus intus cum sitella et sortibus.

nunc nos conlatis signis depugnabimus.

CLEOSTRATA　　　　　　　II 6

Face, Chaline, certiorem me quid méus uir me uelit.

CHALINVS

ille edepol uidere ardentem te extra portam mortuam.

CL. credo ecastor uelle.　CH. at pol ego haud credo,

sed certo scio.　　355

LY. plus artificum est mihi quam rebar; hariolum hunc

habeo domi.

quid si propius attollamus signa eamusque obuiam?

sequere. quid uos agitis?　CH. adsunt quae

imperauisti omnia:

uxor, sortes, situla atque egomet.　OL. te uno adest

plus quam ego uolo.

CH. tibi quidem edepol ita uidetur; stimulus ego nunc

sum tibi,　　360

fodico corculum; adsudascis iam ex metu, mastigia.

LY. táce, Chaline.　CH. comprime istunc.　OL. immo

istunc qui didicit dare.

LY. adpone hic sitellam, sortis cedo mihi; animum

aduortite.

atque ego censui aps te posse hoc me impetrare, uxor mea,

350 st tace *B¹V*: S. (*i.e. SENEX*) tace *B²J*: sed tace *E*　parumper *Camerarius*: parum *B¹VEJ*　352 conlatis *B²J*: consolatis *VE*　depugnabimus *B²J*: depugnauimus *B¹VE*　353 me quid *J*: equide *B¹V*: equidem *B²E*　354 mortuam *Ritschl*: metuam *P*: Metiam *ante Ritschl plerique*　355 credo *B*: crede *VEJ*　uelle *B¹*: uellem *B¹VE*: uellet *J*　CH. *add. Pareus*　356 habeo *V¹J*: abeo *BV¹²E*　357 eamusque *B²*: famusque *B¹VE*: fiamusque *J*　358 imperauisti *B²J*: impetrauisti *cett.*　359 OL. *Ladewig*: LY. *BJ*　361 fodico *Bentley*: eo dico *P*　adsudascis *B⁴*: adsudasis *cett.* (-ssis *J*)　362 LY. *Z*: CL. *BJ*　CH. *add. Camerarius*　(comprime) istunc] istum *Pylades*　qui didicit *Lipsius*: quid dicit *P*　364 atqui *Pius*　me *Lambinus*: mecum *P*

3.2

Casina ut uxor mihi daretur, et nunc etiam censeo.   365
CL. tibi daretur illa? LY. mihi enim – ah, non id
                                        uolui dicere;
dum 'mihi' uolui, 'huic' dixi, atque adeo mihi dum
                                        cupio – perperam
iam dudum hercle fabulor.   CL. pol tu quidem, atque
                                        etiam facis.
LY. huic – immo hercle mihi – uah, tandem redii uix
                                        ueram in uiam.
CL. per pol saepe peccas.   LY. ita fit, ubi quid tanto
                                        opere expetas.   370
sed te uterque tuo pro iure, ego atque hic, oramus.
                                        CL. quid est?
LY. dicam enim, mea mulsa: de istac Casina huic
                                        nostro uilico
gratiam facias.   CL. at pol ego neque fació neque censeo.
LY. tum igitur ego sortis utrimque iam ⟨diribeam⟩.
                                        CL. quis uotat?
LY. optumum atque aequissumum istud esse iure
                                        iudico.   375
postremo, si illuc quod uolumus eueniet, gaudebimus;
sin secus, patiemur animis aequis. téne sortem tibi.
uíde quid scriptum est.   OL. unum.   CH. iniquom
                                        est, quía isti príus quam mihi data est.
LY. accipe hanc sis.   CH. cedo.   OL. mane; unum
                                        uenit in mentem modo.
uíde ne qua illic insit alia sortis sub aqua.
                                        CH. uerbero,   380

369 redii *J*: redi *BVE*   uix ueram *B*: uixeram *VEJ*   371 ego atque
Camerarius: atque ego *P*   374 diribeam *add. Schoell duce Pareo*   376 *u.*
solus habet (in margine) *B*   si *Camerarius: om. B*   378 quid *B*: quod *VEJ*
scriptum est *B²*: scriptum *cett.*   CH. iniquum est *B*: inicus est *VE*: unicus
est *J*   data est *Weise, Geppert*: est *P*: dedit *Leo*   379–81 *personarum notas
correxit F. Groh* (*Listy Filologicke 16* (1889) *340–1*). *B habet* 379 CH. cedo
mane / 380 LY. uerbero / 381 CL. nulla est   380 qua] quae *Prisciani
codd.*   insit *B²*, *Priscian.*: sit *EJ*: sint *V*   alia sortis *Priscian.*: alias oris *B¹VE*:
alia sors *B²J*

men te censes esse? LY. nulla est. habe quietum
                                    animum modo.
OL. quod bonum atque fortunatum sit mihi –
                    CH. magnum malum –
OL. tibi quidem edepol, credo, eueniet; noui pietatem
                                    tuam.
sed mane dúm; num ista aut populna sors aut abiegnast
                                    tua?
CH. quid tu id curas? OL. quia enim metuo né in
                    aqua summa natet.   385
LY. euge! cáue. conicite sortis nunciam ambo huc.
                                    eccere.
uxor, aequa. OL. noli uxori credere. LY. habe
                                animum bonum.
OL. credo hercle, hodie deuotabit sortis, si attigerit.
                                    LY. tace.
OL. taceo. deos quaeso — CH. ut quidem tu hódie
                    cánem et furcam feras.
OL. míhi ut sortito eueniat – CH. ut quidem hercle
                    pedibus pendeas.   390
OL. at tu ut oculos emungare ex capite per nasum tuos.
quid times? paratum oportet esse iam laqueum tibi.
periisti. LY. animum aduortite ambo. OL. taceo.
                    LY. nunc tu, Cleostrata,
ne a me memores malitiose de hac re factum aut suspices,
tibi permitto: tute sorti. OL. perdis me. CH. lucrum
                                    facit.   395
CL. bene facis. CH. deos quaeso ut tua sors ex
                    sitella effugerit.

381 quietum *B²J*: quae tum *B¹VE*   382 quod *Camerarius*: quid *P*
fortunatum *Guyet*: fortunatum tuum *P*   384 mane dum *Z, Priscian.*: ne
dum *P*   386 euge *F*: auge *B¹VE*: aeuge *B²* (*ut uid.*): age *J*   ambo *Pius*:
amabo *P*   388 deuotabit *J*: deuobit *BVE* (*pro* deuouebit? *Leo*): deuorabit
Ital.   389 ut *B²E¹J*: aut *B¹VE¹*   390 sortito *Spengel*: sortitio *B²*(-icio)
VE: sortio *J*   CH. *add. Acidalius*   393 ambo *Pius*: amabo *P*   394 suspices *Pylades*: suspicere *B¹*: suscipere *B¹VEJ*

OL. ain tu? quia tute es fugitiuos, omnis te imitari

cupis?

CH. utinam tua quidem ista, sicut Herculei praedicant

quondam prognatis, in sortiendo sors deliquerit.

OL. tu ut liquescas ipse, actutum uirgis calefactabere.   400

LY. hoc age sis, Olympio. OL. si hic litteratus me

sinat.

LY. quod bonum atque fortunatum mihi sit. OL. ita

uero, et mihi.

CH. non. OL. immo hercle. CH. immo mihi hercle.

CL. hic uincet, tu uiues miser.

LY. percide os tu illi odio. age, ecquid fit? CL. ne

óbiexis manum.

OL. compressan palma an porrecta ferio? LY. age ut

uis. OL. em tibi!   405

CL. quid tibi istunc tactio est? OL. quia Iuppiter

iussit meus.

CL. féri malam, út ille, rursum. OL. perii; pugnis

caedor, Iuppiter.

LY. quid tibi tactio hunc fuit? CH. quia iussit haec

Iuno mea.

LY. patiundum est, siquidem me uiuo mea uxor imperium

exhibet.

CL. tam huic loqui licere oportet quam isti. OL. cur

omen mihi   410

uituperat? LY. malo, Chaline, tibi cauendum censeo.

CH. temperi, postquam oppugnatum est os. LY. age,

uxor, nunciam

398 CH. *J*: om. *B*   ista *Guyet* (*e u.* 399): *om. P*   Herculei *BVE¹*: Herculeis
E²J   399 in sortiendo *Nonius*: ista in sortiendo *P*   400 OL. *Ussing*:
CH. *B*: LY. *J*   402 sit *Pylades*: est *P*   403 *personarum notas in P turbatas
correxit Acidalius*   404 percide *Turnebus* (*cf. Pers. 283*): praecide *P*   odio
Seyffert: hodie *P*   fit *B²*: sit *cett.*   ne] caue *Bothe*   obiexis *Lambinus*: oblexis *P*
(-sis *J*)   405 em *Brix*: rem *BVE¹*: hem *E²J*   410 loqui *E² Ital.*: loqui
qui *P* (cui *J*)   licere *B²E²J*: liceret *B¹*: liceree *VE¹*   412 uxor *Bentley*:
uxor mea *P*   nunciam *Camerarius*: iam nunc *P*

sorti; uos aduortite animum. prae metu ubi sim nescio.
perii; cor lienosum, opinor, habeo; iam dudum salit.
de labore pectus tundit.   CL. teneo sortem.   LY. ecfer
                             foras.   415
CH. iamne mortuós?   OL. ostende. mea est.
                  CH. †mala cruciast† quidem.
CL. uictus es, Chaline.   LY. cum nos di iuuere,
                      Olympio,
gaudeo.   OL. pietate factum est mea atque maiorum
                       meum.
LY. intro abi, uxor, atque adorna nuptias.   CL. faciam
                      ut iubes.
LY. scin tu ruri ésse ad uillam longe quo ducat?
                   CL. scio.   420
LY. intro abi et, quamquam hoc tibi aegre est, támen
                fac accures.   CL. licet. —
LY. eamus nos quoque intro; hortemur ut properent.
               OL. numquid moror? —
LY. nam praesente hoc plura uerba fieri non
                  desidero. —

             CHALINVS   II 7

Si nunc me suspendam, meam operam luserim,
et praeter operam restim sumpti fecerim,   425
et meis inimicis uóluptatem creauerim.
quid opus est, qui sic mortuós equidem tamen?
sorti sum uictus; Casina nubet uilico.
atque id non tam aegrest iam uicisse uilicum,

413 prae metu *Pistoris*: praebe tu *P*   414 iam *Pylades*: iam iam *P*
416 mortuus *P*: mortuo's *Lambinus*: mortuos sum *Geppert*   mea est] mea
haec est *Geppert*   male excrucias *Schoell*: mala crux east *Camerarius*   417 di
iuuere *Spengel*: diu (dum *J*) uiuere *P*   418 meum *Pylades*: mecrum *P*
420 ruri] rus hinc *Langen*   422 hortemur *B²*: hortamur *cett.*   423 LY.
add. Dousa   hoc praesente *Guyet*   fieri *Camerarius*: *om. P*   424 suspendam
me *Reiz*   427 sic] sim *Bierma*   mortuos] mortuus sim *Geppert*: mortuus
sum *Brix*   signum interrogationis post tamen *posuit Acidalius, post* opus est *Z,*
post mortuos *Lambinus*

quam id expetiuisse opere tam magno senem,   430
ne ea míhi daretur atque ut illi nuberet.
ut illé trepidabat, ut festinabat miser,
ut sussultabat postquam uicit uilicus!
attat, concedam huc; audio aperiri fores.
mei béneuolentes atque amici prodeunt.   435
hinc ex insidiis hisce ego insidias dabo.

OLYMPIO   II 8

sine módo rus ueniat; ego remittam ad te uirum
cum furca in urbem tamquam carbonarium.

LYSIDAMVS

ita fieri oportet.   OL. factum et curatum dabo.
LY. uolui Chalinum, si domi esset, mittere   440
'tecum obsonatum, ut etiam in maerore insuper
inimico nostro miseriam hanc adiungerem.
CH. recessim cedam ad parietem; imitabor nepam.
captandust horum clanculum sermo mihi.
nam illorum me alter cruciat, alter macerat.   445
at candidatus cedit hic mastigia,
stimulorum loculi. protollo mortem mihi;
certum est, hunc Acheruntem praemittam prius.
OL. ut tibi ego inuentus sum obsequens! quod maxume
cupiebas, eius copiam feci tibi.   450
erit hódie tecum quod amas clam uxórem.   LY. tace.
ita me di bene ament ut ego uix reprimo labra,
ob istánc rem quin te deosculer, uoluptás mea.
CH. quid, deosculere? quae res? quae uoluptás tua?

---

434 aperiri E^1: opperiri B: operiri E^1J: operari V fores *Merula*: foras P
435 mei *Mueller*: mihi P beneuolentes] beneuolentis BE^1: beneuolenti
VE^1J amici *Gulielmius*: ame BV: amme E: ad me J 436 hisce *Camerarius*:
hic P: his *Pylades*   437 ueniat *Camerarius*: eueniat P 443 recessim]
retrouorsum *Nonius*   cedam P, *Nonius*: dabo me *Festus*   446 ut *Geppert*
447 mortem protollo *Brugmann*   451 tatae *Schoell*   454 deosculere
Meursius: deosculer P res est *Camerarius*   uoluptas quae *Dousa*

†ecfodere hercle hic uolt, credo, uesicam uilico. 455
OL. ecquíd amas nunc me? LY. immo edepol me
                quam te minus.
licetne amplecti te? CH. quid, 'amplecti'?
                OL. licet.
LY. ut, quia te tango, mel mihi uideor lingere.
OL. ultro te, amator! apage te a dorso meo.
CH. illuc est, illuc, quod hic hunc fecit uilicum. 460
et idém me pridem, cum ei aduorsum ueneram,
facere atriensem uoluerat sub ianua.
OL. ut tibi morigerus hodie, ut uóluptati fui!
LY. ut tibi, dum uiuam, bene uelim plus quam mihi.
CH. hodie hercle, opinor, hi conturbabunt pedes; 465
solet híc barbatos sane sectari senex.
LY. ut ego hódie Casinam deosculabor! ut mihi
bona multa faciam clam meam uxorem! CH. attatae!
nunc pol ego demum in rectam redii semitam.
hic ipsus Casinam deperit. habeo uiros. 470
LY. iam hercle amplexari, iam osculari gestio.
OL. sine príus deduci. quid, malum, properas?
                LY. amo.
OL. at non opinor fieri hoc posse hodie. LY. potest,
siquidém cras censes te posse emitti manu.
CH. enim uéro huc aures mágis sunt adhibendae mihi; 475
iam ego uno in saltu lepide apros capiam duos.
LY. apud hunc sodalem meum atque uicinum mihi
locus est paratus; eí ego amorem omnem meum
concredui; is mihi se locum dixit dare.

455 credo hercle ecfodere hic uolt *Bothe* 456 ecquid *B¹*: ecquis *cett.*
461 et idem] cidem (= idem, *cf. Mil. 1207*) *Lambinus*: itidem *Geppert*
465 hi *J¹*, *Lambinus*: iis *BVE*: is *J¹* 468 clam *Pius*: om. *P* CH. attate
B¹J (attat): attate CH. *VE* (artare *E¹*, aptate *E¹*, astute *E³*) 470-1 habeo
uiros. SEN. iam *Pylades*: SEN. abeo. uiros iam *B¹VEJ*: SEN. abeo rus.
iam *B¹* 472 properas *B*: operas *VEJ* 474 posse te *Pylades* emitti
manu *Camerarius*: mitti manu *VE¹J*: manumitti *B* 478 amorem omnem
Pylades: omnem amorem *P*

OL. quid eius uxor? ubi erit?   LY. lepide repperi.   480
mea uxór uocabit huc eam ad se in nuptias,
ut hic sit secum, se adiuuet, secum cubet.
ego iussi, et dixit se facturam uxor mea.
illa hic cubabit; uir aberit faxo domo.
tu rus uxorem duces; id rus hic erit,   485
tantisper dum égo cum Casina faciam nuptias.
hinc tu ante lucem rus cras duces postea.
satin astu?   OL. docte.   CH. áge modo, fabricamini;
malo hercle uostro tam uorsuti uiuitis.
LY. scin quid nunc facias?   OL. loquere.   LY. téne
                                    marsuppium.   490
abi atque obsona, propera, sed lepide uolo,
molliculas escas, út ipsa mollicula est.   OL. licet.
LY emito sepiolas, lopadas, lolligunculas,
hordeias.   CH. immo triticeias, si sapis.
LY. soleas.   CH. qui, quaeso, potius quam sculponeas,   495
quibus báttuatur tibi os, sénex nequissume?
OL. uin lingulacas?   LY. quid opust, quando uxor
                                    domi est?
ea lingulaca est nobis; nam numquam tacet.
OL. in re praesenti ex copia piscaria
consulere potero quid emam.   LY. aéquom oras; abi.   500
argento parci nolo; obsonato ampliter.
nam mihi uicino hoc etiam conuento est opus,
ut quod mandaui curet.   OL. iamne abeo? LY. uolo. —
CH. tribus nón conduci possum libertatibus
quin égo illis hodie comparem magnum malum,   505

482 adiuuet B: adiutet E: aduitet V   484 hic B: huc VEJ   uir aberit
Camerarius: si uir abierit BVE¹   485 hic Gulielmius: hoc P   488 astu
Bothe: at tute BV: arture E¹: astute E²J   OL. docte B¹: om. cett.   satin
docte? OL. astute Leo   493 emito EJ: emitto BV   lopadas Fleckeisen:
lepidas P, Priscian.: lepadas Camerarius   lolligunculas (loli-) J¹, Priscian.:
lolligiungas BVE: lingunculas J¹   496 battuatur Fulgentius: babtuatur P
500 potero B¹: om. cett.   uerbum potero post quid emam transtul. Leo editores-
que recentiores   abi Camerarius: abis P   504 possim Camerarius

quinque hanc omnem rem méae erae iam faciam palam.
manufesto teneo in noxia inimicos meos.
sed si nunc facere uolt era officium suom,
nostra omnis lis est; pulchre praeuortar uiros.
nostro omine it dies; iam uicti uicimus.　　　　　　510
ibo intro, ut id quod alius condiuit coquos
ego nunc uicissim ut alio pacto condiam,
quo id quod paratum est ut paratum ne siet,
sietque íd paratum quod paratum non erat. --

ACTVS III

LYSIDAMVS　　　　　　　　　　III 1

Nunc amici ánne inimici sis imago, Alcesime,　　　515
mihi sciam; nunc specimen specitur, nunc certamen
　　　　　　　　　　　　　　　　　　　　cernitur.
cur amem me castigare, id ponito ad compendium;
'cano capite', 'aetate aliena' eo addito ad
　　　　　　　　　　　　　　　　　compendium;
'cui sit uxor', id quoque illuc ponito ad compendium.

ALCESIMVS

miseriorem ego ex amore quam te uidi neminem.　　　520
LY. fac uacent aedes.　　AL. quin edepol seruos,
　　　　　　　　　　　　　　　　ancillas domo
certum est omnis mittere ad te.　　LY. oh, nimium scite
　　　　　　　　　　　　　　　　　　scitus es.

---

507 roxia *Pylades* (*cf. Merc. 729*): noxa *P*　　509 pulchre *Pius*: pulcra
(-chra) re *BVE*: pulchra *J*　　praeuortam *Lambinus*: peruortam *Langen*
510 omine *BE²*: homine *VE¹*: omne *J*　　513 quo id quod *VE²J*: quod
id quod *B*: quid quod *E¹*: quo id quoi *Mueller*: id quod *Ussing*　　514 sitque
Pylades　id *Ussing*: ei *P*　quoi *Gronovius*　　517 cur amem me *Buecheler*:
cura meme curam exime *VEJ*: curam exime *B*　　518 u. om. *V*　ea *Angelius*
addito *B*: addita *EJ*　　522 oh *Seyffert*: eho *P*

sed facitodum merula †per uorsus quos cantat colas:
'cum cibo cum quiqui' facito ut ueniant, quasi eant
Sutrium.

AL. meminero.   LY. em, nunc énim tu demum nullo
scito scitus es.   525

cura; ego ad forum modo ibo; iam hic ero.   AL. bene
ambula.

LY. fac habeant linguam tuae aedes.   AL. quid ita?
LY. cum ueniam, uocent.

AL. attatae! caedundus tú homo es; nimias delicias facis.
LY. quid me amare refert, nisi sim doctus ac dicaculus?
sed tu cáue in quaesitione mihi sis. — AL. usque adero
domi. —   530

CLEOSTRATA   III 2

Hoc érat ecastor id quod me uir tanto opere orabat meus,
út properarem arcessere hanc huc ad me uicinam meam,
liberae aedes ut sibi essent Casinam quo deducerent.
nunc adeo nequaquam arcessam, ne illis ignauissumis
liberi loci potestas sit, uetulis ueruecibus.   535
séd eccum égreditur senáti columen, praesidium popli,
meus uicinus, meo uiro qui liberum praehibet locum.
non ecastor uilis emptu est, modius qui uenit salis.

523 merula per uersus quod *Festus*: merui aperuorsus quos *P*: maeoni
aper uersus quos *T*: merula parrae (puero *Klock*, pueris *Guyet*) uersus
quos *Scaliger*   tu colas *Lindsay*: Colax *Valla*   524 cum cibo cum
(tum *J*) quiqui *P*: cum suo cuique *Festus*: cum cibo suo quique (=
quisque) *Acidalius*   ut *om. Festus*   525 LY. *add. Camerarius* te demum
nullum scitum scitiust *Dousa*   526 cura *Camerarius*: LY. cura *P*
529 ac dicaculus *Kiessling*: dicax uiuus *B*: dicas uiuis *VEJ*   530 in
quaesitione 'uetus cod.' *Meursii, Buecheler*: inquisitione (-ni *B*) *P*   531–2 *sic
Brix: inuerso ordine P*   531 id *del. Camerarius*   532 huc *Koch: om. P*
533 deducerent *VEJ*: deduceret *B*   534 ne *Saracenus: om. P*   illis *Koch:
om. P*   535–883 *praesto est A*   535 uetulis *A*: uitulis *P*   ueruecibus *P*:
uerbecibus *A (cf. GLK vii 192)*   536 progreditur *Mueller (cf. 796)*   popli
A (ut uid.), Camerarius: populi *P*   537 praehibet *A*: praebet *P*   538
emptu est *Lambinus*: emptus est *PT*: emptus *A*   modio *Dousa*

ALCESIMVS

miror huc iam non arcessi in proxumum uxorem meam,
quae iam dudum, si arcessatur, ornata exspectat domi.   540
sed eccam, opino, arcessit. salue. Cleostrata.   CL. et tu,
                                                    Alcesime.
ubi tua uxor?   AL. intus illa te, si se arcessas, manet;
nam tuos uír me orauit ut eam istuc ad te adiutum
                                                    mitterem.
uin uocem?   CL. sine eam; te nolo, si occupata est.
                                                 AL. otium est.
CL. nil moror; molesta ei esse nolo; post conuenero.   545
AL. non ornatis isti apud uos nuptias?   CL. orno et
                                                    paro.
AL. non ergo opus est adiutrice?   CL. sátis domist;
                                                 ubi nuptiae
fuerint, tum istam conuenibo. nunc uale, atque istanc
                                                    iube.
AL. quid ego nunc faciam? flagitium maxumum feci
                                                    miser
propter operam illius hirqui ímprobí, edentuli,   550
qui hoc mihi contraxit. operam uxoris polliceor foras
quasi catillatum. flagitium hóminis, qui dixit mihi
suam uxorem hanc arcessituram esse; ea se eam négat
                                                    morarier.
atque edepol mirum ni subolet iam hoc huic uicinae meae.
uerum autem altrouorsum quóm eam mecum rationem
                                                    puto,   555

540 iam dudum si arcessatur *AB*: iam si arcessatur dudum *VEJ*
541 opino *Bothe*: opinor *AP*   arcessit *AJ*: accersit *BVE*   542 illa *P*: illam
(*uel* ellam) *A*: ellam *Seyffert*   543 isto *Spengel*   eam *del. Bothe*   ad *del.*
Geppert   mitterem *P*: mitteret *A*   544 eam te *Goetz*: eam i̧i̧ *A*: om. *P*
546 isti *A*: istic *P*   uos *AJ*: nos *BVE*   548 istanc *A*: istam *P*   552 catillatum *ABVE, Fulgentius*: catillae tum *TJ*   553 arcessiturum *Havet* (*cf.*
adn. ad 671)   esse *del. Acidalius*   555 altrouersum *P* (ult-*J*): alterouorsum
A, Gloss. Plaut. (*GLK* iii *58*) cum *P*: quo *A*   rationem *A*: ratione *BVE*:
rationum *J*

si quid eius esset, esset mecum postulatio.
ibo intro, ut subducam nauim rursum in puluinaria. —
CL. iám hic est lepide ludificatus. miseri ut festinant
senes!
nunc ego illúm nihili, decrepitum, meum uirum ueniat
uelim,
ut eum ludificem uicissim, postquam hunc delusi
alterum.   560
nam ego aliquid contrahere cupio litigi inter eos duos.
séd eccum incedit; at quom aspicias tristem, frugi
censeas.

LYSIDAMVS   III 3

Stultitia magna est, mea quidem sententia,
hominém amatorem ullum ad forum procedere,
in eum diem quoi quod amet in mundo siet: 565
sicut ego feci stultus. contriui diem,
dum asto aduocatus cuidam cognato meo.
quem hercle ego litem adeo perdidisse gaudeo,
ne me nequiquam sibi hodie aduocauerit.
nam meo quidem animo qui aduocatos aduocet   570
rogitare oportet prius et percontarier
adsitne ei animus necne adsit quem áduocet.
si neget adesse, exanimatum amittat domum.
sed uxórem ante aedis eccam. eí misero mihi!
metuo ne non sit surda atque haec audiuerit.   575
CL. audiui ecastor cum malo magno tuo.
LY. accedam propius. quid agis, mea festiuitas?
CL. te ecastor praestolabar. LY. iamne ornata res?

556 esset esset *A*: esset *P*   557 nauim *P*: nauem *A*   rursum *P*: rusum *A*
puluinaria *A*: puluinarium *P*   562 at] ut *Ussing*   565 quoi *A*: cui
P: qui *recc.*, *Gulielmius*: quo *Meursius*: quom *Geppert*   amet *P*: amat *A*
568 perdidisse *AB¹* (*ut uid.*) *J*: perdisse *B²VE*   570 *u. om. P*   571 percontarier *Pylades*: contarier *AB*: contrarier *VEJ*   572 adsitne *AJ*
(ass-): at sine *VE*: absitne *B¹*   necne] necne ei *Seyffert*   578 res *Bothe*:
res est *AP*: rest *Pareus* (*cf.* 895)

iamne hanc traduxti huc ad nos uicinam tuam
quae te adiutaret?   CL. arcessiui, ut iusseras.   580
uerum hic sodalis tuos, amicus optumus,
nescioquid se sufflauit uxori suae;
negauit posse, quoniam arcesso, mittere.
LY. uitium tibi istuc maxumum est: blanda es parum.
CL. non matronarum officiumst, sed meretricium,   585
uiris alienis, mi uir, subblandirier.
i tu atque arcesse illam; égo intus quod factost opus
uolo accurare, mi uir.   LY. propera ergo.   CL. licet.
iam pol ego huic aliquem in pectus iniciam metum.
miserrumum hodie ego hunc habebo amasium. —   590

ALCESIMVS   III 4

Viso huc, amator si a foro rediit domum,
qui me atque uxorem ludificatust, larua.
sed eccum ante aedis. ad te hercle ibam commodum.
LY. et hercle ego ad te. quid ais, uir minimi preti?
quid tibi mandaui? quid tecum oraui?   AL. quid est?   595
LY. ut bene uociuas aedis fecisti mihi!
ut traduxisti huc ad nos uxorem tuam!
satin propter te pereo ego atque occasio?
AL. quin tu suspendis te? nempe túte dixeras
tuam árcéssituram esse uxorem uxorem meam.   600
LY. ergo arcessiuisse ait sese, et dixisse te
eam nón missurum.   AL. quin eapse ultro mihi
negauit eius operam se morarier.

579 huc P: om. A   580 arcessiui A: accersiui P   585 officiumst A:
parum ést officium P (parum e u. 584)   587 arcesse P: accerse A   facto
est P: factust A   590 ego hunc A: hunc ego VEJ: hunc B   habebo A:
habeo P   591 ALCESIMVS LYSIDAMVS A: SENES DVO P   594 et
hercle ego A: at ego hercle B: atque ego hercle VE¹J (ego om. E¹)
596 uociuas A: uaciuas BV: uacuas E¹J   599 suspendis A: suspendes P
600 arcessituram VE: arcersituram B: accersituram AJ: arcessiturum
Ernout (cf. adn. ad 671)   esse del. Ernout   uxorem uxorem A: uxorem P
601 arcessiuisse edd.: accersiuisse AVE¹J: arcersiuisse B: accessiuisse E¹
602 eapse ultro Bothe: eapsaltro A: ea (eam BV) ipsa ultro P

LY. quin eapse me adlegauit qui istam arcesserem.
AL. quin nihili facio.   LY. quin me perdis.   AL. quin
                                                benest.   605
quin etiam diu morabor, quin cupio tibi –
quin! – aliquid aegre facere, quin faciam lubens.
numquam tibi hodie 'quin' erit plus quam mihi.
quin hercle di te perdant postremo quidem.
LY. quid nunc? missurusne es ad me uxorem tuam?   610
AL. ducas, easque in maxumam malam crucem
cum hác, cum ístac, cumque amica etiam tua.
abi et áliud cura; ego iam per hortum iussero
meam istúc transire uxorem ad uxorem tuam.
LY. nunc tu mihi amicus es in germanum modum. —   615
qua ego hunc amorem mi esse aui dicam datum?
aut quid ego umquam erga Venerem inique fecerim,
cui sic tot amanti mi obuiam eueniant morae?
                      attat!
quid illúc clamoris, opsecro, in nostrast domo?   620

PARDALISCA   III 5

Nulla sum, nulla sum; tota, tota occidi.
    cor metu mortuomst, membra miserae tremunt.
    nescio unde auxili, praesidi, perfugi,
    mi aut opum copiam comparem aut expetam.
    tanta factu modo mira miris modis   625
    intus uidi, nouam atque integram audaciam.
    cáue tibi, Cleostrata; apscede ab ista, opsecro,
    ne quid in te mali   faxit ira percita.
    eripite isti gladium, quae suist ímpos animi.

604 eapse A: ea ipsa P   arcesserem Merula: arcerserem B: accerserem V𝐽:
accesserem AE   605 quin (nihili) AB¹𝐽: qui B¹VE   606–9 sine personarum notis AP; uide adnotationem   610 missurus ne P: missurunne
A: missurun Schoell   613 aliud P: aliquid A   616 aui A: aut P
617 quid Gronovius: quod AP   618 cui] quom Goetz   tot P: om. A
eueniant P: eueniunt A   620 in nostrast domo A: in nostra domo est P
625 factu Scioppius: factis AP   miris A: ueris P   627 abscede P: apsede A

LY. nam quid est quod haec huc timida   atque

                         éxanimata exsiluit?   630

Pardalisca! PA. perii; unde meae   usúrpant aures

                               sonitum?

LY. respice módo ad me. PA. ó ere mi –   LY. quid

              tíbist? quid timida es? PA. perii.

LY. quid, periisti? PA. perii; ét tu   periisti.

                  LY. ah, perii? quid ita?

PA. uae tibi! LY. immo istuc tibi sit.   PA. ne

              cadam, amabo, tene mé.

  LY. quicquíd est, eloquere mi cito.   PA. contíne

                      pectus.   635-6

face uentum, amabo, pallio. LY. timeo hoc negoti

                    quid siet;   637-8

nisi haec meraclo se uspiam percussit flore Liberi.   639-40

  PA. optine auris, amabo. LY. i in malam a me crucem.

  pectus, auris, caput, teque di perduint.

  nam nisi ex te scio quicquid hoc est cito, hoc

  iam tibi istúc cerebrum dispercutiam, excetra tu,

  ludibrio pessuma adhuc quae me habuisti.   645

PA. ere mi – LY. quid uis, mea tu ancillá? PA. nimium

            saeuis. LY. numero dicis.   646-7

  sed hoc quicquid est eloquere, in pauca confer:

  quid intus tumulti fuit? PA. scibis, audi.

  malum pessumumque hic modo intús apúd nos   650

  tua ancilla hoc pacto exordiri coëpit,

---

630 exsiluit *Merula*: exsiliuit *A*: exsiluit foras *BVE*   631 sonitum *P*:
sonum *A*   632 o *om. P* tibi est *P*: tibi es *A*   633 quid *P*: qui *A*
ah perii *Geppert*: aperi *AP* ita *A*: tibi *P*   634 istuc *P*: uae *A*   ne
cadam amabo *A*: nec ad (necat *B¹E¹J*) amabo *P*   635-6 eloquere *P*:
loquere *A*   637-8 face *P*: fac *A* negoti *A*: negotium *P* siet *A*: est *P*
639-40 meraclo se *T*: meraco se *A*: mera (emera *E¹*, imera *E²*) glose *P*
percussit *AT*: percursit *P* liberi *A*: libico *PT* (-yco)   641 i in *AB*:
in *VEJ* a me *A*: *om. P* 643 est cito hoc *A*: scito *P*   644 dispercuciam
B: dispertiam *VEJ*: *A n.l.* excetra tu *Lipsius*: excitra tu *A*: execrata *P*
(-eta *J*)   646-7 mea tu (*uel* me) *A*: mea *P, Festus*   648 eloquere *A*:
loquere *P* confer *A*: refer *P* (refert *V*)

quod haud Atticam condecet disciplinam.
LY. quid est id? PA. timor praepedit dicta linguae.
LY. possum scire ego istuc ex te quid negoti est?
                                        PA. dícam.
tua ancilla, quam tu tuo uilico uis   655
dare uxorem, ea intus – LY. quid intus? quid est?
PA. imitatur malarum malam disciplinam,
uiro quae suo interminatur, uítam –
LY. quid ergo? PA. ah! LY. quid est?
                    PA. interemeré ait uélle uitam.
gladium – LY. hem? PA. gladium – LY. quid
                                eum gladium?   660
PA. habet.   LY. eí misero mihi! cur eum habet?
PA. insectatur omnis domi per aedis
nec quemquam prope ad se sínit adire;
ita omnes sub arcis, sub lectis latentes
metu mussitant.   LY. occidi atque intérii.   665
quid illi obiéctumst mali tam repente?
PA. insanit.   LY. scelestissumum me esse credo.
PA. immo si scias dicta quae dixit hodie!
LY. istuc expeto scire. quid dixit?   PA. audi.
per omnis deos et deas deierauit   670
occisurum eum hac nocte quicum cubaret.
LY. men occidet?   PA. an quippiam ad te attinet?
                                    LY. vah!
PA. quid cúm ea negoti tibist?   LY. peccáui;
illuc diceré 'uilicum' uolebam.
PA. sciens de uia in semitam degrédere.   675
LY. num quid mihi minatur?   PA. tibi infesta
                                        solist

652 atticam P: attica A   654 possum A: quid est possum P   655 tu A: om.
P   658 quae suo A: suo quae P   666 illic Spengel   mali tam A (ut uid.):
maltiam E¹ (ut uid.): malitiam B(-ciam) V: malitiae J   670 deierauit
Bentley: deiurauit P: delerauit ṣẹ A   671 occisurum B¹VEJ: occisuram
AB¹   672 men A: me P (male J)   673 duos uersus facit A (quid
cum ea | ... peccaui)   674 illuc P: illud A   675 degredire Bentley
676 num P: nam A

plus quam cuiquam.   LY. quamobrem?   PA. quia se

des uxorem Olympioni;

neque se tuam nec se suam neque uíri uitam sinere in

diem   678–9

crastinum protolli. id huc   missa sum tibi ut

dícerem,   680–1

ab ea út caueas tibi.   LY. perii hercle ego miser.

PA. dignus tu.   682–3

LY. neque est neque fuit me senex quisquam amator

adaeque miser.   PA. ludo ego hunc facete;   685

nam quae facta dixi omnia huic falsa dixi.

era atque haec dolum ex proxumo hunc protulerunt;

ego hunc missa sum ludere.   LY. heus, Pardalisca!

PA. quid est?   LY. est –   PA. quid?   LY. est quod

uolo exquirere ex te.

PA. moram offers mihi.   LY. at tu mihi offers

maerorem.   690

sed etiamne habet nunc Cásina gladium?

PA. habet, sed duos.   LY. quid, duos?   PA. altero te

occisurum aít, altero uilicum hodie.

LY. occisissumus sum omnium qui uíuont.

loricam induam mi optumum esse opinor.   695

quid uxor meá? non adiít atque ademit?

PA. nemo audet prope accedere.   LY. exoret.   PA. orat;

negat ponere alio modo ullo profecto,

nisi se sciat uilico non datum iri.

LY. atque ingratiis, quia non uolt, nubet hodie.   700

nam cur non ego id perpetrem quod coëpi,

678–9 nec se suam P: nec suam A   sinere in diem Schoell: sinere in A: sin B¹VE: in B¹: sinet in J   680–1 dicerem A (ut uid.) J: di B¹VE: dicam B¹   682–3 ut] uti Schoell   dignus tu] dig— A (sed dig—u dispexit Schoell in A): dignu's tu Schoell: dignus es Leo: om. P   688 hunc AJ: huc BVE   689 ex te A: a te P (ad te J)   693 occisurum B¹VEJ: occisuram AB¹   696 adiit P: adit A   ademit AJ: adimit BVE   699 nisi A: ni P   700 atque P: atqui A   quia AB¹E: quam B¹V: quem J: quoi Pistoris   701 nam cur P: numquam A (ut uid.)

ut nubet mihi – illud quidem uolebam,
nostro uilico? PA. saepícule peccas.
LY. timor praepedit uerba. uerum, obsecro te,
dic me uxorem oráre, ut éxoret illam   705
gladium ut ponat et redire me intro ut liceat.
                                        PA. nuntiabo.
LY. et tu orato.   PA. ét ego orabo.   LY. at blande
                            orato ut sóles. sed audi.
      si efféxis hoc,
      soleas tibi
      dabo, et anulum in   710
      digito aureum, et
      bona plurumá.
      PA. operam dabo.
      LY. face ut impetres.
      PA. eo núnciam,   715
      nisi quippiam
      remorare me.
      LY. abi et cúra. —
redit eccum tandem opsonatu meus adiutor; pompam
                                              ducit.

Vide, fúr, ut sentis sub signis ducas.

702 uolebam *aliquot codd. Prisciani*: dicere uolebam *A*: uolebam non sed *P*:
uolebam cum *alii codd. Prisciani*   703 saepicule *AP*: saepiuscule *Priscian.*,
Gloss. Plaut. (GLK iii 58)   704 te *A (ut uid.)*: om. *P*   705 me *P*: med
Bothe: *A n.l.*   706 ut liceat *P*: liceat *A*   707 audi *A*: audin *P*
708–12 *duos uersus* (... dabo et | ... pluruma) *faciunt et A et P*   711 digito
P: digitum *Mueller*: *A n.l.*   713–18 *sic A*: *duos uersus facit P* (... iam | ... cura)
715 eo *B*: ed *VE*: sed *J*: *A n.l.*   717 remorare *F*: rememorare *P*: *A n.l.*
719 redit *AB²J*: reddit *B¹VE*   opsonatu meus *AJ²*: opsonatum eius *cett.*
ducit *AB²*: dicit *cett.*   720 OL]YMPIO LYS[IDA]MVS CITRIO *A*:
SERVVS SENEX COCI *P*   signis *A*: signum *P*   qui *P*: quid *A*   hi *A*:
om. *P*   sentis *A*: sentes *P*

CITRIO

qui uero hi sunt sentis? 720
OL. quia quod tetigere ilíco rapiunt; si eás ereptum,
ilíco scindunt.
ita quoquo adueniunt, úbi ubi súnt, duplici damno
dominos multant.
CI. heia! OL. attat! cesso magnufice patricíeque
amicirier atque ita ero
meo ire áduorsum?
LY. bone uir, salue. OL. fateor. LY. quid fit?
OL. tu amás, ego ésurio et sitio. 725
LY. lepide excuratus incéssisti. OL. aha, hodie
* * * * * lus.
LY. mane uéro, quamquam fastidis. OL. fu fu! foetet
tuos míhi sermo.
LY. quae res? OL. haec res. LY. etiamne adstas?
OL. enim uéro πράγματά μοι παρέχεις.
LY. dabo tibi 729a
μέγα κακόν, b
ut ego opinor, nisi resistis. 730
OL. ὦ Ζεῦ, 731a
potin a me abeas, b
nisi me uis 732a

721 scindunt P: scidunt A   722 quoquo AB²J: epioquo VE² dominos
AB¹: om. cett.   723 cum clausula (724) uno uersu AP   CI. Saracenus:
LY. Ital.   patricieque A: patriceque P   amicirier atque A: amice P
725 esurio P: resurio (essurio?) A   726 cessisti Mueller aha hodie
—— lus A: aha hodie P: aha hodie te nolo, ama solus Schoell: aha hodie
sum Sardanapallus Lindsay in app.   727 fu fu Leo: ey ey P: fy fy Spengel:
ede]pol A (ut uid.)   728 personae spat. ante etiamne habet P: om. A ante
enim pers. spat. habet uterque ΠΡΑΓΜΑΤΑ ΜΟΙ ΠΑΡΕΧΕΙΣ A: pragmata moe
perechis VEJ: pragmata meo acacon moe parechis B   729a tibi A:
om. PT   729b ΜΕΓΑ ΚΑΚΟΝ AT: meca cachon J: meo acacon B: me
cacaon V: me cacacon E   731a uerba ὦ Ζεῦ in fine u. 730 locant et A et P
732a me uis B²VEJ: meus A: meus uis B¹

uomere hodie.   b

LY. máne.   OL. quid est? quis hic est hcmo?

LY. érus sum.   OL. quis erus?   LY. cuius tu

                                  seruo's.

OL. seruos ego?   LY. ác meus.   OL. nón sum

                          ego liber?   735–6

memento, memento.   LY. mane atque asta.

                                 OL. omitte.

LY. seruos sum tuós.   OL. optumest.   LY. opsecro te,

Olympisce mi, mi pater, mi patrone.   OL. em,

        sapis sáne.   740a

        LY. tuos sum équidem.   b

OL. quid mi ópust seruo tam nequam?

LY. quid nunc? quam mox recreas me?

OL. cena modo si sit cocta.

LY. hisce ergo abeant.   OL. propere cito íntro ite et

                    cito deproperate.   744–5

ego iam intus ero: facité   cenam mihi ut ebria

                        sit.   746–7

sed lepide nitideque uolo;   nil moror bárbarico

                        bliteo. —

stasne etiam?   LY. i sis; ego hic hábeo.

OL. numquid est ceterum quod morae siet?   750

LY. gladium Casinam intus habere ait,   qui me ác

                      te interimat.

732b uomere P: uomire A (ut uid.)   733 est homo A: homo est P
734–6 uno uersu coniungit A   734 quis AB: qui VEJ   seruo's] seruus es
AP: seruus Bothe   735–6 ac] atque AP   738 te A: om. P
739–40a uno uersu P   739 Olimpisce BVE: Olympice AJ   mi mi P: mi A
741 opust seruo A: seruo opus est P   744–51 initia uersuum mutila in P
744–5 hiscè A: om. P   abeant A: habeant P   cito intro] Citrio intro Schoell
deproperate P: properate A   746–7 ego A: om. P   facito Geppert   cenam
P: cena A   sit A: est P   748 sed A: om. P   bliteo A: ritu P   749–50 uno
uersu A   749 stasne A: ne P   LY. ante i Ussing, ante ego Camerarius: om.
AP   habeo A: habito P   750 OL. add. Camerarius   siet A (ut uid.): sit
VEJ (ceterum…siet om. B)   751 duos uersus facit A (ait | qui)   gladium
A: om. P   ac] atque AP   interimat A: inuitat P

OL. scio: síc sine habere.
nugas agunt; nóui
ego illás malas mérces.
quin tu i modó mecum domúm.　　LY. at pol malum
　　　　　　　　　　　　　　　métuo.　　755
i tu modo; pérspicito prius　　quid intus agatur.
　　OL. tam mihi mea uita　　　　　　757a
　　tua quam tibi carast.　　　　　　　b
uerum i modó.　LY. si tu iubes.　　inibitur técum. —

ACTVS IV

PARDALISCA　　　　　　　　　IV i

Nec pol ego Nemeae credo neque ego Olympiae
neque usquam ludos tam festiuos fieri　　　　　760
quam hic intus fiunt ludi ludificabiles
seni nóstro et nostro Olympioni uilico.
omnes festinant intus totis aedibus;
senex in culina clamat, hortatur coquos:
'quin agitis hodie? quin datis, si quid datis?　　765
properate; cenam iam esse coctam oportuit.'
uilicus is autem cum corona, candide
uestitus, lautus exornatusque ambulat.
illae autem in cubiculo armigerum exornant duae,
quem dent pro Casina nuptum nostro uilico.　　770
sed nimium lepide dissimulant, quasi nil sciant

755 *duos uersus facit* A (mecum | domum)　　756 *duos uersus facit* A (perspicito | prior)　prius P: prior A　757a tam A (*ut uid.*) VEJ: iam B 757b tua quam A: quam tua P　758 *duos uersus facit* A (tu | iubes) *personas correxit Seyffert* (LY. uerum...OL. si P)　i A: *om.* P　inibitur P: em (*uel* im) ibitur A　766–71 *fnes uersuum mutili in* P　766 iam P: *om.* A　oportuit A: oppo BVE¹: opto E²J　767 is A: hic P　768 lautus A: laute VEJ (uestitus...exornatusque *om.* B)　ambulat ABJ: ambulabat VE　769 in cubiculo armigerum P: armigerum ilico A　exornant duae A: ornant P　770 nostro uilico A: nostra P　771 lepide AJ²: ledi VEJ¹: lidi B¹ (pe *suprascr.* B²)　quasi nihil sciant A: *om.* P

fore huius quod futurumst. digne autem coqui
nimis lépide ei rei dant operam, ne cenet senex.
aulas peruortunt, ignem restingunt aqua;
illarum oratu faciunt. illae autem senem   775
cupiunt extrudere incenatum ex aedibus,
ut ipsae solae uentres distendant suos.
noui égo illas ambestrices; corbitam cibi
comesse possunt. sed aperitur ostium.

LYSIDAMVS   IV 2

Si sapitis, uxor, uos tamen cenabitis,   780
cena ubi erit cocta; égo ruri cenauero.
nam nóuom maritum ét nouam nuptam uclo
rus prosequi; noui hominum mores maleficos;
ne quis eam abripiat. facite uostro animo uolup.
sed properate istum atque istam actutum emittere,   785
tandem ut ueniamus luci; égo cras hic ero.
cras habuero, uxor, ego tamen conuiuium.
PA. fit quod futurum dixi; incenatum senem
foras extrudunt mulieres.   LY. quid tu hic agis?
PA. ego eo quo me ipsa misit.   LY. ueron? PA. serio.   790
LY. quid hic speculare?   PA. nil equidem speculor.
                                              LY. abi.
tu hic cunctas; intus alii festinant.   PA. eo.
LY. abi hinc sis ergo, pessumarum pessuma. —
iamne abiit illaec? dicere hic quiduis licet.
qui amát, tamen hercle si esurit nullum esurit.   795
sed eccúm progreditur cum corona et lampade
meus sócius, compar, commaritus, uilicus.

<hr>

773 rei *P*: om. *A*   776 incenatum *A*: incenem *B¹EJ*: incenam *B²V*
778 ambestrices *Loman*: ambas estrices *AP*   corbitam *A*: corbitant *P*   cibi
Turnebus: tibi *B* (*ut uid.*) *VE¹*: ibi *J*: ubi *E¹*: *A n.l.*   779 comesse *A* (*ut
uid.*), *Saracenus*: comes esse *P*   784 abripiat *AB*: arripiat *VE* (ari-) *J*
uolup *A*: uolupe *P*   785 emittere *P*: mittere *A*   791 hic *B*: om. *VEJ*
(*A n.l.*)   792 hic *Acidalius*: hinc *P* (*A n.l.*)   794 quiduis *A* (*ut uid.*) *J*:
quod uis *BVE*   797 socius *A*: socerus *P*

OLYMPIO   IV 3

Age, tibicen, dum illam educunt huc nouam nuptam foras,
suaui cantu concelebra omnem hánc plateam hymenaeo
                                                    meo:
    hymen, hymenaee o hymen.   800
LY. quid agis, mea salus?   OL. esurio hercle, atque
                                adeo hau salubriter.
LY. at ego amó.   OL. at ego hercle nihili facio; tibi
                                amor pro cibost,
mihi ieiunitate iam dudum intestina murmurant.
LY. nam quid illaéc nunc tam diu intus remorantur
                                        remeligines?
quasi ob industriam, quanto ego plus propero, procedit
                                            minus.   805
OL. quid si etiam suffundam hymenaeum, si qui citius
                                            prodeant?
LY. censeo; et ego te adiutabo in nuptiis communibus.
    LY. OL. hymen, hymenaee o hymen.
LY. perii hercle ego miser; dirrumpi cantando
                                    hymenaeum licet:
illo morbo quo dirrumpi cupio non est copiae.   810
OL. edepol ne tu, sí equos esses, esses indomabilis.

799 hymenaeo meo *A. Klotz*: hymenaeo | miωi (*uel* miω #) *A*: himeneo |
meio *P* (himin- *J*): hymenaeo mihi *Ernout*: hymenãẽo *Leo* (*v. Questa,
R.F.I.C. 40 (1962) 359–66*)   800 *Olympioni continuatum P*; ω (*littera
Graeca*; = LY.OL. *uel grex uel cantor*) *Lindsay, Ernout, Paratore (cf. Trin. 1189,
Andrieu 230ff.*)   hymen ae eo *BJ* (himen): himen ac eo *E²*: himen et eo *V*:
hymenaeo *A*   801–6 *fines uersuum mutili aut temere suppleti in P*   801 hau
salubriter *A*: haud sitio *P* (sicio *B*)   802 nihili *A*: nihil *P*   pro cibost *A*:
pericli *P*   803 ieiunitate *Schoell*: iamnunitate *A* (*ut uid.*): inanitate *P*:
iaiunitate *F. Skutsch (cf. 129)*   804 remorantur *A*: remoratur *P*   remeligines *Festus*: remiligines *A*: *om. P*   805 procedit *A*: tanto *P*   806 suffundam *Leo*: si offendam *A*: offendam *P*: offundam *Salmasius (ex. cod.
Helmst.*): occentem *Pius*   si qui citius prodeant *A*: *om. P*   807 adiutabo
P: adiuuabo *A*   808 LY.OL. *edd.*: OL. *BVE*   hymen ae eo *P* (himen
E): hymenaeo *A (cf. 800)*   809 cantando hymenaeum *P*: hymenaeo
cantando *A*: cantando hymenaeo *Schoell*   810 copiae *A*: copia *P*

LY. quo argumento? OL. nímis tenax es.   LY. num
                              me expertu's uspiam?
OL. di melius faciant! sed crepuit ostium; exitur foras.
LY. di hercle me cupiunt seruatum.

PARDALISCA

iam oboluit Casinus procul.

                                              IV 4
Sensim super attolle limen pedes, noua nupta.   815-16
sospes íter incipe hoc, uti uiro tuo
          semper sis superstes,
tuaque ut potior pollentia sit, uincasque uirum
                              uictrixque sies   819-20
     tua uox superet tuomque ímperium;
uir te uestiat,   tu uirum despolies.
noctuque et diu   út uiro subdóla sis,
     opsecro, memento.
OL. malo máxumo suo hercle ilicó, ubi tantillum
                              peccassit.   825
LY. tace. OL. nón taceo. LY. quae res? OL. malá
                              malae male monstrat.
     LY. facies tú hanc rém mi ex parata imparatam.
     id quaerunt uolunt, haec ut infecta faciant.

812 quo *P*: quod *A*   num me *AE*: num ne *B*: non ne *V*   expertu's
Lambinus: expertus *AP*   813 exitur *BEJ*: exit *A*: exigitur *V*   814 PA.
addidimus duce Leo in app.: CH. *Lindsay*: TIBICEN *Schoell*: *neque personae nota
neque spatium in AP*   Casinus *ABVE*: Casina *J*   815-16 super attolle *P*:
superatolle *A*   noua *P*: mea noua *A*   817 incipe *A*: incipere *P*   uti *A*:
ut *P*   819-27 *initia uersuum mutila aut temere suppleta in P*   819-20 tuaque *A*: atque *P*   sit *AB*: ut *VEJ*   821 tua uox *A*: om. *P*   822 uir te
AB²J: uirtute *B¹VE*   tu *del. Lindsay*   823 noctuque *A*: om. *P* sis *A*,
Nonius: sies *P*   825 malo *A*: om. *P*   tantillum *A*: tantulum *P*   826 tace
A: om. *P*   mala male male *P* (-ae -ae *J*): male malae *A*: malae male
Schoell   monstrat *P*: monstrant *A*   827 facies tu *A*: facies tun *Lindsay*:
om. *P*   uerbum id e uersu sequenti ad finem huius u. transtulit Lindsay   828 uo-
lunt *P*: id uolunt *A*

CLEOSTRATA

age, Olympió, quando uis uxorem, accipe hanc ab nobis.

829–30

OL. date ergo, daturae   si umquam estis hodie
uxorem.

LY. abite intro.   CL. amabo, integrae atque
imperitae huic

impercito.   OL. futurum est.

ualete.   LY. ite iám, ite.   CL. iam ualete. —

LY. iamne abscessit uxor?   OL. domist; ne time.

LY. euax!   835

nunc pol demum ego sum liber.

meúm corculum, melculum, uerculum!   OL. heus tu,

malo, sí sapis, cauebis.

meast haec.   LY. scio, sed meus fructus est prior.

OL. tene hanc lampadém.   LY. immo ego hanc
tenebo.   840

Venus multipotens, bona multa mihi

dedisti, huius cum copiam mihi dedisti.   OL. o

corpusculum málacum!

mea uxórcula – quae res?

LY. quid est?   OL. ínstitit plántam
845

quasi luca bos.   LY. tace sis.

829-30 *uno uersu* P, *duobus* A (... uxorem, ... nobis)   CL. *Seyffert, Ussing*: PA. *B²J* ab *A*: a *P*   831 OL. *Pistoris*: LY. *P*   uxorem *P*: *del. Bothe*: uxorem mihi *A*   832 LY. *Pistoris*: OL. *P* CL. *Seyffert*: PA. *P*   833 impercito *AB²*: impera cito *B¹VJ*: impera atque *E*   OL. *Pistoris*: LY. *P*   834 ualete # ite iam # ite # iam ualete *A*: ualete ite iam ualete (*nullis personarum notis*) *P*: *personas uarie attribuerunt edd.; sic.* G–S¹, *Ernout*   835 OL. domi est ne time. LY. euax *P*: # domist # ne time # euax *A*   837 melculum *A, Priscian.*: melliculum *P, Festus*   838 sapis *P*: sapies *A*   839 fructust prior *Lindsay* (*cf.* 378, 571): fructus prior est *Bothe*   840 hanc tenebo *A, Priscian.*: iam tenebo *P*   841 bona multa *Studemund*: bonam uitam *P*: multa bona *A*   842 # o *A*: *om. P*   843 malacum *A*: melliculum *P*: malaculum *Geppert*   844-51 *fines uersuum mutili in* P   844 OL. *praemittit* P   quae res *A*: *om.* P   845 institit *P*: insistit *A*   planta *Fleckeisen*   846 luca bos # tace sis *A*: iocabo *P*

nebula haud est mollis aeque atque huius pectus est.
OL. edepol papillam bellulam – ei misero mihi!
LY. quid est? OL. péctus mi icit non cubito, uerum
ariete.
LY. quid tu ergo hanc, quaeso, tractas tam dura
manu? 850
at mihi, qui belle hanc tracto, non bellum facit.
uah! OL. quid negotist? LY. opsecro, ut ualentulast!
paene exposiuit cubito. OL. cubitum ergo ire uolt.
LY. quin imus ergo? OL. i belle, belliatula. —

ACTVS V

MYRRHINA   V I

Acceptae bene et commode eximus intus 855
ludos uisere huc in uiam nuptialis.
numquam ecastor ullo die risi adaeque,
neque hoc quod relicuom est plus risuram opinor.

PARDALISCA

lúbet Chalinum quid agat scire, nóuom nuptum cum
nóuo marito.
MY. nec fallaciam astutiorem ullus fecit 860
poeta atque ut haec est fabre facta ab nobis.

847 aeque *A*: *om. P*   pectus est *Geppert*: est péçtus *A*: est *P*   848 *personae
spatium ante* ei *in A, nullum in P*   849 icit *A*: agit *P*   uerum ariete *A*: *om. P*
850 dura manu *A* (*ut uid.*): *om. P*   851 bęllum facit *A*: *om. P*
852–3 *personarum notas correxit Loman*   852 uah *A*: OL. uaha *P* (uaaha *V¹*,
uaah *V²*, uahat *E*)   quid *P*: quid id *A*   853 exposiuit *AB*: exposuit *VEJ*
854 LY. *Loman*: OL. *P*   quin imus *AJ*: qui nimis *BVE*   OL. *Lindsay*:
LY. *P* (*Lys. continuat Loman*)   i belle belliatula *A*: bella bellatula *P*
855 MY. *Weise*: CL. *A* (*ut uid.*) *B²* (MUL., *i.e.* CL. *?*): PA. *J*   856 uiam
A (*ut uid.*), *Lambinus*: uia *P*   858 relicuomst *Bothe, Schoell*: reliquom est *AP*
(-quum)   859 PA. *add. Schoell*   861 aeque *Fuhrmann*

CLEOSTRATA

optunso ore nunc peruelim progrediri
senem, quo senex nequior nullus uiuit;
    nisi illum quidem
nequiorem arbitrare esse, qui locum   865
praebet illi ⟨stupri⟩. te nunc praesidem
uolo hic, Pardalisca, esse, qui hinc exeat
    eum ut lúdibrio habeas.
    PA. lubens fecero
et solens. CL. spectato hinc   omnia intus quid
                          agant.   870
⟨adstiteris⟩ pone me, amabo.   MY. et ibi audacius
                          licet 871-2
quae uelis libere proloqui. CL. tace;
    uostra foris crepuit.

OLYMPIO   V 2

Neque quo fugiam, neque ubi lateam, neque hoc
              dedecus quómodo celem, 875
scio; tántum erus atque ego flagitio superauimus
              núptiis nóstris.
ita nunc pudeo atque ita nunc paueo atque ita
          inrídiculo sumus ambo.

862 CL. *add. Schoell*   863-72 *pleraque in A perierunt* (865 N ——, 867
VOLOHICP——, 869 F——, 870 ELE·· STEX (*ita Schoell*: ILE /// AEST
Studemund) ——SOC——)   864 nisi *Brix*: ne *P*: ni *Camerarius*: nec
Mueller   illum *B*: ullum *VEJ*   865 arbitrare *BVE*: arbitrarem *J*: arbitrarer
Camerarius: arbitror *Z*   866-71 *uersus mutili in P*   866 stupri *add.*
Willcock te *Valla*: *om. P* (*spatio in B relicto*)   867 uolo *A* (*ut uid.*): *om. P*
(*spatio relicto*)   868 ludibrio *B¹V²E²J*: dibrio *B¹V¹E¹*   870 spectato *B²*:
e ctato *B¹*: e erato *E¹*: e etato *E²*: etato *V*: ecato *J* intus quid *B*: intus
quid intus *VEJ*   871-2 adstiteris *add. Willcock ex. gr.* pone *B²*: one
B¹VE: ene *J* MY. *Camerarius*: MUL. (*i.e.* CL. ?) *B²* et ibi] et tibi *edd.*
uett. audacius licet] licet audacius *Lindsay*: audacius licebit *Geppert*
873 uelis *A*: uis *P* CL. *Willcock*: PA. *B¹*: MY. *Lindsay*   874 uostra *A*
(uestra) *VEJ*: nostra *B*   876 erus *A*: frus *P*   877 ita (*tertium*) *P*: *om. A*
inridiculo *A*: inridiculum *P*

sed ego insipiens noua nunc facio: pudet quém prius
　　　　　　　　　　nón puditumst umquam.
operam date, dum mea facta itero; est operae pretium
　　　　　　　　　　auribus accipere;
ita ridicula auditu, iteratú ea sunt quae ego íntus turbaui.　　880
ubi intro hánc nouam núptam deduxi, recta uia in
　　　　　　　　　　cónclaue abduxi.
sed támen tenebrae íbi erant tamquam in puteo. dum
　　　　　　　　　　senex ábest, 'decumbe' inquam.
conloco, fulcio, mollio, blandior,
ut prior quam senex nup⟨tias perpetrem⟩.
tardus esse ilico coepi, quoniam　*　*　　　　　　885
respecto identidem, ne senex　*　*
inlecebram stupri príncipio　　eam sáuium pósco.
　　reppulit mihi manum,　　　　　　　　　888a
　　neque enim dare sibi　　　　　　　　　　b
　　sauium me siuit.
enim iám　*　, magis iam ádpropero, magis iám lubet
　　　　　　　　　　ín Casinam inruere;　　890-1
cupio illam operam seni súrriperé; forem óbdo, ne senex
　　　　　　　　　　me ópprimeret.　　892-3
CL. agedum, tu adi hunc.　PA. opsecro,　　ubi tua
　　　　　　　　　　noua nuptast?

878 quem A: que P　puditumst umquam A: puditum umquam est P
879-86 fines uersuum mutili iŋ P　879 operam AJ: opera BVE　pretium
A: om. P　880 turbaui A: tu BVE: tuli J　881 hac Geppert recta uia
A: uia recta P　in conclaue A: clauem P　882 tamen] tam Spengel:
del. Ussing (ut sept. cum diaeresi fiat; v. Questa 233, 240)　tamquam] quam
Spengel　in puteo dum A: om. P: nox B¹　senex ATJ: nex B¹VE: nec B¹
abest Leo: adest A: abs te PT　decumbe inquam A: decumbe in B:
decumbem VEJ: decumbam T　883 blandior A: om. P　884-956 deest A　884 nuptias perpetrem Schoell: nuptias exsequar Lange: nup P
885 taurus Palmerius　quoniam] quom Osbernus　886 identidem ne
senex VEJ (sex): om. B　me opprimat add. Loman　887 inlecebram B¹:
incelebram VEJ: incelebrem B¹　888a reppulit VE: repulit BJ
888b neque enim BE: neque ecum V: nec quietum J　889 siuit BV:
sinit EJ　890-1 iam magis iam P: iam magis Bothe: iam crucior magis
iam Spengel: iam magis insto iam Schoell　894 CL. Saracenus, Schoell: MY.

OL. perii hercle ego; manifesta res.   PA. omnem

                            ordine rem 895

    fateri ergo aequom est.   896a

    quid intus agitur?   b

    quid agit Casiná?   c

    satin mórigera est?   d

    OL. pudet dícere.

    PA. memora ordine,

    ut occéperas.

    OL. pudet hércle.   900

    PA. age audácter.

    postquam decubuisti, inde uolo   902a

    memorare   b

    quid est fáctum.   c

OL. flagitium est.   PA. cauebunt   qui audierint

                                    faciant.

OL.   *   *   †hoc magnus est†.   PA. perdis. quin tu

                     pergis?   OL. ubi   *

*   *   *   †us suptus porro†   *   *   905

PA. quid?   OL. babae!   PA. quid?   OL. papae!

PA.   *   *   *   est?   OL. oh, erat máxumum.

*   *   haberet metui;   id quaérere occépi.   908a

*   *   *   *   *   *   *   *   *   *   *   b

dum gladium quaero ne habeat,   arripio capulum.

Camerarius PA. *Schoell:* CL. *Camerarius usque ad finem scenae personarum notae nullae in P; addiderunt Ital., Cam., qui tamen Pardaliscae partes Cleostratae dederunt; correxit Schoell* 895 res *Geppert:* res est *P:* rest *Schoell (cf.* 578) omnem ordine rem *recc., Leo:* omnem in ordine rem *Z:* omnem ordinem rem *J:* omnem in ordinem rem *BVE* 896–901 *tres uersus facit P* (... agit | ... dicere me | ... audacter) 896a aequom *Camerarius:* aegum *B¹VE:* aegrum *B²:* actum *J* 897–8 dicere. PA. memora *Schoell:* dicere me (*spatium*) mora *P* (discere *E*): dicere me. Memora *Ital.* 902–8 *initia mutila in P* 902a postquam decubuisti *Lambinus:* uam (quam *E²J*) debuisti *P* 902b memorari *cod. G Bothii, Geppert:* memorare te *Becker:* memora *Lindsay* 904 magnus *BVE:* magnum *F* 908a gladium ne haberet *recc.:* ferrum ne haberet *Schoell post* 908a *unius uersus spatium in B, dimidii in V, nullum in EJ* 909 *spatia ante et post* arripio *in VE, prius solum in J, neutrum in B*

sed cum cogito, non habuit gladium; nam esset frigidus. 910
PA. eloquere. OL. at pudet. PA. num radix fúit?
OL. non fuit. PA. num cucumis?
OL. profecto hercle * non fuit quicquam holerum;
nisi, quicquid erat, calamitas profecto attigerat
numquam.
ita, quicquid erat, grande erat.
PA. quid fit denique? edisserta. 915
OL. ubi appéllo Casinam, inquam,
'amabo, mea ⟨tu⟩ uxorcula, cur uírum tuom síc me
spernis? 917-18
nimis tú quidem hercle immerito
meo mi haec facis, qui mihi te expetiui.' 920
illa haud uerbum facit, et saepit ueste id qui estis
⟨mulieres⟩.
ubi illúm saltum uideo opsaeptum, rogo ut áltero ⟨mé⟩
sinat íre.
uolo, ut obuortam, cubitis im * * * * * * *
ullum muttit e * * * * * * * * * *
surgo, ut in eam in * * * * * * * * * * 925
atque illam in * * * * * * * * * *
MY. perlepide narrat * * * * * * * * *
OL. sauium * * * * * * * *
itá quasi saetis labra mihi compungit barba.
continuo in genua ut astiti, pectus mihi pedibus percutit. 930
decído de lecto praecipes; subsílit, optundit os mihi.

910 esset *Ital.*: esse *P*   912 *spatium inter* hercle *et* non *in* BV, nullum in EJ;
an hercle uero?   916 *ibi* Lambinus appello *J*: apello *BVE* Casina
Bothe duce Lambino inquam *Saracenus*: inquit *BJ*: inquid *VE*   917-18 mea
E (*ut uid.*) *J*: me *BV* tu *Willcock*: te *Leo in app.*: *om. P*   920 qui
Guyet: quia *P*   921-8 *fines uersuum mutili in P*   921 illa *J*(?) *Ital.*: illam
BVE(?) estis mulieres *Loman*: feminae estis *Guyet*: estis *P*   922 me sinat
ire *Willcock*: sinat ire *J*: sin adire (*praecedente spatio*) *B*, (*nullo spatio*) *VE*
924 muttite *BVJ*: mittite *E²*   927 MY. *add.* Pius   928 OL. *add.* Pius
929 labra *ζ*: labram *P* *ante* mihi *spatium in* B, nullum in VEJ   930 ut
astiti *Seyffert*: astituti *BVE¹*: astuti *E¹*: adstanti *J*   931 praecipes *Seyffert*:
praeceps *P*

inde foras tacitus profugiens exéo hoc ornatu quo uides,
ut sénex hoc eodem poculo, quo egó bibi, biberet.

                        PA. optume est.
sed ubi est palliolum tuom?   OL. hic intus relíqui.
PA. quid núnc? satin lepide ádita est   uobis manus?
                        OL. mérito.   935
sed concrepuerunt fores.   num illa me nunc sequitur?

                 LYSIDAMVS   V 3

    Maxumo ego ardeo flágitio,
    nec quid agam meis rebus sció,
    nec meam ut uxorem aspiciam
    contra oculis; ita disperii.   940
    omniá palam sunt probra;
   omnibus modis   occidi miser.
*   *   *   *   *   *   ita   manufesto faucibus téneor.
*   *   *   *   quíbus modis   purgem scio mé meae
                               uxóri.
*   *   *   *   *   *   *   que expalliatus sum miser,   945
*   *   *   *   *   *   *   *   clandestinae nuptiae.
    *   *   *   *   *   *   *   *   censeo
    *   *   *   *   *   *   *   mi optumum est.
*   *   *   *   *   *   *   *   intro ad uxorem meam,
sufferamque ei meum tergum ob iniuriam.   950
    séd ecquis est qui homo múnus uelit
     fungier pro me?

932 profugiens *Redslob*: preficiens *BVE* (-t-): proficiens *J*   exeo hoc ornatu
Palmerius: sex eo cor natu *BVE*: exeo cum ornatu *J*   935 adita est
Camerarius: addita est *BVJ*: addita *E*   OL. *add. Acidalius*   936 *totum
uersum Olympioni continuat Acidalius*: OL. num *Camerarius* (*spatio ante* num *in
BV relicto*)   937 ego *J*: ergo *BVE*   941 omnia *Camerarius*: nia *BVE*:
quia *J*   943–50 *initia uersuum mutila in P*   943 faucibus *VEJ*: facibus
B   944 nec quibus *Z*   945 que *recc.*: quae *P*: qui *Z*: atque *Geppert*:
scipionem perdidi atque *Schoell*   946 clandestinae *J*: ndestine *BVE* (-ime)
949 intro ad uxorem meam *Nonius*: ea dux uxorem meam *P*: intro ad
uxorem eam *Gerlach*: intro eam ad uxorem meam *Schoell*   950 *sic Nonius*
(ei *Mercier*: et *codd. Nonii*): riam *P* (*in fine u.* 951 *V*)   951 munus *E¹*:
minus *P*

quid nunc ágam nescío, nisi ut   improbos famulos
                                                       imiter,
      ac domo fugiam.
      nam salus nulla est scapulis,   955
          si domum redeo.
nugas dicere istaéc licet;   uapulo hercle ego inuítus
                                                    tamen,
      etsi malum mérui.
      hac dabo protinam et fugiam.

            CHALINVS

      heus! sta ilico, amator.   960
  LY. occidi! reuocor; quasi
      non audiam, abibo.
                                          V 4
CH. Vbi tu és, qui colere mores Massiliensis postulas?
nunc tu si uis subigitare me, probast occasio.
rédi sis in cubiculum. periisti hercle. age, accede huc
                                        modo;   965
nunc ego tecum aequom arbitrum extra considium
                                       captauero.
LY. perii! fusti defloccabit iam illic homo lumbos meos.
hac iter faciundumst; nam illac lumbifragiumst obuiam.
CL. iubeo te saluere, amator.   LY. ecce autem uxor
                                       obuiamst.
nunc ego intér sacrum saxumque sum, nec quo fugiam
                                        scio.   970

955 scapulis *J*: capulis *BVE*   957–1018 *praesto est A*   957 dicere
istaec *Willcock*: istic dicere *A*: istuc dicere *P*   959 protinam me
Camerarius: me protinam *Roppenecker*   et fugiam] in fugam *Camerarius*
960 CH. *Leo*: OL. *Camerarius*: CL. *Ussing*: *spatium AP*   heus sta ilico *A*: heus
stalicio *B*: heu stalicio *V* (-itio) *EJ*: heu stalino *Z*   961 occidi *AE²*:
occide *P*   963 CH. *add. Lambinus*   964 si uis *A*: siue is *P*   subigitare
Scioppius: subicitare *AP*   965 redi sis in cubiculum *A*: om. *P*   periisti *J*:
perisiti *ABVE*: CL. periisti 'nonnulli' *apud Lambinum*: MY. periisti 'quidam
libri ueteres' secundum eundem   modo *A*: om. *P*   966–72 *habet A* (*uiii uersibus*):
om. *P*, *uiii uersuum spatio in B relicto*   967 f·s·· (fusti *Studemund*) defloccabit
A: flocco habebit *Nonius* (*sed defloccare in lemmate*)   970 *seclusit Leo*

hac lupi, hac canes; lupina scaeua fusti rem gerit.
hercle opinor permutabo ego illuc nunc uerbum uetus:
hac ibo; caninam scaeuam spero meliorem fore.
CL. quid agis, dismarite? mi uir, unde hoc ornatu
                                                aduenis?
quid fecisti scipione aut quod habuisti pallium? 975
MY. in adulterio, dum moechissat Casinam, credo
                                                perdidit.
LY. occidi!   CH. etiamne imus cubitum? Casina sum.
                              LY. i in malam crucem.
CH. non amas me?   CL. quin responde; tuo quid factum
                                            est pallio?
LY. Bacchae hercle, uxor – CL. Bacchae?
      LY. Bacchae hercle, uxor – MY. nugatur sciens.
nam ecastor nunc Bacchae nullae ludunt.   LY. oblitus
                                          fui;   980
sed tamen Bacchae – CL. quid Bacchae?   LY. sin id
                                    fieri non potest –
CL. times ecastor.   LY. egone? mentire hercle.
                        CL. nam palles male.
ṇ * * * * quid me ụẹ * ụṣ * am me rogas?
* * * * * * * malẹ r * * * mihi
* * * * * * * * * * * * gratulor.   985

972 permutabọ *A*: permutaui *Schoell*   973 hac *AB¹J*: ac *B¹VE*
974 CL. *J*: MY. *Leo*   dismarite *A*: tu marite *P*   spatium ante mi uir in *A*,
nullum in *P*: CL. mi uir *Leo*   hoc ornatu *A*: ornatu hoc *P*   975 scipione
Lambinus: scipione⁓ *AP*   976 MY. *Geppert*: PA. *Camerarius*   977 occidi
sequente personae spatio *A*: occidit *P*   i in *AJ*: in *BVE*   978 CH. *add.*
Camerarius   979 Bacchae *A*: Bache ergo *P*   CL. *Studemund*: spat. in *A*,
non in *P*   LY. *Studemund*: spat. in *AB*, non in *VEJ*   MY. *Ital.*: PA. *Camerarius*:
om. *AP*   981 LY. *add. Geppert*   sin id *A*: in id *BVE*: id *J*   982 CL.
add. Luchs   mentire *A nullo personae spatio*: haud mentire *B* (*antecedente personae
spatio*) *VEJ*   CL. *Luchs*: spatium in *B*, nullum in *AVEJ*   palles male *A* (*ut
uid.*): pa *P*   983-91 *ix uersibus paucissima in A leguntur praeter* 991: *om. P*
ix uersuum spatio in B relicto   983 *sic A secundum Studemund, qui tamen*
NONPUDE *in initio paene legit: Schoell sibi persuasit se in A legisse* non pudet
te # quid mentiri usit # etiam me rogas, *unde scripsit* CL. non pudet te?
LY. quid mentiri usu sit? CL. etiam me rogas?

*   *   *   *   *   *   *   *   qu *   *   *   sęnex

họ *   *   *   *   *   *   *   *   *   ọn *   ụ

*   *   *   *   *   *   *   *   *   unç Casinụst   *   *   988-9

quị hịç   *   *   *   *   *   *   lęm frụs *   rạm *   dịs   990

(OL.) qui etiam me miserum famosum fecit flagitiis suis.

LY. non taces?   OL. non hercle uero taceo; nam tu

                              maxumo

me opsecrauisti opere Casinam ut poscerem uxorem mihi

tui amóris causa.   LY. ego istuc feci?   OL. immo

                          Hector Ilius.   994-5

LY. te quidem opprésset. feci ego istaec dicta quae uos

                             dicitis?

CL. rogitas etiam?   LY. si quidem hercle feci, feci

                           nequiter.

CL. rédi modo huc intro; monebo, si qui meministi

                           minus.

LY. hercle, opinor, potius uobis credam quod uos dicitis.

séd, uxor, da uiró hanc ueniam. Myrrhina, ora

                        Cleostratam.   1000

si umquam posthac aut amasso Casinam, aut occepso modo,

ne ut eam amasso, sí ego umquam adeo posthac tale

                         admisero,

nulla causast quin pendentem me, uxor, uirgis uerberes.

MY. censeó ecastor ueniam hanc dandam.   CL. faciam

                        út iubes.

---

991 *adfert Nonius tamquam ex Asinaria*   (OL.) *Schoell*   fecit *A* (*ut uid.*): facit *Nonius*   992 maxumo *A*: maxime *P* (-ume *J*)   993 opere *A*: ob *P*   994-5 OL. *Leo*: CL. *edd. priores*: *spatium in B, nullum in AVEJ*   Hector Ilius *Palmer*: hectore illius *P*: ecastor ilius *A*   996 LY. *add. Lindsay*   oppresset *A*: oppressisset *P*   *ante* feci *personae spatium in A, nullum in P*   istaec *A*: ista haec *P*   998 si qui *A*: si quidem *P*: si quid *Bothe*   1000 da uiro *P*: uero *A*   uiro tuo *Leo*, ueniam mi *Lindsay*, *hiatus uitandi causa*   1002 eam amasso *BE²J*: ea amasso *VE¹*: ęamasso *A* (*ut uid.*; *fort.* ne uti amasso): amasso *Bothe*   *uersum secl. Gruter, Guyet, alii*   1003 me] *del. Camerarius*   1004 mecastor *Mueller*   hanc dandam ueniam *Bothe*   *personae spatium ante* faciam *in A, non in P*: CL. *Saracenus*: Cleustrata (*i.e.* Cleostrata) CL. *Lindsay*   uti *Camerarius*

propter eam rem hanc tibi nunc ueniam mínus grauate
prospero,   1005
hanc ex longa longiorem ne faciamus fabulam.
LY. non irata's?   CL. non sum irata.   LY. tuaen fidei
credo?   CL. meae.
LY. lepidiorem nemo uxorem quisquam quam ego habeo
hanc habet.
CL. age tu, redde huic scipionem et pallium.   CH. tene,
sí lubet.
mihi quidem edepol insignite factast magna iniuria;   1010
duobus nupsi, neuter fecit quod nouae nuptae solet.

spectatores, quod futurumst intus, id memorabimus.
haec Casina huius reperietur filia esse ex proxumo,
eaque nubet Euthynico nostro erili filio.
nunc uos aequomst manibus meritis meritam mercedem
dare.   1015
qui faxit, clam uxorem ducet semper scortum quod uolet;
uerum qui non manibus clare quantum poterit plauserit,
ei pro scorto supponetur hircus unctus nautea.

1005 ueniam *AJ*: rem ueniam *BVE*   1006 ne *A*: ni *P*   1007 tuaen *A*:
tuae *P*   1008 nemo uxorem *A*: uxorem nemo *P*   quisquam *P*: *om. A*
1009 si *Bothe*: se *A*: *om.* P   1010 insignite *A*: insigne te *P*   1012 *seqq.*
Chalino continuant codd., Pardaliscae dat Schoell, gregi Camerarius, ω (= *Cantori,*
cf. ad 799–800) *Ussing*   1012 id *AVE*: hic *F*: *om. J*   memorabimus *AJ*:
memorauimus *VE*   *uersum inde a* futur *om. B*   1014 Euthynico *A*: te ut
hynico *P* (ynico *E*, hinico *J*)   1015 meritam meritis *Schoell in append.*
1016 faxit *AJ*: flaxit *BVE*   ducet *A*: ducat *P*   uolet *AJ*: uole *BVE*
1017 qui *AE*: quae *BVJ*   poterit *AEJ*: proterit *BV*   plauserit *AJ*: pluserit
BVE   1018 nautea *A, Donatus, Festus*: nausea *P*

COMMENTARY

THE CHARACTERS

O̮LȲMPI̮Ō: a slave, the bailiff (*uilicus*) of Lysidamus, i.e. in charge of the family's estate in the country; a high-sounding name for a low character.

CHĂLĪNV̆S: a slave, the valet (*armiger*, see 55) of Euthynicus; the name means 'bridle' in Greek.

CLE͞OSTRĂTĂ: wife of Lysidamus. Her name is always trisyllabic where it appears in the play (393, 540, 627 (in cretics), 1000), so that it is to be scanned with synizesis of the first two vowels. For this reason Lindsay (followed by Paratore) arbitrarily altered the spelling in his edition to Cleustrata.

A character called Kleostratos appears in the *Aspis* of Menander.

PĀRDĂLĪSCĂ: maid of Cleostrata; her name is a diminutive (pet-name) from *pardalis* 'panther'.

MȲRRHĪNĂ: Cleostrata's friend and neighbour, wife of Alcesimus. Her name (which is quite common in comedy, being found in Aristophanes' *Lysistrata*, Terence's *Hecyra*, and three of the partially surviving plays of Menander) means 'myrtle' – a sweet-smelling herb; cf. Casina.

LȲSĬDĀMV̆S: head of the house, and husband of Cleostrata. His name, which is a perfectly good Greek one, is not found anywhere in the text of the play, and has only been known since the progressive decipherment of the Ambrosian palimpsest, around 1870 (the palimpsest has it in the scene headings). Before that, the old man was called Stalino in printed editions of Plautus, a name which arose from textual corruption in lines 347 and 960.

G. E. Duckworth ('The unnamed characters in the plays of Plautus', *C.Ph.* 33 (1938) 279–82) and Andrieu (165¹ and 171) have both argued that we may have been too credulous – that perhaps the old man *was* unnamed by Plautus, and 'Lysidamus' is an invention of the writer of the scene headings in A (who may have felt that he needed a name to complete his normal form of presentation); for the lateness of the scene headings, cf. p. 34 n. 1.

ALCESĪMŪS: neighbour of Lysidamus and husband of Myrrhina. His name might have the meaning 'helpful' in Greek.

CĪTRĬŌ: a cook, his name formed (as Leo says) from Greek χύτρα 'a pot'. His name also does not appear in the text of the play; it is found in A only, in the scene heading of III 6. Duckworth voices the same suspicion of the reliability of this information as in the case of Lysidamus.

CHARACTERS WHO DO NOT APPEAR

CĂSĬNĂ: a girl brought up as a slave in the house of Lysidamus and Cleostrata. Her name is derived from a spice – *casia* 'cinnamon' (see notes on 219, 814); cf. Myrrhina.

EVTHȲNĬCVS: son of Lysidamus and Cleostrata. The name means 'victorious'.

THE SCENE

A street in Athens. At the back of the stage are the houses of Lysidamus and Alcesimus.

ARGVMENTVM

Acrostic plot summaries were added to all the plays in the Plautine tradition, probably towards the end of the second century A.D. They archaize in language, and are free with hiatus, evidently taking the view that it was a Plautine feature. The example before the final cretic in the first line (*conserui | expetunt*) has several parallels in the *argumenta* of other plays (e.g. *Aul. Arg.* II 1 *aulam repertam auri plenam | Euclio*, a line with hiatus at the caesura in addition), and indeed in the text (see *Cas.* 47, 48).

2 allegat: the word is taken from lines 52 and 55.

3 senem adiuuat sors: a reference to the lot-taking scene, which gave its name to the Greek original of the play (31).

5 mulcat 'beats'; the verb is to be distinguished from *multo* (*mulcto*) 'to fine'.

PROLOGUE

1-88

The function of a Plautine prologue is to make contact with the
spectators, to enlist their good will, and to explain what is necessary
for their understanding of the plot. The prologue of the *Casina* has
additional interest: it explains the relation between Plautus' play and
his original, Diphilus' *Kleroumenoi*, and it was written in part for a
revival of the play after Plautus' death. Some of the lines, then, were
composed by a stage director around the middle of the second
century B.C. Scholars have identified three layers of material in these
eighty-eight lines: (1) direct imitation of the prologue of Diphilus'
play (which, being a play of recognition, may be assumed to have had
an expository prologue); (2) Plautus' own composition when he
adapted the play for the Roman stage; (3) lines composed for the
revival performance. (K. Abel, *Die Plautusprologe* (1955) 55–61.)

(1) What derives from Diphilus is the simple and clear exposition
of the situation in 35–63, although within this there are doubtless
Plautine changes and additions (for example, the military imagery
of 50ff., and probably the illness of the slave in 37).

(2) Plautine are the opening lines 1–4, with their direct appeal to
the favour and good humour of the audience; 23–34, with topical
humour about the holiday, and information on the title of the play
and its origin from Diphilus; and 64 to the end, with the explanation
that the young master will not return during the action of the play,
some discussion of customs relating to the marriage of slaves, a brief
synopsis of the conclusion of the plot (which Plautus will not in fact
be using), and some crowd-pleasing obscenity and complimentary
remarks about military success.

(3) The lines composed for the revival seem to be 5–22.

Metre: senarii.

1 saluere iubeo 'I welcome'. The expression is derived from the
common imperative *saluete*.

2 maxumi: genitive of value; 'you who have the highest regard for
fides, and Fides for you'.

   Fides (good faith, truthfulness), the personification of an abstract
quality, was a most ancient divinity at Rome, worshipped with

Jupiter on the Capitoline hill. This line is therefore a fulsome compli-
ment to the audience, although any particular topical allusion, if
there was one, is lost to us. F. Skutsch suggested that *Fides* was the
speaker of the prologue, parallel to divine figures and personifications
who appear in this role in other plays. This has appealed to many,
and may conceivably have some relevance to the discussion of
'credit' in 23–8; it is not however at all clear what this divinity has
to do with the present play (Arcturus in the *Rudens* has both a moral
function and a weather connection; Pan in the *Dyskolos* and the Lar
Familiaris in the *Aulularia* both influence the action of their plays).
Consequently Skutsch's ingenious suggestion remains no more than a
guess, especially as *Fides* (if she it is) does not take the trouble to
identify herself to the audience, at least in the prologue as we have it.

The hiatus between *maxumi* and *et* is perhaps justified by a pause in
speaking (for hiatus, see Appendix 1, section 10).

3 signum clarum date 'clap your hands'.

4 iam inde a principio: the words go together; 'right from the
beginning'.

5–22 These are the lines newly composed for the revival of the play
after Plautus' death. The composer of this passage has a tendency to
use the first person plural, representing himself as speaking for the
whole company (*nos* 11, mostly plural verbs in 11–16, *nostrum* 22);
the speaker of the rest of the prologue uses the first person singular.

5 qui utúntur: the scansion of the first foot is indeterminate –
spondee or anapaest. Either *qui* is elided, producing a spondee
(*qu(i) ūtūntur*), or else it is shortened in prosodic hiatus, and then acts
as the *brevis brevians* to shorten the first syllable of *utuntur* (*quĭ ŭtūntur*,
with iambic shortening of the type of *uŏlŭptās mĕă* (p. 215). Perhaps the
effect of these alternatives would not be so very different in practice.
The same uncertainty applies to the scansion of 37 *qui in mórbo*,
42 *quae illam éxponebat*.

sapientis: -*is* is the correct form for the ending of the accusative
plural in Latin of the Republican period.

7 antiqua: either this word must be pronounced with four syllables,
the last being elided – an improbable solution proposed by Camerarius

and followed by Lindsay – or there is hiatus between *antiqua* and *opera*. The same phenomenon recurs at the beginning of 13.

opera 'workmanship' (it is the plural of *opus*); in *Most.* 828 the word is used for features of a house.

8 aequom: in early Latin *-uo-* stands invariably for later *-uu-*, e.g. *seruos, tuos* for *seruus, tuus.*

9–10 'The new comedies which come on the stage now are much more debased than the new coinage.' Much ingenuity has been shown by numismatists and others in proposing dates for the revival of the play that would fit the reference to new coinage; but nothing convincing has been found. We are ignorant of essential facts. As to the 'new comedies', some have thought that this could not have been written while Terence was alive (he died in 159); but in fact the polemical tone of Terence's prologues shows that there was in some circles considerable disapproval of the type of comedy he was producing, so that the allusion may be to Terence himself.

nequiores: the word *nequam* is used for poor quality coins also in Apul. *Met.* 10.9.

13 antiquam: for the scansion, see 7n.
  eius: scanned as a trochee, $-\cup$.

14–15 give an approximate length of time before the revival, say twenty to thirty years: the older members of the audience enjoyed what was presumably the first performance, but the younger ones do not know the play. Seeing that there are strong arguments for placing the *Casina* among the last of Plautus' plays, and dating it to about 185 B.C. (979–80n.), this suggests a date for the revival of 165–155; cf. 9–10n.

14 probastis = *probauistis.*

15 iuniorum qui sunt 'those who are among the younger men'; the genitive is partitive.
  norunt = *nouerunt.*

16 dabimus operam 'we will take care', a common expression.
  sedulo: adverb.

17 This does not imply the existence of dramatic contests, such as took place at Athens; simply, 'our play was thought the best'.

18 ea: to be scanned either as a monosyllable by synizesis, or as two short syllables by iambic shortening (Appendix 1, section 8); in either case, the ictus of the first foot falls on the first syllable of *tempestate*.

flos poetarum: as well as Plautus himself, and possibly Naevius, this would include Ennius and Caecilius, who were the last representatives of the old school – Ennius famous particularly for epic and tragedy, Caecilius with a reputation for comedy as great as that of Plautus himself. The probable dates of death were

Naevius   201
Plautus   184
Ennius   169
Caecilius   168

19 A traditional euphemism for death – the place where all must go, the *locus communis*.

20 'But, though absent now, they benefit us as though they were here.'

pro praesentibus: not 'on behalf of those present', but 'as if they were present', *tamquam praesentes*; cf. *pro consule. pro*, however, is a modern supplement; the manuscript text is defective.

21 opere magno = *magnopere*.

esse oratos: perfect infinitive passive; 'to hear my appeal' (lit. 'to have been asked').

22 operam detis 'pay attention' (cf. 16). This expression is regular with the dative in Plautus, but not found elsewhere with *ad*.

gregem 'company' of actors.

23 There is nothing wrong with the sense of the line (*alienum aes* means 'borrowed money', 'debt'); but the form is highly suspicious, and has been emended or marked as defective by editors. As presented in the manuscripts, there are two instances of hiatus, between *curam* and *atque* at the caesura of the fourth foot, and between *alienum* and *aes* in the last foot. The former may be acceptable, particularly in a prologue which, for whatever reason, contains numerous examples of hiatus (79n.); but the latter is intolerable. The only alternative to the assumption that a word has dropped out (and no really satisfactory word has been proposed) is Camerarius' suggestion that *aes* may be disyllabic, as in the adjectives formed from it, *ăhēnus* (122) and *ăhēneus*. There is however no evidence at all for disyllabic *ăēs* apart from this line.

24 ne quis: a new main sentence, 'let nobody'.

flagitatorem: *flagitatio* was a procedure whereby a creditor, to recover his money, or any offended party, to get redress, shouted his demands publicly, putting pressure on the debtor or offender by causing him embarrassment (H. Usener, *Rh.M.* 56 (1901) 1-28); cf. *Men.* 46 *illum clamore uidi flagitarier*, *Most.* 603-6.

25 ludi sunt 'it is a public holiday'. Stage productions took place at Rome either on certain regular holidays or at the funeral of a great man. (In the *didascaliae*, which survive for all of Terence's plays and two (*Pseud.* and *Stich.*) of Plautus', we hear of the *ludi Romani, ludi plebeii, ludi Megalenses*, and the *ludi funebres Aemili Pauli*. See Lily Ross Taylor, 'The opportunities for dramatic performances in the time of Plautus and Terence', *T.A.P.A.* 68 (1937) 284-304.)

ludus datus est argentariis: there is a *double entendre*. The word can mean both 'the bankers are given a rest' and 'the bankers are given the slip'.

26 'It is calm; the halcyon festival is being observed around the forum' (the business centre of Rome).

Alcedōnia: a comic formation, as if it were the name of a Greek festival, like the Aphrodisia (*Poen.* 191) or the Eleutheria (used in a similar joking way at *Stich.* 422). The halcyon days (when kingfishers were popularly believed to hatch their eggs in a nest floating on a calm sea) were the seven days on either side of the winter solstice – 14-28 Dec. This is of course merely a passing joke; none of the relevant *ludi* were at that time of the year.

27 ratione utuntur 'they show good sense', in not expecting payment during the holiday.

ludis 'during the games'.

There may, as has been suggested, be other double meanings here. *ratione utuntur* might refer to the bankers making up their accounts, cf. *rationem puto* 555; and *ludis poscunt* might mean 'they demand in sport'.

poscunt neminem: verbs of asking may take the accusative of the person as well as of the thing.

28 A joke against an unpopular class. 'The money-lenders don't ask for their money during the festival; on the other hand, they don't return yours when the festival is over.' At *Curc.* 377–8, the banker says *habent hunc morem plerique argentarii | ut alius alium poscant, reddant nemini.*

autem: normally second word, but sometimes postponed.

29 uociuae: the old spelling of *uaciuae*, later *uacuae*, 'empty', 'receptive'; in 527 there is a pun on *uocare* and *uacare*.

30 comoediaī: *-ai* is the old first declension genitive ending.

uolo 'I will'. *uolo* + infinitive is often close to a pure future tense, exactly like the future in English; this is particularly common with verbs of speaking (J. B. Hofmann and A. Szantyr, *Lateinische Syntax und Stylistik* (1965) 314).

31 Clerumenoe = Κληρούμενοι, 'men drawing lots'. Diphilus' play took its name from one memorable scene (here 353–423).

32 latine Sortientes: it seems probable from this that Plautus called his play *Sortientes*, and that the title *Casina* was given only at the revival. These lines would thus be parallel to *Merc.* 9–10 *graece haec uocatur Emporos Philemonis | eadem latine Mercator Macci Titi.* Alternatively, he may be just translating the Greek word for the benefit of his audience.

33 postid: i.e. *post id* 'thereafter'; cf. *postea.*

denuo = *de nouo*, 'anew'. The word is strictly unnecessary as it means approximately the same as *rursum*. Such tautology is common in Plautine Latin.

34 cum latranti nomine 'with his barking name' – i.e. with a name normally applied to dogs, because the word *plautus* was used to describe a dog 'with soft flat ears', like a basset hound.

35–63 Exposition of the dramatic situation.

35 senex is scanned as two short syllables by iambic shortening (Appendix 1, section 8).

hic 'here', said with a wave of the hand.

ei is scanned here (and in lines 37, 53, 66 of this prologue) as two longs, the second in this instance elided; scansion as one long syllable (*eī*) is rather more common.

36   in illisce aedibus: there are two houses on the stage. Plautus and Terence are generally accurate in their use of the demonstrative pronouns *hic* 'this, near me', *iste* 'that, near you', *ille* 'that, over there'; so much so that one can often deduce the positions of the actors from the pronouns employed. There is an apparent inconsistency here; but *hic* (35) was said in relation to the whole stage ('here, where you see me'), *in illisce* pointing to the house in question.

in illisc(e): the first syllable of the various cases of *ille* and *iste* (less commonly *ipse*) is particularly liable to shortening after a previous monosyllable (Appendix 1, section 8). The general objection to the shortening of the naturally accented syllable of a word does not apply in the case of these pronouns, which it is reasonable to suppose were less strongly accented than other words. So we get scansions like *ăd illam* (79), but not *ăd ŭrbem*. (In the present example, the question of shortening the accented syllable does not arise, because the accent of *illisce* was on -*is*- by the normal 'penultimate' rule, p. 212.)

illisce: all forms of *ille* and *iste* may in Plautus have the stressing suffix -*c(e)* added; so that, in addition to *ille, illa, illud,* we find *illic, illaec, illūc* (for *illud-ce*).

37   The sick slave obviously played a key part in the recognition scene of Diphilus' *Kleroumenoi*. He had the essential information about the identity of the woman who exposed the baby sixteen years ago. Such minor characters appear in many comedies with this sort of plot -- an old nurse, a runaway slave, a passing shepherd. Plautus has however removed the recognition scene entirely from his version of Diphilus' play; and, although he apparently feels that he should mention the slave in deference to his model, he makes no further use of him. Perhaps therefore (though not necessarily) Plautus is responsible for the indisposition of the slave (cf. 64–6).

38   A weak joke, prepared for by the unusual expression *in morbo cubat* of the previous line. *immo hercle uero* corrects what has just been said, 'no, I should have said'.

hercle: Latin everyday speech took emphatic words from the names of the three demigods Hercules, Castor and Pollux; and we find with great frequency in Plautus *hercle, mēhercle, ēcastor, mēcastor, pol, ēdepol*. Of these, by convention those derived from Hercules are used only by men, those derived from Castor only by women (Aul. Gell. 11.6).

quid is internal object of *mentiar*, 'not to tell you a lie'.

39f A natural, if rather colloquial, way of speaking: 'that slave – but it happened sixteen years ago, when he saw'.

39   annos sedecim: it is normal to find the accusative (of duration of time) with *abhinc* (Ter. *Andr.* 69 *abhinc triennium*).

Sixteen is also the age of the girl in the *Eunuchus* of Terence (*Eun.* 526).

40   quom: the old spelling of the conjunction *cum*.

primulo: diminutives were common in colloquial Latin; they often have no special force.

41 If the parents did not wish to rear a child, custom in many Greek states permitted them to abandon it in some place where there was a chance of somebody finding it and looking after it (Harrison 1 71, with many references). This exposing of unwanted babies is a common feature of New Comedy plots, often the necessary prelude to a recognition sixteen or so years later (Gomme and Sandbach 34–5; Ter. *Heaut.* 626ff.).

There is hiatus at the caesura, after *exponi* (cf. 73).

adit, orat, etc.: historic presents, for vivid narrative.

mulierem: presumably Myrrhina, the neighbour's wife (1013), or else a woman acting for her. The baby of course was Casina.

43   exorat 'he persuades her'.

rectā: understand *uiā*, 'straight'.

44 Although the second vowel of e.g. *amat* is long in Plautus (p. 213), *dat* is probably an exception and short (cf. *dăre, dăbo* and especially the passive *dătur*). Thus the first foot is an anapaest, *dăt ĕrāe.*

educet: from *edŭcare*, not *edūcere*.

46 The point of the insistence that Cleostrata has brought Casina up as if she were her own daughter is the assumption in New Comedy plots that a girl who is to marry an Athenian citizen, after being recognized during the play to be free-born herself and Athenian, must be a virgin (except for the special case where she has been raped or seduced by the same young man who eventually marries her). A slave girl brought up in the house would be less likely to have remained *pudica* (81).

quasi si: for *quasi* 'as if'; cf. *nisi si*.

47 Hiatus in the fifth foot.

48 êam or ĕăm (18).
Hiatus in the fifth foot.
hic: with a wave of the hand again, 'the one over here'.

49 amāt: cf. 44n.
efflictim 'desperately', found only with verbs of loving.
contra 'in opposition to him'.
This line has hiatus at the caesura.

50 **sibi** stands as a pyrrhic disyllable in prosodic hiatus (p. 216). This is very common with monosyllables (5n., 66), less so with disyllables (but cf. *uirùm* 58).

legiones parat: Plautus likes to use military imagery, especially in his big 'slave plays' *Bacchides* and *Pseudolus*. This is without doubt an addition to the language of his model; cf. 54, 344, 352, 357 (W. T. MacCary, *Servus gloriosus: A study of military imagery in Plautus* (diss. Stanford, 1969)).

51 Fraenkel's view (*EP* 200) that *que. . .que* was a non-Latin feature introduced by Ennius in his hexameter verse from the Greek τε. . .τε, is contradicted by W. B. Sedgwick *ad Amph.* 7. If it is an innovation, it must have preceded Ennius, as Plautus uses it naturally enough.

The preposition *clam* is here separated from the word it governs.

52 **uilicum**: i.e. Olympio, the slave who acts as overseer or bailiff of the country estate.
qui posceret 'to ask'.

53 **istanc** 'that girl' about whom you (the audience) have been hearing. For *sib(i) istānc*, cf. *in illīsce* 36.
is: the father, Lysidamus.
ei: the slave, Olympio.

54 excubias: a military term, 'night quarters'.
  foris: adverb, 'away from home'.

55 filius: by Hermann's law (p. 219), a dactylic word may not
provide a complete foot in iambic verse, *except in the first foot* where in
general more licence was allowed. The awkwardness is caused by the
clash of metrical ictus with the natural word accent. 767 begins in the
same way, *uilicus is autem*.

  is: unnecessary to the sense, but stressing the subject (the son, in
contrast to the father), as if we were to say, 'the son – *he* has deputed
his *armiger*'. Fraenkel (*IuA* 207) suggested that this was a colloquial
manner of speaking, as it certainly is in English, for it is found most
obviously in ballad-style poetry, e.g. 'The brown girl *she* has house and
lands | Fair Eleanor *she* has none'.

  armigerum: a soldier's servant. So presumably the son had
served in the army.

56 qui poscat: primary sequence of tenses; so *adlegauit* in 55 must
have been a true perfect. In 52 however the same construction after
adlegauit contained an imperfect subjunctive; it is unlikely that any
difference of meaning is intended (Lindsay, *Syntax* 56).

57 quod amat: indicative, although within indirect speech,
because it is independent fact; 'what he loves', 'his love'.
  intra praesepis suas 'in his own home'.

58 uirŭm: prosodic hiatus (50n.).

59 Hiatus after *propterea*.
  So the house is divided. The father and son are competing for the
same girl; each has deputed his personal slave to marry her, and each
with ulterior motives. The mother supports her son, in order to
frustrate her husband. This behaviour would not seem particularly
improper to an ancient audience (although the Romans would no
doubt feel that the father's position was undignified), so long as the
girl was a slave. However much the son loved her, marriage was not
possible. When it is discovered that she is after all of citizen birth, then
of course everything changes.

60 So A. The reading of P (*sensit filium suom*) would break Luchs's
law (p. 219).

61 ēandem īllam amáre et ĕsse ímpedímentó sibí, with synizesis of *eandem*, and shortening of *ess(e)* by the preceding mono-syllable.

62 The son is sent abroad, presumably as a merchant; not to the wars, as he has left his *armiger* behind.

63 absenti tamen: these words go together in a rather elliptical way; 'in spite of his absence'. This is a regular use of *tamen* in Latin.

64-6 Plautus explains that he personally has removed the young man from the plot of his play (cf. 37n.).

66 qui is shortened in prosodic hiatus; *quĭ ĕrāt.*

67-71 Cf. *Stich.* 446-8 *atque id ne uos miremini, homines seruolos | potare, amare atque ad cenam condicere: | licet haec Athenis nobis.*

68 seruiles nuptiae: there could be no such thing as a slave wedding at Rome; nor was there any legal state of marriage for slaves. Some favoured male slave might be allowed to associate with a female slave, by whom he might have offspring; but that was all (Varro, *De re rustica* 1.17).

69 seruin: for *serui-ne*, with loss of the final *e* (p. 213).

70 attulerunt: i.e. the actors.
  gentium: partitive genitive, with *nusquam.*

71-2 The prologue speaker claims that slave weddings took place in Greece, Carthage and Apulia (in Italy). Not enough is known about the treatment of slaves in Carthage or Apulia to corroborate or contradict what is said here, but there is some supporting evidence for Greece: in Men. *Epitrepontes* 91, the slave Syriskos has a wife, and so has the slave Syrus in Ter. *Adelph.* 973; in *Mil.* 1007-9, a slave claims to be engaged to marry. It is in fact improbable that slave marriage had any legal validity in Athens either (Harrison I 177); but slaves were treated with more freedom there, and may have been allowed in practice, though not legally, to imitate the customs of free citizens (so G. Augello, *Plauto* I 655). J.-H. Michel (in *Hommages à Léon Herrmann* (1960) 557) correctly points out that what is being discussed here is not so much the state of marriage as a wedding ceremony (*nuptiae*; cf. 73–4); he takes the view that in any case the whole passage is a joke, and no evidence for social customs, as it depends on the veracity of three nations whose unreliability was proverbial (see 76n.).

71 Carthagini: ablative in -*i* for -*e* is quite common in Plautus, in nouns with consonant stems; cf. *uxori* 318, *sorti* 428.

72 The unmetrical reading of the text is that of both A and P, and must therefore stem from an ancient corruption. There is (as in 23) nothing wrong with the sense; presumably a word has dropped out. The three emendations quoted in the app. crit. each involve the assumption that one of a pair of *terra*'s has been omitted ('haplography'); this is quite a common occurrence, cf. 556, 739, 834.

73 *opera*, the reading of P, would be possible, and there is a parallel for it in *Mil.* 855 *opera maxuma*; it would mean something like 'with greater enthusiasm'. However *opere* is the more usual Plautine form; *maiore opere* is merely the comparative of *opere magno* (21).

It is best to scan the line with hiatus at the caesura – *maioreque opere* | *ibi*. The prevalence of a third foot caesura, coupled with the natural pronunciation of *ibi*, more than counterbalance any doubts about the hiatus; cf. 41, where the same view was taken of *puellam exponi* | *ádit*.

75–6 'If anyone wishes to question the truth of this assertion (*id ni fit*), let him make a bet with me, of a jug of sweet wine.' The expression (with *ni*..., and *pignus dare in aliquid*) is quite common; cf. *Epid.* 700–1 *ni ergo matris filia est,* | *in meum nummum, in tuom talentum, pignus da*, 'Would you like to bet a talent to a *nummus* that she isn't a mother's daughter?'

dato: third person imperative.

76 Poenus...Graecus...Apulus: these are the three races referred to in 71–2; this would cause a laugh, because certainly the Greeks and the Carthaginians, and perhaps also the Apulians, were notorious with the Romans for perfidy. (So J.-H. Michel, op. cit. (71–2n.) 557–61; F. Skutsch suggested that the recent Hannibalic war may have left unfavourable memories among the Romans of Apulian unreliability. From time to time some of them defected to Hannibal, e.g. after Cannae, Livy 22.61.11.)

dum 'provided that'.

siet: the old form of *sit*, found in Plautus normally at the end of a line or of a section of it, like some other archaic forms. It seems that it was preserved for its metrical utility, but not as part of ordinary speech.

77 adeo 'as well'.

mea causa 'so far as I am concerned'.

79 reuortar: probably subjunctive, rather than future; 'let me return'.

puellam: this must be scanned as a disyllable by synizesis (*pu͡ellam*), not *pŭĕllam* by iambic shortening, because it is a fixed principle that the naturally accented syllable of a word may not be so shortened; so also, with the same word, in *Cist.* 124 and *Poen.* 1301 (Drexler, *IK* 242).

There is hiatus between *puellam* and *expositiciam*. Whether because the whole Prologue was subject to change and corruption at the revival, or for whatever other reason, it contains an unusually large number of examples of hiatus. Discounting three cases of prosodic hiatus (50, 58, 66), we find twelve or thirteen others, as follows:

middle of the second foot   7, 13, 59
main (third foot) caesura   41, 49, 73
fourth foot caesura   23, 72 (?), 79
end of fourth foot   2
middle of fifth foot   47, 48
middle of sixth foot   23

No explicable principle or licence emerges.

81 pudica: cf. 46n.

libera, ingenua Atheniensis: full marriage in Athens was only possible if both bride and groom were of free Athenian citizen birth.

The discovery that Casina was in fact fully marriageable to the young son of the house was obviously a feature of Diphilus' play, and without doubt it was effected in a recognition scene like those in other comedies, including the *Rudens* (original by Diphilus). Plautus, being more interested in the farcical aspects, has removed the recognition scene from his play, and with it the slave of 37 and the young man himself. He simply gives us the information here in the Prologue, and repeats it in a brief three-line epilogue at 1012–14.

82 quicquam stupri 'anything in the way of fornication';
defining genitive.

85-6 In fact, Casina does not appear in this play at all; and, if she
did, she would have been played by a man, not a woman, according to
Donatus *ad* Ter. *Andr.* 716. This is merely a scurrilous joke, designed
to please the male audience.

86 nuptum: the common supine in -*um*, used with a verb of
motion: *ire dormitum*, 'to go to bed'; *ire nuptum*, 'to get married'.

non manebit auspices: at a proper Roman wedding, the
auspices were taken on the morning of the ceremony (Cic. *De div.*
1.16.28). *auspices* were the minor priests, or augurs, who performed
this function.

87 tantum est 'that is all'.

The end of the (postponed) prologue of the *Cistellaria* has a similar
complimentary reference to Roman military success, in almost the
same words as 87-8 here: *Cist.* 197-8 *haec sic res gesta est. bene ualete et
uincite | uirtute uera, quod fecistis antidhac.* (The closeness of the parallel
has led many editors to read *et* before *uincite* in 87 here, with P. There
is, however, a difference: in the *Cistellaria* sentence there are two verbs
in parallel; here there are three, and asyndeton is a little more natural.
We therefore follow A, omitting *et*, as does Lindsay.)

The encouragement to victory need not refer to the second Punic
War, as it evidently does in the *Cistellaria* (see *Cist.* 201-2). The
Romans were constantly at war with some enemy or other in these
years. On the other hand, it is quite likely that these lines are taken
over from the *Cist.* passage, as a satisfactorily patriotic and complimentary way of ending the prologue.

Notice the alliteration: *ualete. . .uincite | uirtute uera.*

88 uera: one would perhaps prefer *uestra* (*uostra*); but A P are
unanimous (the reading of F is a Renaissance conjecture), and the
appearance of the same expression in the *Cistellaria* passage makes
uera unassailable.

ACT I

89–143

The play proper begins in an altercation between the two slaves who are rivals for the hand of Casina: Olympio, representing the interests of his master Lysidamus as well as his own, and Chalinus, representing those of his master's son, the absent Euthynicus. There is an added contrast here between the town slave (Chalinus) and the country slave (Olympio), reminiscent of Tranio and Grumio in the first scene of the *Mostellaria*.

Metre: senarii.

89 non mihi licere: exclamatory infinitive: 'that I should not be allowed', 'am I not to be allowed?'.

   me solum: with a common switch from the dative (*mihi*) to the accusative for the subject of the infinitive *loqui*.

90 ted: this and *med*, found for *te* and *me* in both accusative and ablative, are the only relics in the text of Plautus of the ancient -*d*, which used to conclude the ablative of all five declensions, as well as some imperative forms; cf. 143.

91 malum: an interjection used in exasperated questions; *quid*... *malum* = 'why the devil'.

   sequere = *sequeris*, second person singular.

92 quasi umbra: understand *sequitur*.

93 quin: this conjunction, derived from the old ablative *qui* (262) + a negative -*nĕ*, is in later literary Latin almost limited to introducing subordinate clauses after verbs of prohibition; in early and colloquial authors it has two different uses: to correct an inaccurate statement, as here, 'on the contrary', 'indeed'; and as an interrogative, 'why not?' (99).

   edepol: 38n.

   in crucem: because *crux* was the ultimate punishment for slaves, *in* (*malam*) *crucem ire* became slang for 'to go to hell'.

94 decretumst: *es* and *est* of the verb *esse* are very frequently shortened by 'prodelision' (Appendix 1, section 5).

dehinc (with synizesis) **conicito ceterum:** *ceterum* is a neuter object to the verb, not a conjunction or adverb; 'from that you can guess the rest' (Ter. *Phorm.* 166 *tu conicito cetera*).

95   sutelis 'machinations'. *sutela = dolosa astutia a similitudine suentium dicta* (Festus p. 407 L.).

97   negotist: defining genitive with *quid* (cf. 82). For the form, cf. *decretumst* 94.

98   quid in urbe reptas? 'Why are you creeping about in the city?'

haud magni preti: genitive of value (cf. 2 *maxumi*). There is probably a suggestion of a pun on *uilicus* and *uilis*.

99   quin 'Why not?' See 93n. In this sense, *quin* is found with either imperative or present indicative (the latter here and in the next line).

ruri: locative-ablative, cf. *Carthagini* 71; *ruri* again in 105 and 110.

praefectura: that of which he is *praefectus* (put in charge), his 'province'. This official terminology is continued with *legatum* (100), *urbanis rebus* (101), *prouinciam* (103).

102   praereptum: supine of purpose, like *nuptum* 86.

103   ăbĭ with iambic shortening twice, for *diērēctus* is of four syllables (cf. *Most.* 8 *abi rús, abi díerecte*). In the second half of the line, *tŭ(am) ĭn prouinciam* with iambic shortening is preferable to a combination of synizesis and total elision *t(ŭãm) ĭn prouinciam*.

rus: accusative of motion towards, without a preposition, as regularly with this word in later Latin.

dierectus: tr. 'directly', 'immediately'. 'A word of uncertain etymology used predicatively, apparently conveying the sense of peremptory dismissal' (*OLD*). This admission of ignorance about the origin of the word (which is found thirteen times in Plautus and once in a fragment of Varro) is an improvement on older speculation ('crucified' *LS*, following Nonius).

105 = *praefeci (hominem) qui ruri recte tamen (res) curet*.

tamen 'in spite of my absence'; cf. 63 *absenti tamen*.

106   quod: adverbial accusative in its own clause, but referring to the (unexpressed) object of *impetrauero*; 'with respect to which', 'the reason why'.

107 quam deperis: this verb, used colloquially for 'to be desperately in love', came, from its sense, to take an object.

108 bellam et tenellam: the assonance gives an erotic and languishing effect; both words are diminutives, of *bonus* and *tener* respectively.

110 incubabo 'I will sleep secure.'

111 tun = *tune* (cf. *seruin* 69).
  ducas: deliberative subjunctive; 'Are *you* to marry her?'

111–12 = *satius hercle est me suspendio mortuom (fieri) quam (ut) tu eius potior fias.*
  satius: 'better'; comparative of *satis.*
  potior: comparative of *potis*; *potior fias* = *potiaris* 'get possession of', but perhaps with more effect from the comparative 'you rather than me').

113 proin tu te in laqueum induas 'so go and put your head in a noose'.

114 sterculino: this was shown by Bentley (*ad* Ter. *Phorm.* 526) to be the old form of the word; later *sterquilinium*. The choice of insult suits the speaker, a town slave abusing a country slave.
  sit: deliberative subjunctive, like *ducas* 111.

115 uae tibi 'go to hell'.

116 si uiuo 'as sure as I'm alive'.

117 egone: *-ne* is here an *affirmative* particle, occasionally found attached to a personal pronoun in the answer to a question (commonly *egone?* :: *tune*, 'I? :: Yes, you', as at *Capt.* 857). Here the response is made more complicated by itself being in the form of a rhetorical question.

118 lucebis facem 'you will shine a torch'. *lucere* is by nature intransitive; only here and at *Curc.* 9 does it take an object.
  Torches were carried before the bride in the wedding procession.

119 postilla: cf. *postea*, *postid* (33, 120).
  ut semper sis: if the text is correct (see below), there is a change

of construction: 'First, you will hold a torch; secondly you are always to be a worthless nuisance; thirdly, when you get to the villa, you will be given, etc.'

nihili: genitive of value, from *nihilum*.

This line has been condemned as an interpolation by several editors. It certainly interrupts the sentence both logically and grammatically; but in a comic writer even a weak joke may suffice to get a laugh, and this may simply be the surprise item in a list (cf. 121–2n.). Leo corrected the grammatical inconsistency by reading *eris* for *sis*, and putting commas round *ut semper* ('next, as always, you will be, etc.').

120   postid locorum: *locorum*, another partitive genitive, is unnecessary to the sense; the phrase means 'next in order of position', and so 'next'.

121–2   The joke and threat are neatly explained by J. C. B. Foster in *Mnem.* 23 (1970) 362–3. Olympio gives a sort of inventory of equipment which will be issued to Chalinus from the store, including two surprise items for comic effect, and an unexpectedly large final item: one jug (*amphora*), one path, one spring, one copper pail (*ahenum*), and eight vats (*dolia*). The task will be to go along the path, fill the bucket from the spring by means of the jug, return along the path, and pour the water into the vats. Foster well compares a list of requirements for a vineyard in Cato's *De agri cultura* 11, which includes *dolia, amphorae, ahenum*.

ahenum: normally a 'cauldron' for boiling water; here a smaller vessel seems more appropriate.

124 = *ita probe curuom* ('so well bent') *aqua aggerunda te faciam.*

125   postilena 'crupper'; i.e. the strap which goes round the hind quarters of a horse, under the tail.

126   The line causes difficulty. 'Afterwards, in the country, unless you have eaten a *heap*, or earth like a worm, etc.' This raises the obvious question, 'a heap of what?'; and there is hiatus between *aceruom* and *ederis* (in the same position, however, as in lines 47 and 48). Many scholars have suspected that the word *eruom* 'cattle fodder' has either been lost in connection with *aceruom*, or (in the genitive *erui*) been replaced by *ruri*. If we are not convinced by such emendations, we must assume that *aceruom* means 'a heap of hay'.

127 quod: adverbial accusative, as in 106; 'with respect to the fact that', 'in so far as', 'if'.

postules: with accusative and infinitive, not simple infinitive (so also in 141).

128 quicquam: the pronoun is used in negative or virtually negative sentences. Here there is clearly the implication that any food at all is not very probable.

128–9 numquam edepol Ieiunium ieiunumst aeque 'Hunger itself is not so hungry as I'll make you in the country.' This play on words based on the personification of an abstract concept is a favourite with Plautus; cf.

As. 268 *ut ego illos lubentiores faciam quam Lubentiast*

Most. 351 *nec Salus nobis saluti iam esse, si cupiat, potest*

Poen. 846 *qui ipsus hercle ignauiorem potis est facere Ignauiam*

Pseud. 669 *namque ipsa Opportunitas non potuit mi opportunius aduenire.*

Compare 225 *munditiis Munditiam antideo.*

aeque atque 'equally as', 'as much as'.

reddibo: for *reddam.* The penultimate syllable is short, as in the simple verb *dăbo.* This form is found also at *Men.* 1038.

131 te: ablative with *condigne.*

132 concludēre: future passive.

fenestram: the accusative is probably better than the ablative *fenestra,* although either would be possible.

fenestram must either be pronounced as a disyllable or have its second syllable shortened. Although the latter involves the iambic shortening of what we should expect to be the accented syllable of the word (see 79n.), it has a parallel in *Philippus* (the gold coin), and may be justified on the grounds that *fenestra* may have had an abnormal accent as a foreign (Etruscan?) word (Drexler, *IK* 222). Lindsay, however, and some other editors, prefer to print *fenstram* or *festram,* supported by Festus (80, 27 L.) '*Festram antiqui dicebant quam nos fenestram.*' The word occurs twice elsewhere in Plautus (*Mil.* 379, *Rud.* 88), and on both occasions its metrical value is as here.

firmiter = *firme;* cf. *ampliter* 501 (also at the end of a line).

As to the meaning of being 'shut in the window', Lambinus thought a cupboard in the wall was meant; but, assuming that the walls were thick, it would be possible (at any rate in imagination) to squeeze a man into the window opening. Compare 140 *in medio pariete*.

133 auscultare...ausculer (old form of *osculer*): a pun.

Scan *quŏm ĕg(o) ill(am) āuscŭlĕr*, with prosodic hiatus of *quom*.

134 mi: vocative.

animule is the first of nine pet-names spoken by Casina in the imagination of the amorous Olympio. This is typical Plautine linguistic exuberance. Even more exotic terms are found in *As.* 666-7 *dic me igitur tuom passerculum, gallinam, coturnicem, | agnellum, haedillum me tuom dic esse uel uitellum* (cf. 693-4 of the same play).

The second half of this line is to be scanned

$$\cup \; \cup | \cup \underset{\smile}{\cup}| \; \cup \cup \; - | \; \cup \; -$$
m(i) animule, mi Olympio

with *brevis in longo* at the *locus Jacobsohnianus* (p. 217), and an anapaest in the fifth foot, brought about by the prosodic hiatus of *mi*.

136 deosculer: subjunctive (without *ut*) as commonly after *sinere*. The word is trisyllabic, with synizesis (*dĕŏsc-*).

uŏlŭptās mĕă: this is a common term of endearment. For the scansion (by iambic shortening), see p. 215.

137 amabo is used in colloquial Latin for 'please', almost invariably by women (see 917).

ted: cf. 90; *med* 143.

meus: two short syllables; for the uncertainty between iambic shortening and loss of final *-s*, see p. 214.

139 furcifer: a *furca* (fork) was a wooden yoke placed over the neck of a slave who was to be beaten, his hands then being tied to it (Plutarch, *Coriolanus* 24). So *furcifer* is a term of abuse, 'villain'.

140 pariete may stand as another example (cf. 134) of *brevis in longo* at the *locus Jacobsohnianus*. Alternatively, *parieti* like *Carthagini* 71.

uorsabere 'you will keep changing position', 'wriggle', 'squirm'.

141 = *ne tu postules te mihi respondere*. This is a negative purpose clause ('so that you can't claim that you should reply to me'). For the construction after *postules*, cf. 127-8.

143 With *med* (cf. 90) the fourth foot of this line is a proceleusmatic – *ăgĕs sĭnĕ*. This seems awkward and unnecessary to a modern reader, because elided *me* would make the line easier to scan. We should not of course on that account depart from the manuscript tradition.

Chalinus follows Olympio into the house. (In the text of the play, the sign — is used to indicate that a character leaves the stage.)

ACT II

Scene 1   144–164

Cleostrata emerges from her house with her maid Pardalisca. She proposes to complain to her neighbour about her husband's behaviour.

This is the beginning of a long canticum sequence, going on to 251; it consists of a solo by Cleostrata (with one line sung by Pardalisca), a duet between Cleostrata and Myrrhina, a solo by Lysidamus, and a duet between him and his wife.

Metrical analysis

144	– – – ∪ – – ∪ – – ∪ – –	ba⁴
145	∪ – – ∪ – – ∪ – – – –	ba⁴
146	– – – ∪ – – ∪ ∪ – – – –	ba⁴
147	– ∪ – – ∪ – ∪ ∪ ∪ – ∪ – –	cr² ith
148	–	
149	∪ ∪ ∪ – ∪ ∪ ∪ – ∪ ∪ ∪ – ∪ – –	cr² ith
150	– – – – ∪ – | – – – – ∪ –	cr⁴
151	∪ ∪ ∪ – – ∪ – – ∪ –	cr³
152	– ∪ ∪ ∪ | – ∪ ∪ ∪ –	ia⁴ᴧ
153	∪ ∪ – ∪ –	ia²
154	∪ ∪ – ∪ –	ia²
155	∪ ∪ – – ∪ ∪ – – ∪ – – – –	ba⁴
156	∪ ∪ ∪ ∪ – ∪ – – ∪ – – – –	ba⁴
157	∪ ∪ ∪ – – ∪ – – ∪ – – ∪ –	cr⁴
158	– ∪ – – – ∪ –	tr⁴ᴧ
159	– ∪ ∪ – ∪ – –	ith
160	∪ ∪ – – ∪ ∪ –	crᶜ
161-2	– – ∪ – – – – ∪ ∪ – ∪ | – – – –	ia⁴ᴧ ia⁴ᴧ
163	– ∪ ∪ – ∪ ∪ – – ∪ ∪ – – ∪ ∪ – ∪ –	cʳ ia⁴
164	– – – – ∪ ∪ ∪ – – – –	cʳ cʳ

General

1. In the metrical analyses, an ictus mark (´) is put over the relevant syllable only where it is thought helpful for the purpose of showing the rhythm.

2. Hiatus is indicated by |.

3. For technical reasons it is convenient to mark a closed syllable at the end of a line (i.e. a syllable ending in a consonant) as *long* in the metrical analyses, even if the vowel in the syllable is known to be short (146, 149). This includes syllables ending in -*m* (145, 156, 161–2). If on the other hand a syllable ending in -*m* is left in hiatus at some point in the line, it is shown as *short* (152, 161–2).

4. For the abbreviated metrical descriptions, see Appendix 1, pp. 221–32. ith is to be found among the trochaic *cola* there (p. 225); c^r denotes the *colon Reizianum* (p. 228).

Notes

145   **meâm**
150   hiatus at the central diaeresis
152   ia⁴ᴬ with hiatus – *flăgĭtiŭm* | *illŭd hŏminĭs*, mirroring the hiatus which is for some reason normal in the phrase *flagitium hóminis* (*As.* 473, *Cas.* 552, *Men.* 489, 709)
157   **dignŭ'**
159   with iambic shortening of a cretic word to a dactyl in the first foot
161–2   with iambic shortening of *eo* and hiatus after *questum*

144 The instructions in this line and in 146 are addressed to slaves within the house.

  cellas 'larders', which are to be shut up, and sealed with a signet ring (*ănulus*), so that the door cannot be opened without her knowledge.

145 in proxumum 'next door'.

146 quid and **me** are both objects of *uolet*.

  facite (*ut*) **accersatis** = *arcessite*.

  (Both *arcesso* and *accerso* are found frequently in the manuscripts of Plautus.)

148   The interjection *st* (the only word in Latin to contain no vowel, as the grammarians inform us) is *extra metrum*, and so in a modern text printed on a line of its own; so also in 212.

149   **tăc(e) ătqu(e) ăbī**: this is one of the incontrovertible examples of iambic shortening in cretics or bacchiacs in Plautus (another is *căuē tibī* in 627). In general, it seems that iambic shortening was avoided in these metres (G. Jachmann, *Glotta* 7 (1916) 39ff.).

coquetur: impersonal passive; 'there will be no cooking today'.

151   **animi causa** 'to please himself'; the phrase is found also at *Trin.* 334.

152   **flagitium illud hominis** 'that disgrace of a man'; *hominis* is genitive of description.

153–4   The two short cola have the rhythm ∪ ∪ – ∪ –, which appears later in a long sequence from 708 to 717. It is best described as an iambic monometer.

One of the ways by which Cleostrata delays and frustrates her husband's improper designs is by her control of the kitchen. He never gets a meal, and even has to forgo the wedding feast (780ff.); cf. 219n.

156   **ĕgŏ pŏl īllūm** is an awkward bacchius, with two resolutions.
probe 'properly'; cf. 124.

This line expands *maledictis* of 155; 157 does the same for *malefactis*.

158–60   Three short lines of abuse. By the scansion adopted here, although one would hardly guess it from the terminology, each line is simply one syllable shorter than its predecessor. Schematically (see Appendix 1, pp. 219ff.), they are

⏔ × ⏔ × ⏔ ∪ ⏑́   tr⁴ᴬ
⏔ × ⏔ × ⏔ ⌒   ith
⏔ × ⏔ ⏖ ⏑́   crᶜ

158   **Acheruntis pabulum** 'hell-fodder', i.e. with one foot in the grave; cf. *Merc.* 290 *Acherunticus,* | *senex uetus, decrepitus.* (*Acheruns* has a long *a* in Plautus, short in later Latin.)

159 flagiti persequentem: although one might expect the objective genitive with a present participle to be a late development in Latin, it is found elsewhere also in Plautus, e.g. *As.* 857 *amantem uxoris maxume, Mil.* 997 *huius cupiens corporist.* It appears that genitive with a present participle expresses a permanent quality, accusative a momentary action (Ernout–Thomas 57).

The words mean something like 'pursuer of disgrace'. *persequentem* is accusative (and so therefore are *pabulum* and *stabulum*) referring to *illum* (156).

160 stabulum nequitiae 'dwelling-place of infamy'; cf. *Truc.* 587 *stabulum flagiti.*

161–2 questum: supine (86).

163 sed foris concrepuit 'but I hear the door' – a common way of announcing the arrival of a new character.

eccam: for *ecce eam* 'look at her', i.e. 'see, here she is', with *ecce* taking an accusative object as if it were a verb.

foras: adverb, 'out'.

164 per tempus 'at the right time', 'opportunely'. Cleostrata fears that she may have chosen an inconvenient time to go across for a chat, as Myrrhina is on her way out. The reason for all this is that the stage represents the street and conversation must take place there; there are no indoor scenes.

Scene 2   165–216

Cleostrata discusses her husband's behaviour with her neighbour Myrrhina, who urges her to accept her dependent position and put up with his infidelities.

Metrical analysis

165–6	∪∪∪∪∪∪ – – – ∪∪ ‿ – – ∪∪ – – ∪∪ – –	an^8
167	∪∪∪∪ – – – ∪∪ – –	an^4
168–9	∪∪∪ – – ∪ – ∪∪∪ – – ∪ –	cr^4
170–1	– – ∪ – – – ∪ – – ∪∪ – –	ia^4 an^2
172–3	– ‿ – ‿ – – – – – ∪∪ – –	c^r an$^{4\wedge}$
174–5	∪∪∪∪ – – – – ∪∪ – –	an^2 c^r
176–7	∪ – ∪∪ ‿ – – – ∪∪ – ∪ –	ia$^{4\wedge}$ ia^2

178	∪ ∪ ´ – – ∪ ∪ – – – –	c^r c^r
179	– ∪ ∪ – ∪∪ – ∪ ∪ – –	an⁴
180–1	– – ∪ ∪ ´ – | ∪ ∪ ∪ ∪ – – ∪ ∪ –	c^r c^r
182	– – – –. – – – – ∪ ∪ – ∪ ∪ – ∪ ∪ – –	an⁸
183a	– – – ∪ –	ba²ᴧ
b	∪ – ∪ ∪ ∪ –	ba²ᴧ
184–5	∪ – – – – – ∪ – – ∪ – –	ba⁴
186–94		9 × cr⁴
195	– ∪ – ∪∪ – ∪ ∪	tr⁴ᴧ
196	∪ ∪ ∪ ∪ ∪ – – ∪ –	tr⁴ᴧ
197	∪ ∪ – – ∪ ∪ – ∪ ∪	tr⁴ᴧ
198	– ∪ ∪ ∪ – – ∪ ∪ ∪ –	ia⁴
199–202		4 × cr⁴
203	– ∪ ∪ – – ∪ ∪ – – ∪ ∪ ∪ ∪ –	chor² cr^c
204	∪ ∪ ´ – – – – – –	an⁴ᴧ
205	– – – – – – – –	an⁴
206–7	∪ ∪ – ∪ ∪ – ∪ ∪ – ∪ ∪ – – – ∪ ∪ – ∪ ∪ –	an⁸
	∪ ∪ –	
208–9	∪ ∪ – – – ∪ ∪ – – – ∪ ∪ – – ∪ ∪ – ∪ ∪ –	an⁸ᴧ
210–11	– – – – – – – – ∪∪ ∪ ∪ – – – ∪ ∪ ∪ ∪ –	an⁸
212	–	
213	∪ ∪ ∪ – – ∪ – – ∪ – ∪ – –	cr² ith
214	– ∪ – ∪ ∪ ∪ ∪ – – | – ∪ – ∪ ∪ –	gl(?) cr²ᴧ
215	– ∪ – – ∪ – ∪ ∪ | – ∪ ∪ | ∪ –	cr² + cr^c
216	∪ ∪ – – – ∪ – – ∪ – ∪ ∪ –	cr² + cr²ᴧ

Notes

165–7 Six examples of iambic shortening in two lines demonstrate the greater licence of anapaests

165–6 **sequimíni:** it is rare, and almost unknown outside anapaests, for a four-syllabled word beginning with three shorts to have the metrical ictus on the third syllable; cf. 723 *patriciequ(e)*
ecquis: the first syllable is scanned short by enclisis (p. 214); cf. 208–9

190 hiatus at the diaeresis

200 hiatus at the end of the first cretic

208–9 **tŭquidem:** enclisis (p. 214)

214   glyconic scansion is rendered improbable by the irregular long penultimate element. See app. crit.

215   prosodic hiatus after *mihi* and *tibi*; cf. 50.

165–6   comites: her slave women; a Roman matron would not normally go into the street unaccompanied.
   heus uos 'Hey you!' *uos* is vocative; cf. *heus Pardalisca* 688. Here Myrrhina speaks to a different group, the servants inside the house.
   ecquis 'does anyone?'

167   hic 'here'; with a wave of the hand to Cleostrata's house.

168–9   caluitur: this very rare word is thus explained by the grammarian Nonius: *caluitur dictum est frustratur* (p. 10 L.), and he quotes our present line. 'Sleepiness makes my hands slow.'

170–1   iussin: 'Did I not tell you?'; for the final *n*, cf. 69 *seruin*.
   colum: from *cōlus* 'distaff', not *cŏlum* 'sieve'. Spinning thread from wool was the endless task of the women of the household. Myrrhina intends to take her knitting (as it were) over to her neighbour's house.

172–3   mecastor: 38n. Also 182 *ecastor*.
   amabo: 137n.

176–7 'There is always enough to upset them indoors and out.'
   aegre quod sit: Latin may use an adverb with the verb 'to be' where we would expect the neuter of the adjective. This particular phrase (*aegre est*) is repeated in 179 and 180–1.

178   nam 'in fact'. *nam*, like *enim*, is an asseverative particle in early Latin.

181   diuidiae: predicative dative of this rare noun, which means 'sadness'. 'What upsets you disturbs me too.'

182   merito 'deservedly'; the word is used as an adverb.

183   The text has been suspected; however, with the not too difficult understanding of *est*, we may translate, 'nor is there any neighbour in whom there are more of the feelings towards me that I should wish'; cf. *Capt.* 700 *nec quisquam est mihi aeque melius cui uelim.*
   qua in: 'anastrophe' of the preposition, as it is called, is rare with *in*, but examples are found with the relative pronoun (as with *cum*;

e.g. 671 *quicum*). The fragments of the early poet Lucilius show *quo in* (5.182 M.), *quis in* (1327 M.); cf. Kühner–Stegmann I 585–6.

186–90 Textual corruption in both A and P probably arose from the same cause, the difficulty of *despicatur* in 186. A has added *uir* at the end of the previous line, to treat *despicatur* as deponent, and give it a subject; P replaced 186 by the very similar 189, which took 190 with it. Perhaps also it was felt that *dic idem* in 187 asked for exact repetition.

186 despicatur: this is to be explained as a transitive impersonal passive: *me despicatur* 'contempt is shown for me' (Lindsay, *Syntax* 53). The closest parallel is a fragment of the dramatist T. Quinctius Atta, quoted by Nonius (p. 797 L.), *nihilne te populi ueretur* 'Are you not at all embarrassed before the people?' (Kühner–Stegmann I 468).

187 hem, quid est? the question follows naturally from the exclamation, which itself is interrogative in effect.

189 uir 'my husband'.

190 optio 'choice', 'opportunity'. *copia* would be the more natural word, but *optio* has evidently been chosen for the word play with *optinendi*.

191 mira sunt: singular *mirum est* is of course normal. For reasons which are not quite clear, a kind of generalizing plural is found with this particular word (E. Löfstedt, *Syntactica* I 63); cf. 625 *miris modis*.

192 ius suom ad mulieres 'their marital rights'. In other words, 'We women always manage in practice to control our husbands.'

193 quin 'Why!' (cf. 93n.).
  mihi: dative of disadvantage; 'this is what he has done to me'.
  ingratiis 'against my will'; negative of *gratiis*, which is ablative plural of *gratia* used adverbially.

194 educta: used in almost the same way as *educata*. The two verbs are frequently confused.
  quae. . . siet: the subjunctive in the second relative clause seems at first sight strange after *est* in the first. Perhaps the effect is concessive (*quae siet = quamuis sit*); so Ussing.

195   For the construction after *postulat*, cf. 127, 141.

196   ipsus = *ipse*.

197–8   Acidalius' brilliant correction of the speakers in these lines (accepted by Leo and G–S²) is far the simplest way to make sense. Lindsay's arbitrary change of *tace* to *dice* (!) was followed by Ernout and Paratore.

197   nam 'but surely'; cf. 178n.

198   nos sumus 'we are alone'. This looks very like a latinization of the Greek expression αὐταί ἐσμεν (e.g. Ar. *Thesm.* 472).
     unde ea tibi est? 'How *can* she be yours?' That this is the meaning, and not 'Where did you get her from?', is shown by Myrrhina's next sentence. Several scholars, beginning with P. Legrand in *R.E.G.* 15 (1902) 376, have assumed the second meaning, and thought that this question appeared also in the Greek original, and the answer to it led eventually to the recognition of Casina as Myrrhina's own child. (For an equally far-fetched attempt to divine the recognition scene in Diphilus' play, see 71on.)

199   peculi 'private property'. The word is more commonly found for the personal savings of a slave, but it can also indicate the limited ownership permitted to the subordinate members (the children, for example) in a Roman family. Myrrhina's assumption that Cleostrata cannot properly have a slave girl as her own, independent of her husband, reflects Roman law, not Greek (Watson 29–31). It is at first sight inconsistent with 371, where Lysidamus concedes that his wife has rights in connection with Casina (*tuo pro iure*); perhaps even in Rome the situation in practice would differ from what was strictly legal.
     Myrrhina's argument for wifely submission has seemed to some commentators inconsistent with her later support for Cleostrata's intrigue against her husband. The explanation is dramatic. At this stage in the play the poet requires the strong statement of two opposing points of view (the prerogative of the husband and the resentment of the wife), and he uses the available characters to bring this out; later the play becomes a male/female confrontation, and Myrrhina takes her natural place beside her friend and neighbour.

200   et quae habet: *quae* refers to the following *ei*; 'If a wife has her own possessions, she cannot have got them properly.'

201   quin 'but that', 'without'. This is close to the later limited use with verbs of prevention.
   uiro: with *subtrahat*.

204   sis = *si uis*. Also 205.
   stulta...**ausculta:** assonance (p. 27).

206–7   delicuom 'lacking'.

208–9   satin = *satisne*.
   tuam rem 'your own interests'.
   istaec = *ista*; object of *loquere*.

210–11   huic uerbo: the dative is regular with *uitare* in Plautus.
   i foras mulier: a formula of divorce. In *Amph.* 928 we hear another formula, spoken there by the wife: *ualeas, tibi habeas res tuas, reddas meas.*

212   st: 148n. Here again it is *extra metrum*.

213   em 'Look!' This exclamation is confused in the manuscripts with the interrogative *hem* (187).
   uir 'my husband'.
   eccum: 163n.

214   age 'come'.
   amabo: 137n.
   The clausula to this line (*impetras, abeo*) has clearly the same rhythm as that of 216 (*nunc uale*. MY. *ualeas*). cr²^ ($\perp \cup \perp \cup \cup -$) seems the best description, because it allows the natural word accents of *ábeo* and *uáleas* to be reflected in the scansion.

216   igitur: this word can have temporal significance; 'then'.
   Myrrhina re-enters her house.

Scene 3   217–278

Lysidamus returns home in a perfumed and euphoric state, thinking of his love for Casina. His wife awaits him.

Metre: The scene falls into three parts –

(a) **217–28** Anapaests
(b) **229–51** *Mutatis modis canticum*
(c) **252–78** Trochaic septenarii

(a) **217–28** Anapaests (Octonarii 217 (?), 219 (?), 222–7
                              Septenarii 218 (?), 220, 221, 228)

Notes

217 **ămŏrém** and **nĭtŏríbŭs** both cause offence, even in anapaests.
219 The weak 'fall-over word' *habeat* arouses suspicion.

217–21 The text of the Palatine recension has suffered some distortion, and unfortunately we have not here the readings of the Ambrosian palimpsest to act as a control. The metre is certainly anapaestic, but in every line there is some doubt about the exact wording.

217 nitoribus nitidis: this kind of word play is called the *figura etymologica*; cf. *munditiis Munditiam* 225, *unguentum unguor* 226.
  omnibus rebus...nitoribus nitidis make an awkward pair.
  anteuenire 'surpass'.

218 potis (*est*) = *potest*. This old adjective is usually (as here) indeclinable.
  salis 'wit', 'taste'.

219 habeat: subjunctive because of the hypothetical, conditional, sense of the sentence; 'which could have'.
  condimentis 'herbs and flavourings in cooking'. One has a strong suspicion that somewhere here (or in 225; cf. also 814), there is an allusion to *casia* 'cinnamon', from which the girl Casina's name is derived.
  Apart from that, a relationship between food and sex is a continual theme in this play (Introduction, p. 32). The *senex* gets neither his food (cf. 152–4) nor his intended sexual pleasure. Compare also 725, 801–2, etc.

220 utier = *uti*, infinitive.

221 placiturum: referring to the whole *ubi* clause; 'it will please'. See however the app. crit.

223 fel...mel: assonance.

224 de me 'from my own experience', which is also the meaning of *domi*. This line, from *hanc* to *facio*, is also found at *Cist.* 204.

225 The text is uncertain (see app. crit.). Schoell's version, which keeps close to the manuscripts, introduces a pun on the name of Casina (cf. 219n.).

    munditiis Munditiam antideo (= *anteeo*): for this kind of Plautine exaggeration cf. the passages cited at 128n.

226 mўrŏpōlās: Greek μυροπώλας, 'perfume sellers'.

    This was incautious of Lysidamus, as his wife smells the perfume in 236, and naturally asks what he has been up to.

227 ut uideor 'as I think'.

    uxor me excruciat, quia uiuit: extreme humour against wives and marriage is common in the plays (e.g. *Aul.* 155-6), and indeed in the fragments of Greek New Comedy, so that it cannot be ascribed simply to Roman vulgarity. It would presumably please the crowd; cf. 234, 354.

228 tristem: 'scowling', 'unwelcoming', rather than 'sad'; cf. 282. The adjective is predicative, to be taken with the verb.

    mala res 'disaster' – i.e. his wife.

    Here the sequence of anapaestic octonarii ends suitably with a catalectic line (sept.). The metre now changes; Lysidamus' soliloquy is over, and he starts a duet with his wife.

(b) 229-51 Mutatis modis canticum

Metrical analysis

229-31 $3 \times ia^8$

(**229** **tŭ:** prosodic hiatus

    ăb(i) ătqu(e): iambic shortening

    ābstĭnĕ: perhaps a unique example in iambics of the shortening of a cretic word-form to a dactyl in other than the first foot of a line or half-line (Questa 44). An objection even to the dactyl is that it breaks Hermann's law (p. 219)

230, 231 *ess'* and *mitt'* by syncope (p. 213) provide an alternative scansion, perhaps to be preferred.)

232–5		$4 \times cr^4$
236	— — ∪ — — — ∪ — — ∪ ∪ —	ia^4 $ia^{2\wedge}$
237	∪ ∪ — — ∪ ∪ ∪ ∪ — — — ∪ ∪ — ∪ ∪ — — — ∪	$an^{8\wedge}$
238–46		$9 \times tr^8$

(These are full of metrical irregularities. Some (e.g. F. Skutsch) have found anapaests instead.)

239   **cănă cŭléx:** the divided anapaest breaks Ritschl's law (p. 219); similarly after *myropola* 238, *lustra* 242

240   **sĕnĕct(a) aetáte:** the accented syllable of *senecta* is apparently shortened by iambic shortening (a phenomenon which occurs with this word also in *Most.* 217 *in sénecta mále querére*). There is hiatus after *aetate*

242   **omnia:** a dactylic word which fills a foot breaks Hermann's law (cf. 229)

244   **⟨senum⟩ senem:** an attractive supplement, but suspect because the consequent line has no central diaeresis, a feature almost invariable in tr^8, as the element at the diaeresis may not be disyllabic (cf. 406 and p. 224).)

247	∪ ∪ ∪ — ∪ ∪ ∪ — — — — — ∪ —	cr^4
248	— ∪ — ∪ — ∪ ∪ — — ∪ —	cr^c cr^c
249–50	∪ ∪ — ∪ ∪ — — — — ∪ ∪ — ∪ ∪ — — —	ith $ia^{4\wedge}$
251		ia^8

229   **quid agis** 'How are you?'

230   **heia** 'Now then!' This exclamation almost always indicates a kind of ironical surprise (Hofmann 25); cf. 723.

Iuno, Ioui: allusion to Jupiter and Juno is a repeated theme in this play, representing the master and mistress of the house, and also perhaps the conflict and jealousy of the married pair; so also 331ff., 406ff. This extravagance is typically Plautine, and probably introduced by him (i.e. not from Diphilus). It is found also in the *Mercator* (690, 956).

231   **mitte me** 'Leave me alone.'

232   **sanŭn** = *sanusne*.

233   **nolo ames:** subordinate subjunctive without *ut*, as commonly in colloquial Latin; cf. *dicas uelim* in the next line.

234 uelim 'I should like'.

Lysidamus refers (in an aside, which she however overhears) to his wife's last remark: CL. *enecas* 'You're killing me' (with annoyance). LY. 'I wish you were speaking literally.' CL. 'I believe you there.' For the comic husband's death-wish for his wife, cf. 227.

235 mi lepos 'my sweet'; not to be confused with *mi lepus* (138). = *ita (lepos tibi sum) ut tu mihi es.*

236 perii 'I'm done for.'

237 manufesto: adverb.
  teneor 'I'm caught.'
  cesso 'Why am I slow to?'
  detergēre: second conjugation.

238 ut: jussive; 'May he ruin you.'
  Mercurius: god of tradesmen.

239 eho: an exclamation of surprise and indignation, 'What?'
  nihili: 119; also 245.
  cana culex 'grey-haired gnat' – the term of abuse being chosen no doubt because of the notorious lechery of flies.

240 ignaue 'you slug'.

241 dedi operam 'I have been assisting.'
  ēmit: present indicative, as regularly with *dum*.

242 in lustra iacuisti: we should expect *in lustris*. Early Latin is not so careful of this distinction; cf. *Amph.* 180 *mihi in mentem fuit.*

245 lustratū's = *lustratus es* (prodelision, p. 214).

The rhythm of the line is worth remark. Eight trochaic feet fall into four equal phrases. This puts great weight on the repeated *ubi*'s; and evidently hiatus is not objectionable between these cola. There is also assonance (in this case rhyme) between the diaeresis and the line end.

246 mades 'you're drunk', a brilliant emendation by Schoell.
  rūgat 'is crushed'. The indicative may be found in indirect questions in Plautus.

248 es: imperative of *ĕdo* 'eat'.
  rem 'your money', 'the family estate'.

249–50 ohe: *interiectio est satietatem usque ad fastidium designans* (Donatus). *ohe iam satis (est)* is common for 'Stop! that's enough' (*Stich.* 734, Hor. *Sat.* 1.5.12).

nimium tinnis: cf. *Pseud.* 889 *nimium iam tinnis; tace.*

251 'Leave yourself something to nag about tomorrow.'
This is the end of the second section of the scene. The metre now changes again, as Lysidamus tries to discuss the situation rationally with his wife.

(*c*) **252–78**   Trochaic septenarii

252   quid ais: this introduces a question; 'tell me'.

254   detur nuptum: cf. 86 *ibit nuptum.*

255   frugi: *bonae frugi* was originally a predicative dative describing the soil, 'fruitful', 'good'. From that, the two words, or *frugi* alone, came to be used as an indeclinable adjective meaning 'honest'.

ubi: in effect, 'with whom'.

The subjunctives *sit* and *educat* (256) are effectively of purpose, within the *ubi* clause, but affected by *ut detur* (254). The ablatives *ligno, aqua,* etc. qualify *bene sit*; 'where she may be well supplied with...'.

56   educat: from *educere*; cf. 194.
A word has dropped out at the end of this line. No really satisfactory supplement has been found.

257   nequam 'worthless' is indeclinable.

armigero atque improbo: Lysidamus treats *armigero* as a term of abuse; cf. 262 *scutigerulo*. Chalinus is a 'soldier's servant' (55n., 62n.). For the coupling of a descriptive noun and an adjective, cf. Cic. *Pro Arch.* 10.24 *fortes uiri, sed rustici ac milites.*

258   peculi: 199n. The genitive depends on *nummus.*
plumbeus: i.e. valueless.
The hiatus between *homini* and *hodie* in this line is at the less common of the two *loci Jacobsohniani* (p. 217), after the initial cretic of a trochaic septenarius. For some reason phrases similar to this seem to attract hiatus in septenarii at this point:

Poen. 824   *cui hominí* | *erus est consimilis*
Most. 948   *cui hominí?* | *ero nóstro quaeso*
Capt. 828   *quo hominé* | *adaeque nemo.*

259   mirum: understand *est.*

senecta aetate officium: this is normally treated as an example of the common hiatus at the diaeresis of a long line (*senécta* | *aétate*); it is probably more correct to mark the hiatus at the end of the word-group (*senécta aetáte* | *ófficium*); cf. 240 *sénecta aetáte* | *únguentatus, Amph.* 1032.

260   quid iam? 'Why so?'

261   quae: the relative, referring to *curare ancillas*, is attracted into agreement with *curatio.*

262   qui malum 'why the devil'. For *qui*, cf. 93n.; for *malum*, 91n.
dăre̊ lŭbĕt: proceleusmatic.
enim: asseverative (178n.); 'in fact'; also in 268.

263   Does she mean, 'we should support our son by giving Casina to his personal servant', or 'by providing amatory opportunities for him'? Cleostrata's motives in respect to her son seem ill-defined in Plautus' play; her prime motive, however, is clearly to frustrate her husband (59).

264   Scan, *unicus est ill' mihi*. The word-break after *unicus* violates Hermann's law (p. 219), unless *est* is treated as enclitic (Appendix 1, section 2 (iii)).

266   homo 'my good man', with sarcasm.
malam rem 'trouble'.

267   nam: explanatory here, as in later Latin.
friguttis: an obscure word; apparently, 'twitter', 'stutter'.

268   frugi: 255n.

269–70   impetro, exoro: present indicatives for vividness.

271   impetrassere: a form equivalent to a future infinitive. See on *decolassit* (307n.). (There are six examples of the infinitive in *-sere* in Plautus, all at the verse end, four of them being this word *impetrassere*; Happ 90 n. 2.)

272 tuis uerbis 'on your instructions', 'from you'.

274 nostrum uter 'which of us'.
Cleostrata leaves the stage.

275 istam: used with a tone of spite (as happens frequently with *iste*), although she is no longer on the stage.
  quod: referring to the previous words, 'a thing which'.
  liceat: jussive subjunctive, 'may I be allowed', 'let me'.

276 ob industriam here, but the commoner *de industria* (with the same meaning) in 278.

Scene 4 279-308

Lysidamus, failing to persuade Chalinus to give up his claim to Casina, makes arrangements for the taking of lots to decide whose bride she is to be.
Metre: trochaic septenarii.
(The conventional scene division here gives a wrong impression. Lysidamus is already speaking in 278, and continues in 279. All that happens is that the slave Chalinus comes out of the house on to the stage.)

279 qui (the old ablative, 'by which', 'how', 'why', 99, 262) is used in curses as if it were *utinam*. The expressions in which it is found are like ours here, with an accusative pronoun immediately following the particle: *Men.* 931 *qui te Iuppiter dique omnes perduint, Pers.* 783 *qui illum Persam. . .male di omnes perdant.*
  deaeque: synizesis.
  te uxor aiebat tua: Plautus cleverly portrays the supercilious attitude of the slave to his master.
  Many editors assume a verbal joke here, by printing *te – uxor aiebat tua*, thus making Chalinus begin as if he is offering *te* as an alternative object to *di omnes deaeque perdant*, and then (after a pause) continue the sentence differently. There are several parallels for this in the text of Plautus; it would be a matter for the producer and actor.

280 enim 'indeed' (178n.).

281 *porrecta frons* would be the opposite of *contracta frons* 'a frown'. So *porrectiore fronte* = 'in a more respectful way'.

282   tristem 'surly', cf. 230.

cuius: monosyllabic.

potestas plus potest: repetition of syllables and alliteration show Plautus' usual appreciation of the sound of words.

283-4   The manuscripts offer a corrupted text at the beginning of this line. Seyffert's correction seems best; cf. *Trin.* 320 *is probus est quem paenitet quam probus sit et frugi bonae.*

frugi: 255n.

iam pridem 'for a long time now', used with the present tense *esse*, is an idiom for which parallels are easy to find in other languages, e.g. French *je suis depuis longtemps...*

intellego: ironical.

285   quin 'why not', 99n.

emittere manu = 'to set a slave free', 'manumit'.

quin 'nay', 93n.

286   nihil est 'it is no use'.

me cupere factum 'that I wish it done'.

287   The line cannot end with two iambic words (*egó loquár*) by Luchs's law (p. 219). We therefore scan with hiatus after *scire* or after *ausculta*, and end *égŏ lŏquár*.

290-1   *caelibem* and *liberum* are balanced by *maritum* and *seruom*. The former word in each case is in apposition to *te*, the latter is predicative (*liberum esse, seruom aetatem degere* 'to live your life as a slave').

gnatos = *natos*.

293   periclo more or less equals 'expense'. Behind the cross-talk, there is a real fact about the slave world, that the condition of a slave could be preferable to that of a poor free (or freed) man; at least the slave would be fed and housed.

294   nato: tautological, 'to no mother's son'. Olympio goes one further (323), and says he would not yield Casina even to Jupiter.

296   There was an ancient custom of taking decisions by drawing marked 'lots' (*sortes*) from an urn (*sitella*) filled with water. The *sortes* would be pebbles, or pieces of some hard wood which does not float. The purpose of the water was presumably to prevent the marks on the lots from being legible while they lay on the bottom (cf. 380 *uide ne quae illic insit alia sortis sub aqua*).

This practice was used for public decisions at Rome (Livy, 25.3, 41.18), especially in connection with the voting order of the tribes in the assembly (Lily Ross Taylor in *Roman voting assemblies* (1966) 70ff.; she seems however to misinterpret the evidence from the *Casina*). R. Düll (*Zeitschr. der Savigny-Stiftung* 58 (1938) 17–35) argued that it was a specifically Roman practice, introduced by Plautus in place of some other method of lot-taking in his original; the mythological reference in 398–9, however, shows that the method was known in the Greek tradition as well. For the actual procedure, see 387n.

efferto 'bring out'. This alternative form of the second person imperative is used with some consistency by Plautus for commands relating to future time (Lindsay, *Syntax* 72).

satis placet 'I have no objection', 'certainly'.

297　aliquouorsum 'one way or another'.

tragulam: this word, which means a javelin, is used by Plautus for a plot or trick (*Epid.* 690 and *Pseud.* 407). In both those passages, however, the metaphor is easily understood, because the phrase is *tragulam inicere*. Here, *decidero* must mean that he will 'parry', 'knock out of the way', the 'javelin' or trick that is being aimed at himself.

298　sic: i.e. by the methods that he has used so far, persuasion and pressure.

300　pereas cruciatu malo: for allusions to the possibility of brutal punishment for slaves, cf. 93, 139.

302　abin = *abisne*, 'Aren't you going?'
Chalinus leaves the stage.

303　-ne often plays the part of *nonne* in Plautus (Lindsay, *Syntax* 128).

304　mĕ́(a) ŭxŏ́r or **m(ea) ŭ́xŏr**? Questa and Drexler assume that the latter, with synizesis and total elision, is the only possible scansion here and at 329, 409, 481, because the former involves the iambic shortening of the accented syllable of *uxor*. This is not certain; the same explanation cannot be used for *sed uxor* in 1000 (tr^{8A}) and 227 (an⁸), nor indeed is it clear that there would be an audible difference of pronunciation between the two scansions – they might in fact sound very much alike (cf. the note on 5 *qui utuntur*).

305   ecce me: cf. 163 *eccam*; also *eccum* (308).

nullum 'of no value', 'done for'; cf. 621 *nulla sum*.

306   spēcula 'a little hope'.

spḗcŭl(a) ĭn sŏrtītūst: the trochaic break is permissible in the first foot of a line or half line, but would otherwise break Ritschl's law (p. 219). The operation of iambic shortening on syllables in quite separate words (*in s-* being shortened by *-cŭl-*) appears to be possible if there is elision between the words (Questa 57ff.). The rather complicated rhythm is the same as that in 970, which begins *nŭnc ĕg(o) intĕr sacrum saxumque*.

307   decolassit 'trickle away' (from *cŏlum* 'sieve'; contrast *cŏlus* 'distaff' 170–1).

Early Latin offers a large number of examples of '*s*-forms' which were later given up. Commonest is a tense in *-so, -sĭs, -sĭt, -sĭmus, -sĭtis, -sint*, these endings being added either to a consonantal stem (e.g. *faxo*) or to a first conjugation verb (e.g. *amasso*). The tense is thought to have originated as an aorist subjunctive (cf. Greek πράξω), but it is used in practice as a future (usually future simple, sometimes as here future perfect). Parallel to *decolassit* in this play are *faxo* 484, *effexis* 708, *peccassit* 825, *amasso* 1001 and 1002, *occepso* 1001, *faxit* 1016. An infinitive was even created from this tense (*impetrassere* 271). (The latest discussion is by Happ 87–92; for the other '*s*-tense' in *-sim, -sĭs, -sĭt*, see note on 324 *seruassint*.)

'I will take a sword for my bed and lie on it.' These are comic heroics, with parody of tragedy (e.g. *Ajax*).

308   eumque incumbam: *eum* is governed by the preposition at the beginning of the verb (Lindsay, *Syntax* 28). Later Latin would have *in eum* or *ei*.

Scene 5   309–352

A conference of the two conspirators, Olympio and Lysidamus. Cleostrata has been no more successful in trying to persuade Olympio than Lysidamus was with Chalinus.

Metre: senarii.

309–11 una opera...qua opera 'as well (put me in an oven), as...'.
Olympio comes out of the house still speaking to Cleostrata, who remains inside.

309 condito: 'put', from *condere*; for the form, cf. 296 *efferto*.

310 pro 'as', 'in place of', 'like'; cf. *pro praesentibus* 20.
  pane rubido: probably dark red, having been twice baked, like a biscuit. (The vowel length *rūbidus* here and at *Stich.* 230, contrasting with *rŭber, rŭbicundus, rŭbeo*, etc., is unexplained.)

311 istuc: antecedent of *quod*.

313 She is frightening him with talk of his prospects of manumission, trying to blackmail him.

314 qui: referring to *me*.
  si = *etsi*, as often.

315 ingratiis: 193n. The genitive *amborum* shows the noun origin of *ingratiis*.

316 una libella: a very small coin, an *as*, the tenth part of a *denarius*. Olympio can get his freedom at a nominal price provided he pleases his master; cf. *Capt.* 947 *at ob eam rem mihi libellam pro eo argenti ne duis*, which also refers to the price of a slave.

317 quicum 'with whom'.

318 cum eadem qua: i.e. *cum eadem cum qua*. Understand *litigas* again in the relative clause.
  uxori: ablative; cf. 71n.

319 quam tu mi uxorem (*dicis*)? 'What do you mean, your wife?' This type of expression is quite common in Plautus (e.g. *Poen.* 972 *quid tu mihi testis?*) and Cicero (e.g. *In Verr.* 2.2.32.79 *quem mihi tu Bulbum, quem Staienum?*). Here it prepares for the alternative identification offered in the following joke.

320 cane: there is a long history of 'dog' or 'bitch' as a pejorative term for women. Helen applies it to herself in the *Iliad* (6.344, 356), and Hecuba in the myth was actually turned into a dog, providing a warning lesson in *Men.* 716–18, *idem faciebat Hecuba quod tu nunc facis:* | *omnia mala ingerebat quemquem aspexerat.* | *itaque adeo iure coepta appellari est Canes.*

321 quid agit? 'What is she up to?'

323 The heroic constancy of the human lover even when his rival is a god also has a long literary background (e.g. Idas in *Iliad* 9.559–60). Irony is added to the use of the theme here by the repeated identification of Lysidamus, Olympio's master, with Jupiter (230, 331ff.). When the time comes (884), Olympio does indeed try not to yield place to 'Jupiter' himself.

324 si is mecum oraret 'if he should ask me'. Perhaps *mecum* (instead of *me*) is to be explained as a survival from the original meaning of *orare*, 'speak' (cf. *orator*); so Hofmann 129.

seruassint: in addition to the '*s*-form' tenses in *-so*, which are used as futures (307n.), early Latin also had a tense in *-sim, -sīs, -sīt, -sīmus, sītis, -sint*, these endings being added either to a consonantal stem (*faxim*) or to a first conjugation verb (*amassim*). The tense is parallel to a Greek aorist optative, and is used in practice as equivalent to a present or perfect subjunctive in Latin. It is found in wishes, as here; in prohibitions, as 404 *ne obiexis*, 628 *caue ne faxit*; in a potential, as 347 *non empsim* 'I would not buy'. So *di te seruassint* = 'May heaven preserve you.'

325–7 A build-up to an obscene joke.

325 Cf. *Merc.* 959 *nam mea uxor… tota in fermento iacet*, *Most.* 699 *tota turget mihi uxor, scio, domi. fermentum* is yeast, which causes fermentation.

326–30 edepol appears in the same position in three successive lines; there follows the rhetorical placing of *inimica, inimicus, inimici* at the beginning of successive clauses. This exemplifies the vigour and artistry of Plautine language.

326 Backchat to *in fermento* and *turget* – 'I wish she'd burst in two', 'split herself'. The same joke is found at *Bacch.* 603 PA. *sufflatus ille huc ueniet*. PI. *dirrumptum uelim*.

327 esse: i.e. *mediam dirruptam esse*; 'I presume she already has been.'

siquidem tu frugi bonae es 'if you are any good as a husband'. For *frugi bonae*, see 255n.

sĭquidem: enclisis, p. 214.

328 uerum: coming back to the point after a joke – as a modern comedian might say, 'but, seriously,...'.

330 familiares: members of the household, fellow slaves.

tuā: this is the regular usage with *rēfert*, either the genitive of the person or the ablative feminine singular of the possessive adjective (agreeing with *rē* in the verb); 'What is that to you?'

331–7 For the theme of master = Jupiter, see 230n.

332 minutos deos 'little gods' (cf. 336 *deos minores*). In Greek popular religion there was a second order of gods called 'daemons'. They may be referred to here, and at *Cist.* 512 *di deaeque, superi atque inferi et medioxumi*, and 522 *di omnes, magni minutique et etiam patellarii*; and are certainly alluded to by Arcturus in the Prologue to the *Rudens* (*Rud.* 9ff.).

caue feceris (perfect subjunctive) 'do not consider'.

(*non*) *flocci facere* means to consider worthless, (not even) worth a tuft of wool. *flocci* is genitive of value.

333 'What you are saying (*istae*) is great nonsense.'

334 ut 'how'.

humani Ioues: imaginative scholars have seen a topical allusion, either to the death of Alexander the Great (F. Skutsch, who uses this hypothesis to help date the play of Diphilus), or to that of Scipio Africanus (Buck, De Lorenzi), or distributively to both (Arnaldi). Others have remained sceptical.

It is a clever line, even without a topical allusion. Human gods unexpectedly die.

335 The connection of thought has worried some commentators. Perhaps *sed tandem* means 'to come to the point', after the moralizing reflection.

336 redierit: future perfect, the exact tense; 'when that has happened, who will etc.'.

337 tergo aut capiti aut cruribus: datives in the same relationship to *subueniet* as *mihi*. The back for beating, the legs for chains, the head perhaps for other fearful punishments (391n.), or to represent the whole living person (cf. *Amph.* 741 *uae capiti tuo* and often).

338 opinione melius 'better than you think'.
    res tibi habet: this intransitive use of *habeo* is found, although *se habet* would be more regular; cf. *Epid.* 696 *bene hoc habet*, *Pseud.* 935a *optume habet*.

342 sitellam: 296n.

343 ita rem natam 'things have so turned out'. Donatus (on *e re nata* in Ter. *Ad.* 295) *sic proprie dicimus de iis quae contra uoluntatem nostram acciderunt*.

344 necessum = *necesse*.
    uorsis gladiis: the expression has caused difficulty. The expanded Servius commentary on Virgil, *Georg.* 3.222 quotes this line as evidence that *uersa* can mean *infesta*. But in fact the sense here demands that the words mean 'with changed weapons' – *mutatis armis*.
    depugnarier: the alternative form of the passive infinitive (cf. 220 *utier*) is usually found (for metrical reasons) at the end of the line.

346 benedice: Greek εὐφήμει; 'hush', 'don't blaspheme'.
    deos sperare = *dis confidere*.

347 istud 'what you have just said'.
    empsim: for the form, see note on 324 *seruassint*. It is the equivalent of a perfect subjunctive used potentially, 'I would not buy'.
    tittibilicio: a nonsense word ('*nullius significationis est*' Festus); ablative of price. 'I would not pay a farthing for'. This obscure word not surprisingly caused difficulty to scribes. It was accurately preserved in the tradition of the grammarians Festus and Fulgentius, but the manuscript tradition of Plautus developed (under the influence of the mistake in 960) to *ut tibi est Stalino* (see 960n.).

350   st: 148n. Here the exclamation is not *extra metrum*, but counts as a monosyllable in the scansion.

eccum exit foras: cf. 163.

351   intus 'from inside'. This is common; cf. 855 *eximus intus*.

352   conlatis signis: Plautus favours military imagery (50n.; cf. 344, 357). It usually appears in the mouth of the dominant slave; in our play Lysidamus takes over some features of the regular slave role (cf. 950n.).

Scene 6   353-423

This is the drawing of lots, performed by the four interested parties – the master and mistress and their two slave supporters. It is of course the scene which gave its name to Diphilus' play *Kleroumenoi* (*latine Sortientes* 32), and is one of the three 'spectacular scenes' (*Introduction*, p. 35). There are many resemblances here, especially in the interchanges between master and slave, to the arbitration scene in the *Rudens* (*Rud.* 1045ff.); this is without doubt the result of the Diphilean origin of both plays.

After much verbal skirmishing, the lot for the lucky man who is to marry Casina is drawn by Cleostrata in 415; it is Olympio's.

Metre: trochaic septenarii.

353   face: classical Latin uses only *fac*.
   Cleostrata is alluding to the instructions which her husband gave to Chalinus in 295-6; Chalinus pretends to misunderstand her.

354   extra portam: funerals took place outside the gates of the city, whether by cremation (*ardentem*) or by burial. Cicero quotes a law from the Twelve Tables: *hominem mortuum in urbe ne sepelito neue urito* (*De leg.* 2.58).

355   'CL. I well believe that that is what he wants.   CH. Believe! I *know* it is.'

356   artificum: genitive depending on *plus*. ' I have more professional staff than I thought.'
   hariolum 'seer', 'soothsayer', 'prophet'. The *hariolus*, like the *haruspex*, divined the future by inspecting the entrails of sacrificial victims.

Lysidamus means that there is something uncanny about the exactness of the slave's knowledge (355 *certo scio*).

357 attollamus signa: cf. 352n.

358 sequere: imperative, addressed to Olympio.
quae imperauisti omnia: in 295–6.

359 situla = *sitella*.
te uno: ablative of 'the degree of difference', with *plus*, as in *nihilo plus*; 'Tu es seul de trop' (Naudet). Cf. *Stich.* 498 *uno Gelasimo minus est quam dudum fuit* 'We are short by one Gelasimus of what we had just now.'

360 stimulus 'goad'. The metaphor in this word leads naturally to *fŏdico* in the next line; cf. *Bacch.* 63 *aculeata sunt* (the attractions of a *meretrix*), | *animum fodicant*.

361 corculum: colloquial diminutive.

362 'LY. Be quiet, Chalinus. CH. Force *him* to be quiet. OL. You'd do better to force *him*. He is accustomed to that sort of thing.'
comprime: this verb is very commonly used by Plautus with a double meaning – 'control' (e.g. 250) and 'force sexually'; cf. *Amph.* 348–9 ME. *ego tibi istam hodie, sceleste, comprimam linguam.* SO. *haud potes:* | *bene pudiceque adseruatur.*
immo istunc 'No, him.'
qui didicit dare: *dare* has here an obscene sense, in effect to 'yield', 'allow'. Olympio, the rustic slave, accuses the house slave Chalinus of having been subjected to 'unnatural practices'. (There is the same sense with *datare*, the frequentative of *dare,* in *Aul.* 637.) This allegation of a homosexual relationship between master and slave is repeated in the scene 452ff., especially 460–2; cf. *Most.* 890 *erus te amat* (said by one slave to another).
(There is an odd metrical problem in this line. It will only scan if *immo* may have a short first syllable, so that (by iambic shortening) *ĭmm(o) ĭstŭnc* forms the fifth foot. There are several doubtful parallels for *immo* in the text of Plautus, and no fewer than five examples in Terence, mostly senarii beginning *immo uéro*. The phenomenon is mysterious, as Questa says (78).

The alternative is to make the easy change of the first *istunc* to *istum*, as do all modern editors except Lindsay. This however has two drawbacks: it destroys the repetition *istunc...istunc*, and it destroys also the natural end of the speech at the diaeresis of the line.)

363 cĕdo 'give', imperative of a verb of which only this form and the rarer plural *cette* are found.

364 atque: Plautus uses this form in an adversative sense later limited to *atqui*; 'and yet'.

365 Lysidamus makes a 'Freudian' slip of the tongue.

366 enim: affirmative (178n.); 'Yes, to me.'
uolui dicere 'I meant to say'.

367 Lysidamus still cannot get it right.

368 atque etiam facis (*perperam*) 'and you're also *acting* wrongly'.

370 per pol saepe: i.e. *persaepe pol*.
quid: indefinite in the *ubi* clause.
expetas: indefinite subject, 'you', 'one'. The verb is in the potential subjunctive, as it would be if the introductory conjunction were *si*.

371 tuo pro iure: Lysidamus here admits that Cleostrata has the right to take the decision about Casina (cf. 199n.).

373 gratiam facias 'do a favour to'.
= *neque facio* (*gratiam*) *neque censeo* (*gratiam faciendam esse*).

374 There is a word missing from the text in the manuscripts, most probably after *iam*. The supplement accepted here (*diribeam*), a technical word for the sorting of votes, might have been omitted because it was unfamiliar.
utrimque 'on both sides'.

375 iure 'rightly'.

376 This line is added in the margin of B, and does not appear in any other manuscript – a clear proof, if it were needed, that the corrector of B had access to an independent source for the text (Appendix 2, p. 233).

377 **sin secus** (*eueniet*).

378 **unum:** this is the mark on the lot given to Olympio.

379 **sis** = *si uis* (204).
  cedo: 363n.

379–81 The attribution of the speeches in these lines was much improved by F. Groh (see app. crit.). Olympio is the surly, suspicious, slave; and *mane* (379) introduces the same sort of comic objection as *mane dum* does in 384. Lysidamus, on the other hand, is at this point outwardly judicious and restrained; 381 *habe quietum animur* suits 387 *habe animum bonum*. Throughout this scene there is uncertainty about the speakers; the evidence of the manuscripts on this is unreliable.

380 **qua:** indefinite, 'any'.
  sortis: an old form of the nominative *sors*, not found elsewhere, but specifically quoted from this line by Priscian (*GLK* II 320).
  uerbero: Latin for *mastigia* (361).

381 **men** (i.e. *mene*) **te censes esse?** 'Do you think that I am like you?' This question suits Chalinus. He had brought out the *sitella*, and was the person who could most easily have interfered with it.
  modo 'only'.

382 **quod bonum atque fortunatum sit:** a typical Latin solemn formula, aimed to get a good omen for the beginning of an enterprise, and said by Olympio as he is about to put his lot into the *sitella*. Chalinus spoils the effect (cf. 410 *cur omen mihi uituperat?*) by interrupting.

383 **noui pietatem tuam:** the gods will certainly not help Chalinus, in Olympio's opinion. When he himself wins, he ascribes the victory to his own *pietas* and that of his ancestors (418).

384 **mane dum:** 'just wait'; *dum* is a sort of enclitic (p. 213). Compare 523 *facitodum*, 894 *agedum*; editors print as one word or two depending on the effect it may have on the scansion of the line; F. Ritschl, *Opusc. phil.* II 567f.
  The suspicious Olympio finds another ground for objection (cf. 379). These are lighter woods; the usual lots were perhaps made of hard wood, which would sink.

386   euge: 'Bravo!', 'Well said!' (Greek εὖγε). But the excited
Lysidamus immediately changes his tone, 'Watch it!'

   nunciam: when this is printed as one word, it is trisyllabic (here
elided – *nūncĭ(am)*).

   eccerē 'There you are.' The lots are now in the jar.

387   aequa: this is part of the procedure of lot-taking, as is shown by
a fragment from Cicero's lost speech *Pro Cornelio*, where he lists the
occasions when a veto may be applied during the passing of a bill,
dum sitella defertur, dum aequantur sortes, dum sortitio fit (*Pro Cornelio*
fr. 30 Schoell). The only intelligible explanation is that *aequare*
involves doing something to the urn, probably shaking it, to make sure
that the positions of the lots inside are random (this action seems to be
described by Cicero at *De div.* 2.86 as *sortes miscere*). The actual
sortitio takes place in 413–15, with Cleostrata dipping her hand in and
taking out one lot (415 *teneo sortem*). Compare 296n.

388   deuotabit 'she will bewitch'.

389   canem: some kind of chain, commonly called *catulus* (Festus
p. 39 L.). The Greek is σκύλαξ, which also means a dog.

   furcam: 139.

390   sortito: adverbial, 'by lot'.

   eueniat 'it may come'.

   pedibus pendeas 'that you should hang feet-down'. When a
slave was beaten, his hands were manacled and raised to a beam, so
that he hung with his feet off the ground. There are many allusions
to this in Plautus (e.g. 1003, *Truc.* 777 *rogitaui ego uos uerberatas ambas
pendentis simul*). The question here is whether *pedibus pendeas* can simply
mean 'hang with feet dangling', or whether it must mean 'hang by
the feet', i.e. upside down. There is a parallel passage in *As.* 301–5,
where the relevant phrase is *quando pendes per pedes*; there it certainly
appears that a heavy weight is attached to the feet of the slave as he
hangs, although the passage is not wholly clear. It seems preferable to
take both as meaning 'hang with feet dangling'; not that there
appears to have been any limit to the brutality of the Roman treatment of their slaves, but that this position would be more practical for
the purpose. (For slave punishments, see J. Marquardt, *Das Privat-
leben der Römer* (1879) 179.)

391 Olympio is characteristically the more violent and brutal. It was not unknown for a slave's eyes to be put out, and the threat is fairly common in Plautus (e.g. *Aul.* 53, 189). The expression here is simply exaggerated and vulgar – that he should blow his eyes out of his head down his nose. Ussing compares *Most.* 1110, where the old man says (with an allusion to the metaphorical use of blowing a person's nose for him, meaning to treat him like a child, and so deceive him) *immo etiam cerebrum quoque omne é capite emunxti meo.*

oculos: sometimes called a Greek accusative, as if *emungare* were the Greek middle, not passive; 'that you may have your eyes blown down your nose for you'.

392 quid times implies some by-play on the stage. Olympio's violent language may have made Chalinus quail.

laqueum evidently refers back to Chalinus' words in 111–12 and Olympio's reply in 113.

393 periisti 'You're done for.'

tu: attracted to the case required for the following purpose clause; it is later picked up by *tibi*.

Cléòstrata: with synizesis, as always. See the remarks on p. 95.

394 suspices: active form, for the usual deponent *suspiceris*. Similarly *sorti* in 395 and 413 is active in form, although from a verb which is normally deponent.

395 tute: strengthened form of *tu*.

lucrum facit 'he's getting a bargain' (by losing you). Chalinus affects to misunderstand Olympio's *perdis me* 'You're ruining me.'

(There has been some anxiety among scholars that *lŭcrum facit* breaks Luchs's law (p. 219). This is answered either by the argument that the two words go so closely together that they count as a quadri-syllable (cf. *Most.* 670 *bona fide, Cas.* 611 and often, *malam crucem*); or that the first syllable of *lucrum*, while certainly remaining short from the scansional point of view before 'mute and liquid' (p. 211), is nevertheless not absolutely short (cf. *Curc.* 477 *supra lacum*).

396 ut effugerit 'that it may have escaped'; perfect tense.

397 ain (*aisne*) **tu?** 'Really?'

fugitiuos: nominative masculine singular; cf. 8n. The fact that a slave who had done something wrong might take the extreme step of running away made *fugitiuos* a term of abuse, like *furcifer* (139).

omnis: i.e. including even inanimate lots.

398–9 An obscure mythological allusion has caused some confusion in the text, including an exceptional trochaic septenarius (399), with neither central diaeresis nor caesura; but there is no difficulty in the meaning. 'I hope your lot has dissolved in the lot-taking process, as they say happened once to the descendants of Hercules.'

Herculei: accepting this form with the older manuscripts, we must take it to be genitive of *Hercules* treated as a fifth declension noun (the usual Latin genitive is either *Herculis* or *Herculi*). Lindsay, following Wackernagel, believed this declension correct for Greek names in Plautus, and indeed replaced it in other lines (*ELV* 157).

praedicant: understand *accidisse* or even *sortes deliquisse*.

deliquerit: perfect subjunctive of *deliquesco*.

The story is told (with some variation) in Apollodorus (2.8.4) and Pausanias (4.3.3-5). It refers to the division of the chief areas of the Peloponnese between the 'Children of Hercules' after their successful invasion (known to us as the Dorian invasion).

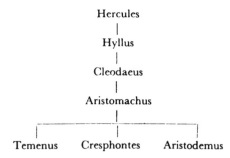

Pausanias' version, which is evidently the same as that alluded to here, is that Cresphontes and the sons of Aristodemus were drawing lots as to which should have Messenia. Because Cresphontes very much wanted to get Messenia, Temenus put in two lots of clay, one dried in the sun for his nephews, and one baked by fire for his brother. The sun-dried one dissolved in the water, so that Cresphontes' lot came out first, and he got what he wanted. The parallel is well chosen.

400 Another bullying remark from Olympio. *liquescas* of course picks up *deliquerit* of the previous line.

401 hoc age 'pay attention'.
litteratus 'scholar', referring to the mythological parallel just quoted. (Cic. *Brut.* 26.99 *alii a C. Persio litterato homine scriptam esse* (a speech) *aiunt*.)

402 Cf. 382.
ita uero 'exactly'.

403 immo 'on the contrary'.

404 illi odio 'that horror'.
age, ecquid fit? 'Come on, let's have some action.'
ne obiexis (= *obieceris*) **manum** 'Don't you touch him'; Cleostrata intervenes. For the tense-form, cf. note on *seruassint* 324.

405 compressan an porrecta 'with the fist or with an open hand'.
ferio: as in English, 'do I strike', meaning 'am I to strike'.
em tibi 'Take that'; to Chalinus.

406 quid tibi istunc tactio est?: this is a peculiar and quite frequent Plautine idiom, with a verbal noun taking an accusative object; cf. *Amph.* 519 *quid tibi hanc curatio est rem?* So also in 408.
quid 'in what way', 'why'; adverbial accusative.
Iuppiter: repetition of the previous identification of Lysidamus and Cleostrata with Jupiter and Juno; 230, 331–7.
(In this line, as also in 408, the eighth element is resolved into two shorts, which is not permitted if there is the regular central diaeresis of the line. There is a caesura after the seventh element, therefore, in these two cases, in place of the diaeresis after the eighth.)

407 rursum 'back'; i.e. return the blow.

408 tactio hunc: cf. 406.
haec: feminine singular, not neuter plural.

409 sïquidem: enclisis, p. 214.
mea uxor: for the scansion, see 304n.

410 'My supporter ought to be allowed to speak just as much as yours.'

cur omen mihi: Olympio's surly reply refers back to Chalinus' interruption of his formal prayers in 382 and 403. The Romans always believed that it ruined a ceremonial occasion if there was an interruption to the set form of words.

411 'I advise you to beware of trouble' – a real, if mildly worded, threat.

412 temperi: adverb meaning 'in good time'; here sarcastic for 'A bit late in the day!', cf. *Aul.* 454 *temperi, postquam oppleuisti fusti fissorum caput.*

oppugnatum: with a play on words, for he is *pugnis caesum* (407).

414 lïenosum: with synizesis, as the *e* is long.

The meaning of *cor lienosum* is obscure. Naudet says that those suffering from disease of the spleen are liable to palpitations of the heart; but this is probably a deduction from our passage, rather than an explanation. There is perhaps a connection with the words of an out-of-breath slave in *Merc.* 124 *perii, seditionem facit lien, occupat praecordia.* The spleen can be greatly enlarged by disease; but how, even in that case, one can speak of a *cor lienosum* remains unclear.

415 *cor* is the subject of *tundit, pectus* the object.

de labore 'from distress'.

foras 'out' (of the *sitella*).

416 iamne mortuos? 'Done for now?' Chalinus is standing by Cleostrata (408, 410), and so naturally catches sight of the lot before Olympio. *sum* is to be understood. Chalinus repeats this unusual expression in 427 *quid opus est, qui sic mortuos?* Modern editors accept Lambinus' change to *mortuo's* (*mortuos es*), addressed to Olympio. But it is not in character for Chalinus, with whom the audience is expected to sympathize, to boast prematurely and mistakenly.

mortuós (= *mortuus*, 8n.) has *brevis in longo* at the change of speaker.

The text of the second half of this line is corrupt. Leo and Lindsay print Camerarius' rhythmically awkward *mala crux éast* for *mala crucias.* (*mala crux* is found in the nominative meaning 'an infernal nuisance' at *Aul.* 522 *aliqua mala crux semper est quae aliquid petat*; cf. also *Aul.* 631.) But this still requires a second emendation (*mea ⟨haec⟩ est*) to achieve proper scansion.

417   cum nos di iuuere, Olympio, gaudeo: a formal expression of congratulation, frequent in Plautus and Terence; cf. *Men.* 1148 *cum tu es liber, gaudeo, Messenio.*

418   Cf. 383. Additional humour is given to Olympio's remark by the fact that a slave, being legally no more than a piece of property, could not properly have *ancestors* at all. The same joke is found at *Mil.* 373, *Pseud.* 581, *Stich.* 303, in each of which a slave refers to his 'forefathers'.

420   'Do you not know that it is a long way off to the villa in the country where he is to take his bride?' But the text is suspect.

   longe esse: for the adverb with *esse*, cf. *aegre est* in the following line (176–7n.).

421   licet 'All right.'

422   eāmus: with synizesis.
   numquid moror 'I'm not stopping you.'

423   hoc: Chalinus.
   Three of the participants in this scene have now entered the house, leaving Chalinus alone on the stage.

Scene 7   424–36

Chalinus soliloquizes on the result of the drawing of lots.

Metre: senarii.

424   meam operam luserim 'I should have wasted my effort.' Perfect subjunctive in the main clause after present subjunctive in the conditional clause is quite common in 'potential' conditions. The verbs in the following two lines continue the same tense.

425   sumpti fecerim 'I should have gone to the expense of'; cf. *Most.* 354 and elsewhere *lucri facere.* Lindsay gives numerous examples of this kind of genitive in *Syntax* 15.
   sumpti: for *sumptus.*

427   'What is the point, seeing that I am done for as it is?' For *qui sic mortuos* (understanding *sum*), cf. 416. For *tamen* used elliptically, cf. 63, 105.
   For the scansion of this line, see under *loci Jacobsohniani* (p. 217).

428   sorti: ablative (71n.).

430   opere tam magno: 21.

432   ŭt ĭllĕ trĕpĭdābāt: the ictus falls on the second syllable of *ille*; cf. *Poen.* 620 *et illé chlamydatus*, also 564 below *hominém amatorem*; Drexler, *Lizenzen* 80.

434   attat: exclamation of surprise at a sudden appearance; so also 619 and 723. It is a shortened form of *attatae* (468, 528).

436   hisce: not agreeing with *insidiis*, but dative plural, 'to these men' (Lysidamus and Olympio).
    Chalinus withdraws to the back of the stage.

Scene 8   437-514

Chalinus, overhearing a conversation between Lysidamus and Olympio, begins to understand their plan. Lysidamus shows signs of over-excitement. Olympio is sent to buy food for the wedding feast.

Metre: senarii.

437 Olympio and Lysidamus come on stage speaking about Chalinus, and how they would like to punish their rival.
    sine modo 'just let him'.

438   cum furca: as a punishment, cf. 139. But the image also suggests itself to Olympio of the charcoal-seller bringing his wares to town slung from a forked stick over his shoulder.

439   dabo factum 'I will see that it is done.'

440   uolui (for *uoluissem*) **mittere** 'I should have liked to send'. The auxiliary verb is idiomatically left in the indicative.

441   obsonatum: supine of purpose, 'to get food'.

443   nepam 'crab'. He withdraws to the back of the stage.

444   captandust horum sermo 'I must catch their conversation.'
    clanculum: diminutive, cf. 361.

445   cruciat, macerat: the words are effectively synonymous.

446 candidatus: Olympio, as bridegroom, is dressed in white.

cedit 'comes': This is an unusual meaning for the simple verb; *incedit* would be commoner.

hic: probably the pronoun, not the adverb.

mastigia: 361. Here it is nominative.

447 stimulorum loculi: *stimuli* are goads, pointed sticks for driving or beating. *loculi* most commonly means a money-box. It was evidently a popular form of Plautine humour to invent outrageous terms of abuse addressed to slaves, alluding to beatings, etc. So, 'you treasure-chest of goads'; cf. *Aul.* 45 *stimulorum seges* 'you crop of goads', *Pers.* 795 *stimulorum tritor* 'you wearer-out of goads'.

protollo mortem 'I postpone my death', alluding to his statement of 424-7. He now has something to do first.

protollo: it is rare in Plautine senarii (and unknown in the iambic lines of later writers such as Seneca and Phaedrus) for a molossus-shaped word (– – –) to fill this position from the sixth to the eighth element in the line. The reason without doubt is the strong clash of metrical ictus and word accent. F. W. Hall (*C.Q.* 15 (1921) 99-105) finds some twenty examples in the plays (another is *Cas.* 59, in the Prologue). In the present case, he thinks the explanation is that there is an air of tragic parody – Chalinus is striking an attitude; compare the high-flown language of the following line.

448 Acheruntem (with long first vowel, 159): accusative of motion towards.

449-70 A comic set-piece. Lysidamus is so pleased with Olympio that he makes what seem to be amorous advances to him. Olympio for his part does his best to be ingratiating. Chalinus, who is eaves-dropping, comes for a time to the wrong conclusion.

449 ut: exclamatory, 'how'; also in 458 and 463.

453 dēōscŭlēr, uŏlŭptās mĕă: for the scansion, cf. 136 (*dĕŏsc-* with synizesis is found also at 454 and 467).

454 quid, deosculere? 'What do you mean, kiss?' The sub-junctive repeats the mood of *deosculer* in Lysidamus' speech; the change to second person is natural, as *tua* for *mea* at the end of the line.

quae res?: probably a reference to *ob istanc rem* (453). The words could also mean 'What's all this', as in 728.

455 A grossly worded reference to homosexual assault. The line, as given by the manuscripts, will not scan, as *uesica* begins with two long vowels.

456 ecquid 'at all'.

ecquíd amas: the break after the trochaic word would violate Ritschl's law (p. 219) if it were not in the first foot; cf. 566 *sicút ego*.

459 ultro te 'Away with you', 'Get away'. We may understand an imperative with *ultro*, to govern *te*.

apage: Greek ἄπαγε, 'Get away.'

This line would be one of the most hilarious in the play, through the opportunity for suggestive action on the stage due to the comic misunderstanding of Lysidamus' motives by Chalinus and (momentarily) Olympio.

460 illuc est quod 'that is the reason why'. *quod* is adverbial accusative, as in 106, 127. Chalinus alleges that this behaviour of Lysidamus explains why he made Olympio his bailiff.

461 et idem: if this mean 'he also', there is unusual iambic shortening of a naturally accented syllable, for the masculine of this pronoun is *ídem*. It seems hardly possible to take *idem* as neuter (*idem*), an adverbial accusative like *quod* in the previous line, 'and in the same way' (so Lindsay, *Syntax* 24).

cum ei aduorsum ueneram: a regular duty of slaves was to go to meet their master and escort him home from a party; they were called *aduorsitores*, and the usual expression for their activity is *aduorsum ire* (*Most.* 876, 897, Ter. *Ad.* 27).

462 The joke is hardly transferable to English. 'He wanted to make me his door-keeper down by the door itself.' The *atriensis* had a position of authority comparable to that of the *uilicus*; he was the steward, major-domo.

463 In his excited language Olympio repeats the exclamatory *ut*; Lysidamus does the same in 467. *morigera* is often used of a wife: cf. note on 896d.

464 **ut** this time is consecutive, as is fairly conclusively shown by the subjunctive verb; 'so much so that'.

465 **hi conturbabunt pedes:** i.e. 'will sleep together'.

466 i.e. he practises homosexuality with adults.

468 **attatae:** Greek ἀτταταῖ, exclamation of surprise.

470 **ipsus** = *ipse* (196).
 deperit: 107n.
 deperit. habeo uiros: see under *loci Jacobsohniani* (p. 217).

472 **deduci** 'her to be married'.
 quid malum 'why the devil' (91).

474 **emitti manu:** Lysidamus holds out this prospect to Olympio, as he had previously to Chalinus (285), and Cleostrata to Olympio (3:3).

476 'Two boars in one thicket' seems like a proverb. The male animals have also sexual connotations, cf. the goat in 550 (*illius hirqui improbi, edentuli*) and the stallion in 811.

477 **hunc:** pointing at the other house on the stage.

479 **concredui:** alternative form of the perfect.
 dare: for *daturum*; cf. the present *ferio* in 405.

481 **uocabit** 'will invite'.
 huc: from here to 487, Lysidamus uses various forms of *hic* indiscriminately for his own house and his neighbour's. A wave of the hand would make it clear.

484 **faxo:** equivalent to the future *faciam* (307n.): 'I will see to it'. *faxo* is coordinate with *aberit*; i.e. neither verb is subordinate to the other.

485 The first *rus* is accusative of motion towards, 'to the country'; so also in 487.

486 **faciam nuptias:** i.e. 'go to bed with'.

488 age 'Come!' This has become so much of an exclamation that it has lost the sense of being second person singular, and can be used with a plural verb.

fabricamini: imperative.

489 malo uostro 'to your disadvantage'.

uiuitis (chosen for the alliteration) is almost colourless, 'are'.

490 scin quid nunc facias? 'Do you know what you are to do now?' This is probably a Grecism, οἶσθ' οὖν ὃ δρᾶσον.

491 Olympio is sent off to buy delicacies for the wedding feast.

propera: in parenthesis, 'be quick'.

492 molliculas: diminutive, as are *sepiolas* and *lolligunculas* in the next line.

licet: 421.

493 emito: future imperative (309) of *emo*.

sepiolas, lolligunculas: small cuttlefish and squids, the same as are now found in the Italian dish *fritto misto di mare*. They are called *seppie* and *calamari* in modern Italian.

lopadas 'limpets'. The Greek word is λεπάς, but *lopas* seems to be the Plautine form. It is found at *Rud.* 297 and in fr. 3 of the lost play *Parasitus Medicus*.

Shellfish are popularly believed to have aphrodisiac powers.

494 hordeias: an unknown fish. Schoell suggested that the name may be hidden in an entry in the *Corpus Glossariorum Latinorum* (2.480): ψῆσσα (thought to be turbot) ὁ ἰχθύς: *ordatia*.

The word suggests barley (*hordeum*) to Chalinus, who – heard only of course by the spectators – says that he prefers wheat (*triticum*), inventing a 'wheat-fish' *triticeia*.

495 soleas 'soles'; but the word also means slippers (709).

qui 'how', 'why'.

sculponeas: wooden 'clogs', worn by slaves. Cato, *De agri cultura* 59, *sculponeas bonas alternis annis dare oportet* (to one's slaves).

496 Cf. Gnatho to Thraso in Ter. *Eun.* 1028: *utinam tibi commitigari uideam sandalio caput* 'I wish I could see your head softened up with a slipper.'

COMMENTARY: 497–514   155

497 lingulacas: *genus piscis uel mulier argutatrix* (Festus p. 104 L.);
another pun.

499 in re praesenti 'when I am on the spot'.

500 aequom oras: Lysidamus answers the implied request in
Olympio's words, which is 'May I go now?' Or *oras* may be little
more than *dicis* (324).

501 parci: impersonal passive; lit. 'I do not want there to be any
sparing of money.'
  ampliter: cf. *firmiter* 132.

502 nam: elliptical use. It gives the reason why he does not wish to
continue the conversation with Olympio.
  opus est mihi hoc (with a wave of the hand) **uicino conuento**
'I need to get together with my neighbour over here.' This use of the
ablative of the perfect participle passive is a common idiom with
opus est; cf. 587 *quod factost opus*, *Merc.* 330 *hoc nunc mihi uiso opus est*
'I need to see him now.'

503 iamne abeo 'May I go now?' For the present tense, cf. 405
ferio.

504 'Not even if I were given my freedom three times over.'
Chalinus thus begins another soliloquy after the others have left the
stage, Olympio in the direction of the market, Lysidamus to call on
his neighbour Alcesimus.

509–10 P. Langen (*Plautinische Studien* (1886) 29) noted how Plautus
makes Chalinus say the same thing ('we've won') four times in these
two lines.

509 praeuortar 'I will outstrip, by-pass, get ahead of'. This is an
unusual use of the passive with an accusative object. Leo suggests that
it is a Latin imitation of the Greek construction with φθήσομαι (future
of φθάνω 'anticipate').

510 nostro omine = *fauste, feliciter*.

511–12 The *ut* is tautologically repeated, as occasionally happens
(e.g. *Bacch.* 777–9).

513–14 The final couplet, reminiscent of rhyming couplets at the
ends of acts in early Shakespeare plays, gets Chalinus off the stage.

513   quo...ut...ne: a plethora of final conjunctions, more striking (and unusual) than the repeated *ut* of 511-12.

ACT III

Scene 1   515-530

Lysidamus makes the arrangement with his neighbour Alcesimus for the latter's house to be vacant and ready for him to take Casina there after the wedding. He then leaves for the forum.

Metre: trochaic septenarii.

516   The use of the *figura etymologica* (217) is typically Plautine. Most of the line is repeated from *Bacch.* 399 *nunc, Mnesiloche, specimen specitur, nunc certamen cernitur.*

   specitur 'is seen' (*conspicitur*).
   cernitur 'is decided' (*decernitur*).

517-19   Rhetorical effect is given by the repeated line endings – *ponito ad compendium, addito ad compendium, ponito ad compendium.*

517   ponito (imperative, second person) **ad compendium** 'save it up', 'don't bother'. The metaphor is financial. *id*, which is the object of *ponito*, picks up the infinitive-noun *castigare*. Literally, 'As to finding fault with my being in love, put that in your savings.' (Both *compendium facere* (with the genitive) and *compendi facere* (*aliquid*) are common in Plautus; the closest parallel to our present example is *Mil.* 781 *quam potis tam uerba confer maxume ad compendium*, i.e. 'be brief'.)

518-19   'cano capite', 'aetate aliena', 'cui sit uxor': these are the arguments a friend might naturally use against Lysidamus' infatuation. They will be vain.

518   eo: adverb; 'add to it', i.e. to the *castigatio* which he is to dispense with in the previous line. So also *illuc* (519).

519   sit: concessive, 'though you have a wife'.
   id: as in 517.
   illuc: adverb, as *eo* in 518.

521   fac uacent 'make them empty'; cf. 146 *facite accersatis.*
   quin: correcting the other's statement (93); 'indeed'.

522 certum est: impersonal passive; in effect, 'I have decided'.

oh: the manuscripts' *eho* is unsuitable here (see 239, and Hofmann 16f.).

scitus 'clever'. Here is further Plautine word-play, 'you are too cleverly clever'.

523–4 'But see to it that you fulfil what the blackbird sings in his lines; make them come with provisions and all, as if they were marching to Sutrium.' The text is corrupt, but the essential point is clear enough in the second half of 524. We are told that *quasi eant Sutrium* had become a proverb derived from a forced march by an army taking its provisions with it. Sutrium was a frontier city in Etruria, where the Romans on occasion had to face hostile Etruscans (Livy 6.2 and 9) and Gauls. Festus (406.30 L.), with supplements by Scaliger: '*Su⟨trium quasi eant⟩ ut⟩ique in prouerbium ⟨abiit ex hac⟩ causa. Gallico tu⟨multu quon⟩dam edictum est, legiones Sutrii ut praesto essent cum cibo suo. quod usurpari coeptum est in is, qui suis rebus opibusque offici id (officii quid* Bothe, *officium* Lambinus) *praestarent quibus deberent. Plautus, 'sed facito dum, merula per uersus quod cantat, colas; cum suo cuique facito ueniant quasi eant Sutrium.'*

So all that Lysidamus is saying is that Alcesimus' household staff should come across on time as arranged.

The explanation of the first part of the couplet, as suggested by Lindsay in *C.R.* 6 (1892) 124, is that the proverb had become part of a popular song, in which it was ascribed to a blackbird (*merula*); and that the words *cum cibo cum quiqui* were thought to sound like the song of the blackbird.

523 facitodum: enclitic *dum* (cf. 384 *mane dum*).

merula: this word is not in the manuscripts of Plautus here, but comes from Festus; it is supported by *cantat*.

†**per:** it seems at least possible that this hides the audience of the blackbird in the popular song, if there was one (e.g. *pueris*, as proposed by Guyet).

colas 'practise'.

524 cum cibo cum quiqui: *quiqui* must be an old ablative, like the common *qui*, from *quisquis*, used indefinitely; 'with food and anything else'. A similar phrase occurs twice in the *Poenulus*: *Poen.* 536

sed tamen cum eo cum quiqui [i.e. 'for all that'] *quamquam sumus pauper-
culi, | est domi quod edimus*; cf. *Poen.* 588; Lindsay, *Syntax* 50.

Lindsay's suggestion (see above, 523-4n.) that these words are an
imitation of a bird-song (cf. pee-wit, whip-poor-will) receives some
modest support from *Men.* 653-4 MEN. *egon dedi?* MA. *tu, tu istic,
inquam.* PEN. *uin adferri noctuam* (an owl) | *quae 'tu tu' usque dicat tibi?*

cum cibo…ut ueniant: this was the sort of instruction issued to
the citizen armies of the ancient world, often with the addition of the
number of days' rations required; e.g. Aristophanes, *Peace* 312 ἔχοντες
ἥκειν σιτί' ἡμερῶν τριῶν, 'to come with three days' provisions'.

525   em 'There!'

tu…nullo scito scitus es: the words clearly refer back to the end
of 522, and apparently mean, 'you are clever, with no need of a
decree' – a pun, as *scitum* means a decision by an authoritative body,
cf. *plebiscitum.* But this is awkwardly expressed, and Dousa's emendation
te…nullum scitum scitiust 'no *scitum* is cleverer than you' is attractive;
it is derived from *Pseud.* 748 PS. *ecquid is homo scitust?* CH. *plebi
scitum non est scitius.*

526   ad forum: the place of public business is the natural place for
a senior citizen to go, and is thus used in the plays to motivate a
temporary absence of the *senex.*

527   habeant linguam…uocent: this is a pun based on the fact
that in old Latin *uocare*, besides meaning 'to invite', was an alternative spelling of *uacare* 'to be empty'; cf. 29 *uociuae.*

528   attatae: 468.

caedundus: gerundive, 'you must be cut down to size', as we
might say.

nimias delicias facis 'you are too excited', 'getting above
yourself'.

530 'Don't make me have to look for you.' *quaestio* is the usual form,
cf. *Persa* 51 *caue fuas mi in quaestione.*

usque adero domi: i.e. until the arrangements are complete.
Then presumably Alcesimus also will leave his house (484), so that
it will be empty for his neighbour.

Both men now leave the stage.

Scene 2   531–562

Cleostrata first shows in a soliloquy that she understands what is going on. She then sows the seeds of dissension between the colluding old men, by insisting that she does not need the help of Alcesimus' wife.

Metre: a single iambic octonarius, followed by trochaic septenarii.

531 All editors change this line into a trochaic septenarius to fit the rest of the scene, by the removal of *id*. The result is rhythmically unattractive – *hóc erat écastór quod mé uir* | (cf. however *Truc.* 949 *lépidus écastór*). A mixture of ia⁸ and tr⁸ᴬ is quite common in both Plautus and Terence (e.g. *Capt.* 533ff.); a single ia⁸ preceding a long run of tr⁸ᴬ is more doubtful, but cf. 251.

532 **hanc** (pointing to Myrrhina's house) **huc** (pointing to her own).

533 **sibi:** plural, in view of *deducerent*.

534 **adeo** 'for this reason', antecedent to *ne*.
   ignauissumis: cf. 240 *ignaue*.

535 **ueruecibus** 'wethers', i.e. castrated rams, old creatures unsuited for the pleasures of love. The word is used abusively for an old man also at *Merc.* 567.

536 **eccum:** 163. The hiatus after it may be that permitted after interjections (p. 216).
   senati: alternative to *senatūs*. We also may describe a person as a 'pillar' of an institution.

537 **praehibet:** scan as a spondee by contraction or synizesis; the word is on the way to becoming *praebet*.

538 'He is not cheap at the price at which a bushel of salt is sold'; i.e. he would be expensive at that price. Salt being proverbially cheap, this means that Alcesimus' worth is minimal. *emptu* is supine with *uilis* (as in *mirabile dictu*). *modius* is the subject of *uenit*, which comes from *uěneo, uěnire* 'to be sold'. *qui* is the ablative of price. For *qui uenit*, cf. *Persa* 661 *qui datur, tanti indica* 'Tell me at what price she is for sale.'

For the whole expression, cf. *Persa* 668 *non edepol minis trecentis carast* 'She is not dear [i.e. she would be cheap] at a price of three hundred *minae*.'

539   huc...in proxumum 'here, next door'.

540   si arcessatur, exspectat 'is waiting to see if she is going to be called over'. This use of *si* is close to an indirect question; so also in 542.
   ornata 'all dressed up'.

541   opino: the active form is found in early Latin.
   Cleostrata: for the scansion, cf. 393n.
   et tu = *etiam tu, tu quoque*.

543 The middle of the line presents a metrical problem. To scan
$-|\overset{\cup}{-}\cup\cup|\overset{\cup}{\cup}\qquad\cup-|$
orauit ut e(am) istuc breaks Ritschl's law (p. 219; *ōrāuĭt | ŭt*); so there seems a syllable too many.
   (1) Lachmann (*ad* Lucr. 5.396) and Buecheler (*Carm. Lat. Epig.* 56.3), followed by Leo, argued that the perfect of the first conjugation was occasionally contracted (*orât* for *orauit*, like *adît* (read by some at 696) for *adiit, adiuit*). The strongest parallels are *Asin.* 501 *adnúmerauit ét mihi crédidit*, *Pers.* 834, *Mil.* 1038, all of which have naturally been emended by most editors.
   (2) Lindsay and more recent editors accept Spengel's modest alteration of *istuc* (A P) to *isto*, the rarer form of the adverb.
   ad te: with *mitterem*.
   adiutum: supine; cf. 86 *ibit nuptum*.

544   uin uocem: cf. 521 *fac uacent*.
   te nolo 'Don't bother.'

545   nil moror 'I don't mind.'

547   satis domist 'We have enough at home.'

548   conuenibo = *conueniam*.
   istanc iube: understand *ualere*.
   At the end of this line Cleostrata withdraws from the front of the stage to allow Alcesimus his parting soliloquy. She comes forward again in 558 for a soliloquy herself.

550 Hiatus both at the diaeresis and at the *locus Jacobsohnianus* (p. 217).

hirqui 'he-goat', a lecherous and smelly animal.

552 catillatum: supine, 'to lick plates', like a parasite. The word comes from *catillus*, diminutive of *catinus* 'a plate', not from a diminutive of *catulus* 'puppy'.

flagitium hominis: see metrical note on 152. The hiatus here would in any case be 'legitimate', as it is at the diaeresis.

553 hanc 'her', i.e. 'my wife'.

morarier: cf. 545. For the ending, cf. 344n.

554 mirum ni 'it is surprising if it doesn't', 'I fear it does'.

subolet: 266.

555 rationem puto 'reckon up the account', a metaphor from book-keeping (cf. 27n.).

556 eius 'of that sort'.

'If she felt like that, she would be finding fault with me.'

557 nauim = *nauem*.

puluinaria: *puluini* were the wooden supports which kept a ship upright and off the ground when it was drawn up on land, now called a 'cradle'.

'To haul the ship [i.e. his wife] back to her berth' (Nixon).

559 nihili: 119.

meum uirum ueniat uelim 'I should like my husband to come.' *uir*, subject of *ueniat*, is made the object of *uelim*; this is a Greek construction, as in the well known οἶδά σε τίς εἶ, 'I know thee who thou art' (Mark 1.24); cf. 859.

561 litigi depends on *aliquid*.

intĕr ĕōs: these two words do not break Ritschl's law (p. 219), because they go closely together.

562 quom aspicias: the subjunctive in the temporal clause has a generalizing force; cf. *Epid.* 718 *sed ut acerbum est pro bene factis quom mali messim metas*, 'How unfair it is when you reap a harvest of

trouble in return for good deeds.' Translate, 'to see him looking so
serious, anyone would think him virtuous'.

frugi: 255n.

Scene 3   563–590

Lysidamus returns from the forum; Cleostrata, who has remained on
stage, continues her efforts to disrupt.

Metre: senarii.

564   hominem amatorem: there is hiatus between the words.
Fraenkel (*IuA* 135, 260) pointed out that *hominém | amatórem* should
have the same rhythm as *hominés captíuos* (*Capt.* 100). This can be
achieved in two ways: either with a proceleusmatic in the first foot –
$\cup$ $\cup\cup$ $\cup$ |−− |
hominem amatorem, involving a very unusual break as well as the hiatus
(Questa 133, 139), or with *brevis in longo* at the hiatus, and an anapaest
| $\cup$ $\cup\cup$ | $\cup$ $\cup$−|
(obtained by iambic shortening) in the second foot – *hominem amatorem*
(so Drexler, *Lizenzen* 83); cf. 432 *ut illé trepidábat.*

565   Reading the dative *quoi*, we must take *in eum diem* with *in mundo
siet,* and *quoi* as referring back to *hominem,* not to *diem.* Lit., 'who has
available something to love for that day'.

in mundo: a phrase found some nine times in Plautus, meaning
'ready', 'at hand'. (Festus p. 97 L. *in mundo dicebant antiqui, cum aliquid
in promptu esse crediderunt,* Charisius p. 261.17 Barwick *in mundo pro
palam, et in expedito ac cito.*) Most authorities derive it from *mundus*
'clean', 'neat'; and this is perhaps correct. S. B. Gulick, however, in
H.S.C.P. 7 (1896) 242, made the interesting suggestion that it
originated from a term in augury, the noun *mundus* used in the technical
sense of *templum,* i.e. a marked-off area of the sky; so for him *in mundo*
means 'on the horizon'.

566   sicút ego: for the trochaic break in the first foot, cf. 456.

567   aduocatus: Fraenkel (*EP* 152f.) points out that Greek practice
is referred to here – an *aduocatus* (Gr. συνήγορος) assisting a relative,
not a Roman *patronus* helping a client. *aduocati* appear on the stage in
the *Poenulus* and Ter. *Phormio.* In the *Menaechmi* (571ff.), a parallel
passage to our present one, Plautus has transposed into a Roman
situation and speaks of time wasted by *patroni* in looking after the
interests of their *clientes.*

568 adeo: 534n.

569 ne me aduocauerit 'so that he may not have asked for my help'.
 nequiquam = *impune* here.

570 aduocet: generalizing subjunctive, cf. 562. For Plautine freedom in the choice of indicative or subjunctive in subordinate clauses, see Lindsay, *Syntax* 65, 69.

572 *amatoris enim animus ibi est, ubi est quod amat* (Naudet). The 'separable soul' is a common conceit of love and friendship (cf. Q. Lutatius Catulus, in *Fragmenta Poetarum Latinorum* ed. Morel p. 43, *aufugit mi animus; credo, ut solet, ad Theotimum | deuenit*; E. Bréguet in *Hommages à L. Herrmann* (1960) 205-14).

573 neget: potential subjunctive; 'if he should say that it is not with him'.
 adesse: understand *animum*.
 exanimatum: 'lacking *animus*', but the word also means 'dead'.

574 uxorem: accusative, governed by *ecce*, which itself has been modified to *eccam* (= *ecce eam* 163).
 ei: exclamation of pain, commonly with *mihi*.

578 ornata 'arranged'.

579 traduxti = *traduxisti*.

580 quae adiutaret 'to help'; subjunctive of purpose.

582 nescioquid 'somehow'; adverbial accusative.
 se sufflauit 'has taken umbrage', 'become annoyed', with his wife. For the expression, with its image of swelling up, cf. 325 *nunc in fermento tota est, ita turget mihi*.

583 quoniam 'when'. '*quoniam* is nothing but *quom iam*; the addition of *iam* makes the present the appropriate tense...After Plautus' time the conjunction dropped its temporal and retained its causal sense' (Lindsay, *Syntax* 135). Take *quoniam arcesso*, therefore, as a subordinate temporal clause to *negauit*.

585-6 *blanda* is the exact epithet for a *meretrix* (Ovid, *Am.* 1.15.18), because it was the characteristic of women of that profession to be always getting presents from their lovers, for the necessary upkeep of their establishment.

585 officium 'function', rather than 'duty'. It derives from *ob-facio* (Skutsch 388).
  meretricium: genitive plural, not neuter of the adjective.

586 uiris alienis 'other people's husbands'.
  subblandirier 'to make up to'.

587 quod factost opus 'what needs to be done'; cf. 502 *mihi uicino...conuento est opus*. Here the *quod*, which would normally be ablative agreeing with *facto*, has been attracted to be the subject of *opus est*.

588 mi uir: already said in 586. The effect is the same as a repeated and sarcastic 'darling' between husband and wife in a modern play.
  licet: cf. 421.

590 amasium 'lover-boy'. Osbernus (author of a medieval Latin glossary): *amasius: ille qui immoderate amat, uel etiam qui intemperate amatur*, quoting this line.
  Cleostrata re-enters her house.

Scene 4   591-620
Alcesimus comes out of his house and confers with Lysidamus.

Metre: senarii.

591 uiso huc 'I have come here to see.'
  si...rediit: indirect question, with the verb nevertheless in the indicative, as commonly in Plautus.

592 lārŭă: trisyllabic (so always in Plautus); 'madman', 'possessed by devils'; as a term of abuse, it has the same meaning as *laruatus*.

593 commodum 'this very moment'; adverb.

595 tecum oraui: cf. 324n.

596 ut...fecisti: sarcastic, 'How very welcoming!'
  uociuas: cf. 29, 527.

598 i.e. *et ego pereo et occasio perit*.

599 **nempe** is always one long syllable in Plautus. This means that if it precedes a word beginning with a consonant, it is subject to syncope (p. 213), *nemp'*.

602 **eapse:** Plautine Latin can decline the first syllable of *ipse*, at least in certain cases. Many editors print *eapse* also in 163, following Bothe; the Ambrosian palimpsest does not however support it there, as it does here and in 604.

quin: the first of eleven rapid repetitions of this word. Similar comic repetition is used twice in the *Rudens* (with *licet* in 1212-27, and with *censeo* in 1269-79), which suggests that the device may come from Diphilus, although it is found in other Plautine plays also, e.g. *Trin.* 583ff.

603 **negauit...se morarier:** in 545.

604 i.e. in 587.

605 **nihili facio** 'I don't care.' For *nihili* cf. 119.
me perdis 'You're ruining me' (cf. 395).
benest: *te perdere*; cf. 395 *lucrum facit.*

606-9 From AL. *quin benest* in 605 to the end of 609, no changes of speaker are indicated in A or P. What the manuscripts offer is a long, angry speech by Alcesimus, the *quin*'s tumbling over each other in his annoyance. As such it was described by Janus Dousa (rightly) as hilariously funny. Bothe, however, thought that quick-fire repartee would be more effective and Plautine, and he divided the expressions between the two characters. In this he has been followed, with variations in the actual attributions, by almost all subsequent editors. A. Thierfelder (*De rationibus interpolationum Plautinarum* (1929) 45 n. 1) gave good reasons for returning to the manuscripts, and restoring the whole sequence to Alcesimus. The only difficulty is the *quin* at the beginning of 607 (which in fact has to be an isolated interjection however the speakers are arranged); it must be considered merely an addition to the comic incoherence of the speech (for which cf. *Poen.* 435ff.).

606 **morabor:** understand *meam uxorem*.

607 **quin! –:** see above (606-9n.); Alcesimus is inarticulate with fury.

609   postremo quidem: i.e. this is the last *quin*.

610   es: long in Plautus; also in 615.

611   ducas 'take her'; 'marry her' if you like.
   eas: from *ire*.
   malam crucem: 'perdition', 'destruction'; this pair of words has through frequency become the equivalent of a single word (consequently it does not break Luchs's law, p. 219), and can now be qualified by an adjective, *maxumam*.

612   A very expressive line. *hac* is Alcesimus' own wife Myrrhina; *istac* is Cleostrata; *amica tua* is Casina.
   cum hác, cum ístac: double hiatus, not yet convincingly explained, but clearly not to be emended. This is not a question of the common prosodic hiatus, because there the monosyllable becomes the first of a pair of shorts (e.g. 66 *qui ĕrat*). Some scholars explain in terms of a preposition forming one word with the word it governs, so that *cum hac* no more needs to elide than *circumit* or *quamobrem* (677); so Questa 93. G. Maurach, in *Acta Classica* 14 (1971) 50, thinks rather of the abrupt enunciation of an angry man. On the other hand, the closest apparent parallel to the present case is *Truc.* 38 *dum húc, dum illuc*; and this is explicable neither in terms of a preposition adhering to its noun nor on the grounds of any strong feeling in the words.

613   per hortum: we should imagine a narrow street running behind the houses, reached by way of their gardens (*Asin.* 741–2, *Pers.* 678–9; Duckworth 87). Thus the dramatist can get Myrrhina into Cleostrata's house, where she is needed for the coming buffoonery, without bringing her across the stage.

615   in germanum modum 'genuinely'.
   Alcesimus re-enters his house.

616   qua...aui 'with what inauspicious omen', *auis* 'bird' being a source of augury.
   dicam 'am I to say'; deliberative subjunctive.
   The slightly untidy, though idiomatic, expression (instead of 'Where has this love come from?', he says 'Where am I to say that this love has come from?') causes difficulty to the formulation of the second question, in the next line.

For the whole passage, cf. Ovid, *Am.* 3.12.1–4 *quis fuit ille dies, quo tristia semper amanti | omina non albae concinuistis aues? | quodue putem sidus nostris occurrere fatis, | quosue deos in me bella mouere querar?*

617 aut quid…fecerim: for *aut quid dicam me fecisse*, with a change of construction from the previous line (see note there).

inique fecerim 'I have offended'. Unhappiness in love might well, as the ancients saw it, be the consequence of some offence against the goddess of love.

618 mi: the antecedent (*ego* 617) is unnecessarily repeated inside the relative clause, attracted to the case of *cui*. Literally, 'to whom, being in love, so many delays come in my way'.

eueniant: subjunctive, because there is a causal implication.

619 attat: *extra metrum*, as *st* in 148, 212. For the meaning, cf. 434.

620 clamoris: defining genitive depending on *illuc*, which is the nominative neuter of the pronoun (cf. 36n.).

Scene 5 621–719

In a long and brilliant canticum, the maid Pardalisca informs her master with pretended terror that Casina has gone mad inside the house and threatens to kill whoever sleeps with her this night.

Metrical Analysis

(This, one of the most extensive cantica in Plautus, has received special treatment in recent years from G. Maurach in *Untersuchungen zum Aufbau plautinischer Lieder* (1964) 44–56, and (lines 630–45 only) by C. Questa in *Due cantica delle Bacchides e altre analisi metriche* (1967) 57–72.)

The general structure is:

Monody A **621–9**   cretics, leading to variations

Duet   B **630–47**
          (*a*) **630–40** obscure metre (trochees and anapaests?), ending with iambics
          (*b*) **641–7** cretics, leading to variations, and ending with anapaests

c **648–707**

    (a) **648–61** bacchiacs, ending with anapaests
    (b) **662–83** bacchiacs, ending with trochees
    (c) **684–707** bacchiacs, ending with trochees

D **708–18** iambic sequence

A

621–7		$7 \times cr^4$
628	— ∪ — — ∪ — — — — — — ∪ ∪	cr^2 $tr^{4\wedge}$
629	— ∪ ∪ — — ∪ ∪ — — ∪ ∪ — — ∪ ∪ —	$chor^4$
	(**sŭĭst**: iambic shortening **impōs**: cf. *ēs* 610)	

B (a)

630	— ∪ — ∪ — — ∪ ∪ ∪ | — ◡́ ∪ ∪ —	tr^4 $an^{4\wedge}$
	— ◡ ∪ —	
631	— ∪ — ∪ ∪ ∪ — ∪ ∪ — | — ◡́ — —	tr^4 $an^{4\wedge}$
	— ◡ ∪ —	
632	— ∪ ∪ ∪ ∪ — | — ∪ ∪ —	$tr^{4\wedge}$ $an^{4\wedge}$
	— ◡ ∪ — ∪ ∪ — ◡ ∪ —	
633	— ∪ ∪ — — ∪ ∪ — | ◡́ —	tr^4 $an^{4\wedge}$
	∪ ∪ ◡́ — ∪ ∪ — ◡ ∪ ∪	
634	— ∪ — — — ∪ — — — ◡ ∪ — — ∪ ∪ —	tr^4 an^3
635–6	— ◡ ∪ — ∪ ∪ ∪ — ∪ — — ◡ ∪ — ◡́	ia^4 an^2
637–40		$2 \times ia^8$

(b)

641–3		$3 \times cr^4$
644	— ∪ ∪ — ∪ ∪ — — — ∪ ∪ — ∪ ∪ —	$da^{3\wedge}$ — $da^{3\wedge}$
		(Diphilean)
645	— ∪ ∪ — — ∪ ∪ — — ∪ ∪ — —	$chor^2$ adoneus
646–7		an^8

c (a)

648–59	bacchiacs	
648–53		$6 \times ba^4$
654	— — — ∪ — — — — — ∪ ◡́ — ◡́ —	$ba^3 + ba^c$
655	∪ — — ∪ — — ∪ — — ∪ — —	ba^4
656	∪ — — ∪ — — ∪ — — ∪ —	$ba^2 + ba^{2\wedge}$

657	∪ ∪ – – ∪ – – ∪ – – ∪ – –	ba^4
658	∪ – – ∪ – – ∪ $\underline{\prime}$ – $\underline{\prime}$ –	$ba^2 + ba^c$
659	∪ – – ∪ – – ∪ ∪ ∪ ∪ │ ∪ ∪ $\underline{\prime}$ ∪ $\underline{\prime}$ –	$ba^3 + ba^c$

(**650, 659** *brevis in longo* at end of third bacchius
659 *hiatus* at the same place)

660–1		$2 \times an^4$

(*b*)

662–76	bacchiacs	
662	– – – ∪ – – ∪ $\underline{\prime}$ ∪ $\underline{\prime}$ –	$ba^2 + ba^c$
663	– – – ∪ $\underline{\prime}$ – ∪ ∪ ∪ $\underline{\prime}$ ∪	$ba^{2\wedge} + ba^c$
664	∪ – – ∪ – – – – – ∪ – –	ba^4
665	∪ – – ∪ – – ∪ $\underline{\prime}$ – ∪ ∪ –	$ba^2 + ba^c$
666	∪ $\underline{\prime}$ – $\underline{\prime}$ – ∪ – – ∪ – –	$ba^c + ba^2$
667–72		$6 \times ba^4$
673–5	⏕ ∪∪ – ∪ – – ∪ $\underline{\prime}$ ⏕ ∪∪ ∪	$3 \times (ba^2 + ba^c)$
676	– – ∪ ∪ ∪ – – ∪ – – ∪ – –	ba^4

(**674** *brevis in longo* at caesura)

677		tr^8
678–9		ia^8
680–1	– ∪ – – – ∪ – – ∪ – ∪ ∪ – ∪ –	$tr^{4\wedge}$ $tr^{4\wedge}$
682–3	∪ ∪ – │ – ∪ ∪ – ∪ –	$tr^{4\wedge}$ tr^4
	∪ ∪ – ∪ ∪ ∪ – – – –	

(*c*)

684–705	bacchiacs	
684	∪ – ∪ ∪ ∪ – – ∪ – – ∪ – –	ba^4
685	∪ – – ∪ – – ∪ $\underline{\prime}$ ∪ $\underline{\prime}$ –	$ba^2 + ba^c$
686–90		$5 \times ba^4$
691	∪ ∪ ∪ – ∪ $\underline{\prime}$ – ∪ ∪ ∪ ∪ ∪ –	$ba^{2\wedge} + ba^c$
692–3		$2 \times ba^4$
694–5	– – – ∪ – – ∪ $\underline{\prime}$ ⏜ $\underline{\prime}$ –	$2 \times (ba^2 + ba^c)$
696–701		$6 \times ba^4$
702	– – – ∪ – – ∪ $\underline{\prime}$ ∪ $\underline{\prime}$ –	$ba^2 + ba^c$
703	– – – ∪ $\underline{\prime}$ – ∪ ∪ – $\underline{\prime}$ –	$ba^{2\wedge} + ba^c$
704–5		$2 \times ba^4$

(**693, 696** *brevis in longo* at caesura
705 *hiatus* and *brevis in longo* at diaeresis)

706–7		$2 \times tr^8$

D

708-17   10 × ia²

(The form of ia² here is ∪ ∪ − ∪ −; see
commentary, 708-18n., for discussion)

718   ∪ ∪ − −   ia²^

719   an⁸

621-9 This cretic opening is evidently a parody of the entrance of a
distraught female figure in tragedy; it is closely reminiscent of
Andromache's lament in cretic tetrameters in Ennius (81ff. Jocelyn)
*quid petam praesidi aut exsequar? quoue nunc | auxilio exili aut fugae freta
sim? | arce et urbe orba sum. quo accedam? quo applicem?* Compare also the
lament of the shipwrecked Palaestra in *Rudens* 664-5 *nunc id est cum
omnium copiarum atque opum, | auxili, praesidi uiduitas nos tenet.*

The language is rich in figures of speech: repetition (621 *nulla...
nulla, tota...tota*), alliteration (622, 624, 625), assonance (623 *auxili,
praesidi, perfugi*).

621 nulla sum 'I'm done for', 'I'm finished'; cf. 305 *ecce me
nullum senem.*

624 opum 'help'; cf. *Rud.* 664, quoted above.
    comparem aut expetam 'I may find or (even) look for.'

625 factu: supine with *mira*; cf. 538 *uilis emptu.*

626 integram 'unheard of'.

628 mali: partitive genitive with *quid*.
    faxīt: subjunctive; see 324n.

629 isti: dative; in English, '*from her*'.
    impos 'out of control'.
    Bothe pointed out that the choriambs give an effect of excitement.
A very similar line is *Men.* 110 *ni mala, ni stulta sies, ni indomita imposque
animi.*

630-3 These lines are metrically the most difficult in the play.
Many scansions have been proposed, to which may be added that
suggested here, 'asynarteta' (i.e. lines consisting of unconnected and
dissimilar metres), composed of trochaic and anapaestic cola.

630 nam quid est 'Why! What is the reason'; for the asseverative *nam*, cf. 178.

631 perii: 236.
  unde meae usurpant aures sonitum: the turgid phrase suggests tragic parody again.

632 mi: vocative.

634 istuc: i.e. *uae*.
  amabo 'please' (137).

635–6 contine pectus 'hold me up'; 'put your hands round my waist' (Nixon).

637–8 hoc negoti: defining genitive, cf. 620 *illuc clamoris*; also 649 *quid tumulti*.

639–40 meraclo: agreeing with *flore*. It is diminutive of *meracus*, from *merus*, 'unmixed' or 'neat', of wine. The ancients normally drank their wine diluted with water.
  se...percussit 'has confused herself'.
  flore Liberi 'with the flower of Bacchus', a periphrasis for wine. *flore* probably refers to the 'fragrance', 'bouquet'. We may compare *Curc.* 96 *flos ueteris uini meis naribus obiectust*, *Cist.* 127 *me compleui flore Liberi*.

641 optine auris 'hold my ears', a position for kissing; cf. *As.* 668 *prehende auriculis*. Pardalisca is extracting the maximum amusement from the situation.
  in malam crucem: 611.

642 perduint: alternative form for *perdant*, present subjunctive.

643 hoc (end of the line) 'with this', i.e. his stick (cf. 975 *scipione*).

644 dispercutiam: the compound is found only here.
  excetra 'snake'; used as a term of abuse also at *Pseud.* 218.

645 ludibrio: predicative dative with *habuisti*; 'you have treated me as a joke', 'made fun of me'.
  adhuc: with *habuisti*.

646-7 numero: ablative used adverbially in archaic Latin. Grammarians (Festus p. 174 L., quoting this very line; Nonius p. 558 L.) are unanimous that the word means 'quickly' or 'too quickly'; and they are followed by most modern scholars. So, 'you speak too soon', 'you've seen nothing yet'.

(This certainly seems to be the meaning at *Mil.* 1400 PY. *perii!* PE. *haud etiam, numero hoc dicis.* Others (e.g. Lindemann *ad Mil.* 1400) think that the word more properly means 'precisely', 'exactly', which would make perfectly good sense in our line.)

649 tumulti: cf. 536 *senati.*
   scibis = *scies*; cf. 548 *conuenibo.*

650 malum pessumumque 'bad, indeed very bad'; object of *exordiri.*

651 hoc pacto: antecedent of *quod.*
   cŏēpĭt: trisyllabic, as also at 701, and at *Cist.* 687, *Merc.* 533, Lucr. 4.619.

652 disciplinam 'upbringing', as also at 657.

653 timor praepedit dicta linguae: the high-flown language suggests tragic parody again (Haffter 89). The phrase is imitated by Lysidamus in 704.

658 interminor is intransitive in Plautus; thus *uitam* is not its object, but the beginning of a clause depending on it (e.g. *uitam eius se interempturam esse*). The sense of this is repeated after Lysidamus' interruption.

659 quid ergo: understand *interminatur.*
   interemere...uitam: cf. *Epid.* 594 *uitam tuam ego interimam.*

660-1 The metre switches to fast-moving anapaests, mirroring the excitement of the moment (Maurach).

660 gladium: with great force at the beginning of the line; 'A sword!'
   hem 'What?'; cf. 187.
   quid eum gladium 'What about that sword?'

661 ei misero mihi: cf. 574.

662   omnis: accusative plural.

  domi: 'in the house'; locative.

  per aedes 'through every room'; cf. 763 *totis aedibus*.

664   arcis 'chests'.

666   quid: with *mali*.

  illi: dative.

667   scelestissumum 'most wretched of men'. If a man suffers, he must have offended the gods; he must have done something which they consider wrong; by this train of thought it comes about that the word *scelestus* can mean 'unlucky'; cf. 617n.

668   immo si scias 'if you only knew'.

671   occisurum: the future infinitive in Latin was originally an indeclinable form in *-urum*. Later, because this looked like an accusative·masculine, it came to be declined as the future participle, and *esse* was added to make the infinitive (A. Meillet and J. Vendryes, *Traité de grammaire comparée des langues classiques*² (1948) 363; Lindsay, *Syntax* 76). The ancient evidence is in Aulus Gellius 1.7 and Priscian 9 (*GLK* II 475); the examples quoted include such striking cases as *credo ego inimicos meos hoc dicturum* from C. Gracchus, and *illi polliciti sese facturum omnia* from Cato. The old form is found in the Palatine manuscripts here, but not in the Ambrosianus; the same is true at 693.

  quicum = *quocum*.

  With further parody of tragedy (cf. 621–9n.), Casina is now described as in the frame of mind of the Danaids, who killed their husbands on the wedding night. This is a nasty shock for Lysidamus.

672   Richly comic.

  vah: expression of surprise; 'Oh!'

674   illuc dicere 'uilicum' uolebam: *illuc* ('that other thing') is explained by *uilicum*; 'I meant to say the bailiff.' This method of self-correction is common, e.g. *Mil.* 27 PY. *quid bracchium?* AR. *illud dicere uolui 'femur'*. So also in 702 below.

675   de uia in semitam: the road (*uia*) is straight and true; a narrow path is winding. So Pardalisca says that her master is knowingly leaving the straight way and turning aside into a defile.

(This is without doubt the meaning, but 369 *redii uix ueram in uiam* and 469 *in rectam redii semitam* show that metaphorically speaking both words can be used for the right road.)

677   cuiquam 'anybody'. There is an implied negative in 'you more than anyone else', which explains the use of *quisquam* (cf. 128n.).

   des: subjunctive because this is the reason attributed to Casina ('the alleged reason'). The reflexive *se* appears properly here, in virtual indirect speech, referring to the subject of the main verb (*infesta est*).

678–83   Text and metre are unsure. The Palatine manuscripts have lost the ends of the lines; and A is not wholly legible. The simplest correction of both metre and sense is to assume with Schoell that the word *diem* has dropped out of both recensions at the end of 678–9.

678–9   neque se...sinere: this is what Casina is alleged to be saying; it therefore formally depends on *minatur* (676) or one of the earlier verbs of speaking.

   in ⟨diem⟩ | crastinum: Plautus uses the phrase with and without *dies* (*Pseud.* 1334 *in crastinum uos uocabo*; *Stich.* 638 *in crastinum...diem*).

680–1   id: with *dicerem*.

682–3   dignús tu: the rhythm is not very comfortable, although it may be paralleled in *Truc.* 595 *dignúst mecastor*. Leo's *dignus es* would be more Plautine, and would allow the easier, if perhaps not more appropriate, scansion of the line as tr^{8A}. See however the app. crit.

684   me: ablative of comparison, as if *adaeque miser* were *miserior*.

685   ludo ego hunc facete: an aside to the audience.

687   era atque haec ex proxumo 'my mistress and our neighbour from over here'.

   Logically, Pardalisca could hardly assert that Myrrhina was in the plot unless there was quite a long break after 620, because it was only in 613 that Alcesimus said he would send his wife across by way of the garden. This slight inconsistency is, however, acceptable within the conventions of drama.

688   ludere: infinitive of purpose, not rare in Plautus.

689–704 Jachmann 110 n. 1 argued that these lines betray themselves as typical Plautine expansion of his model. They repeat and exaggerate the jokes of 660–74, about the sword and Lysidamus' slip of the tongue.

690   moram offers...offers maerorem: with play on the similar sounding words, and chiastic word order.

   offers maerorem 'You make me weep'; an invented phrase.

692   habet, sed duos: farcical, as if two swords make the situation twice as bad.

693   occisurum: for the indeclinable future infinitive, see 671n. This line is quoted by Aulus Gellius as one of his examples of the phenomenon.

694 A fine 'Irishism': 'I'm the deadest man alive.'

695   induam: subjunctive dependent on *optumum esse*, without *ut*.

697   exoret 'she should persuade her' to give it up.

698   ponere = *se posituram esse* (cf. 479 *dare*).

699   datum iri: future infinitive passive, rare in Plautus.

700   atque: cf. 364.

   quia non uolt: she'll marry whether she likes it or not (*ingratiis*); in fact, she'll marry *because* she doesn't wish to.

701–2 A 'Freudian' slip of the tongue again, as in 365 and 672. Plautus' view, no doubt, was that you cannot have too much of a good thing.

702   illud uolebam 'I meant to say', cf. 674.

703   saepicule 'a little often'.

704   timor praepedit uerba: Lysidamus ingeniously uses Pardalisca's own words (653) for his excuse.

706   gladium: Lysidamus has of course not taken seriously the allegation in 692 that Casina has two swords.

708–18 The long canticum ends with a unique feature, a sequence of ten short cola of the shape $\cup \cup - \cup -$ (a form of ia²), rounded off by the catalectic ∪ ∪ – –. (The closest parallel for this sequence may be *Capt.* 506 *rogo sýngraphum: datur mi ilico: dedi Týndaro: ille abiít domum,* where however the metre is disputed; cf. also *Cas.* 155 *ego illúm fame, ego illúm siti,* Ter. *Hec.* 621 *sumus Pámphile, 'senex átque anus'.*) It has seemed best to print the whole sequence as separate lines, so as to show its rhythm most clearly.

Even without the music, we may recognize that this made a light and vivacious ending to the canticum.

708 effexis: for the tense, equivalent to a future perfect, see 307n.

709 soleas 'slippers' (495), softer than the *sculponeae* normally worn by slaves. 'Slippers and a gold ring', being what free people wore, may suggest manumission of the slave.

710 anulum in digito 'a ring on your finger'. The prepositional phrase depending on a noun is no stranger than *haec ex proxumo* (687).

Jachmann suggested (119) that this ring played a part in the recognition scene towards the end of Diphilus' play, comparable to tokens of various kinds employed to effect the recognition of long-lost daughters in other plays. Perhaps (he says) later in the play this ring was actually produced, and Myrrhina, being present, recognized it as one she had left with the baby sixteen years ago (39–41), with the result that Casina's identity was discovered. This is no more than guesswork; cf. the theory based on *unde ea tibi est* in 198.

713 operam dabo 'I will see to it.'

718 Pardalisca enters the house.

719 In the manuscripts this line comes before the rubric for the change of scene, although its metre is that of the opening of the following scene. This apparent anomaly is caused by the fact that the rubrics in the manuscripts indicate primarily the entrance of a new character; the fact that we call it a new scene is to some extent accidental.

redit opsonatu: with the ablative of the supine (verbal noun) for the return journey. The setting out would have been expressed by the accusative (the supine in *-um*); cf. 440–1 *mittere | tecum obsonatum.*

pompam ducit: Olympio is returning with a whole procession, the cook and his assistants.

Scene 6 720–758

The cooks arrive with Olympio. After some by-play between him and Lysidamus, they all enter the house.

Metrical analysis

The general structure is:

A **720–8** anapaests – a marching rhythm, as the procession (*pompa* 719) comes on the stage

B **729–50** mixed metre, with short lines; a lively duet and dance

C **751–8** Reiziana – repeated short cola form a rhythmical conclusion to the duet

A

720–3 $4 \times an^8$

   (**723 pătrīcīēque:** this scansion, with iambic shortening, is marginally preferable to *pătrīcīēque* by synizesis; cf. *sequimíni* 165–6)

724 $- - - -$ an^2

725–8 $4 \times an^8$

   (**725** prosodic hiatus after *ego*

   726 text defective

   excurātūs incessisti: very doubtful iambic shortening; see Commentary)

B

729a $\cup \cup \cup -$ cr^1

   b $\cup \cup \cup -$ cr^1

730 $\cup \cup \cup - -$ $\cup \cup \cup - -$ $tr^2 \quad tr^2$

731a $- -$

   b $\cup \cup - \cup \cup -$ an^2

732a $\cup \cup - -$ $an^{2\wedge}$

   b $\cup \cup \cup \cup -$ $an^{2\wedge}$

733 $\cup \cup \cup - \cup \cup - \cup -$ $tr^{4\wedge}$

734 $\cup \cup - \cup \cup - - - -$ tr^4

735–6 $- \cup \cup - \cup \cup - \cup \cup - -$ tr^4

737–9 $3 \times ba^4$

   (**738** *brevis in longo* at caesura)

Line	Scansion	Metre
740a	∪ ∪ – –	an²ᴬ
b	∪ ∪ ∪ ∪ –	an²ᴬ
741	– ∪ ∪ – – – – –	an⁴ᴬ
742	– – – – ∪ ∪ – –	an⁴ᴬ
743	– ∪ ∪ – – – – ∪	an⁴ᴬ
744–5	– – ∪ ∪ – ∪ ∪ – ∪ ∪ | – – – ∪ ∪ – ∪ ∪ – ∪	an⁸ᴬ
746–7	∪ ∪ – ∪ ∪ – ∪ ∪ ∪ – – ∪ ∪ – ∪ ∪ –	an³ an³
748	– ∪ ∪ – ∪ ∪ – ∪ ∪ – – ∪ ∪ – ∪ ∪ – ∪ ∪ –	gl (da⁴ᴬ)
		gl (da⁴ᴬ)
749	– ∪ ∪ – – ∪ ∪ ∪ ∪ –	an⁴ᴬ
750	– ∪ – – ∪ – – ∪ – ∪ –	cr² + crᶜ
c		
751	∪ ∪ – ∪ ∪ – ∪ ∪ – ∪ – – ⏑̲ – ∪ ∪ –	Vʳ
752	∪ ∪ – ∪ ∪ – ∪	cʳ
753	– – ∪ ∪ – –	cʳ
754	∪ ∪ – ∪ ∪ – –	cʳ
755	– – ∪ – – – ∪ ∪ | – – ∪ ∪ ∪ ∪ –	Vʳ
756	– – ∪ ∪ – ∪ ∪ – ∪ – ∪ – ∪ ∪ – –	Vʳ
757a	– ∪ ∪ ∪ ∪ – ∪	cʳ
b	∪ ∪ – ∪ ∪ – –	cʳ
758	– – ∪ – – – ∪ – ∪ – ∪ ∪ – –	Vʳ

720 fur: there was a long tradition of 'cook-humour', going back through Greek New Comedy to Middle Comedy. The thieving propensities of cooks (who would of course have the opportunity, being allowed into the house) are a major subject in the *Aulularia*. Here we have merely a brief allusion and a joke.

sub signis: a military metaphor; 'see that you keep your thorns in line'. *uide ut*, when it means 'see how', normally takes the indicative in Plautus; *uide ut* with the subjunctive is a command.

qui: ablative, 'How?'

hi 'these slaves'. There are obviously several; cf. 719 *pombam ducit*, and 764, 772 *coqui*.

sentis: the nominative plural is normally in *-es*, but the spelling in *-is*, transmitted by A, is retained by most modern editors, because it may have been used by Plautus to mimic the earlier occurrence in the line.

721 ilico 'immediately'. This word is still occasionally local in sense in Plautus, 'on the spot', suiting its origin from *in loco*; more commonly, however, it is temporal, as in classical Latin.

si eas ereptum 'if you go to take it back'.

722 ubi ubi 'wherever', like *quoquo*.

duplici damno 'double damage' (theft and violence, *rapiunt et scindunt*). Compare *Truc.* 227–8 *meretricem similem sentis esse condecet, | quemquem hominem attigerit, profecto ei aut malum aut damnum dare* 'It is proper for a *meretrix* to be like a thorn, to cause either harm or loss to whatever man she touches.'

dominos: i.e. those who have hired them.

723 heia: cf. 230. The exclamation is the cook's response (ironical applause) to Olympio's joke; 'Come off it!'

attat: cf. 434. Olympio has just seen Lysidamus.

cesso 'why am I slow to': cf. 237.

patricie 'aristocratically'. The Palatine manuscripts have *patrice* 'paternally', which was believed by early editors (e.g. Lambinus) to be standing for *patricie*, even before the reading of the Ambrosian palimpsest was known.

Olympio puts on a flowing cloak and struts about the stage, affecting to be too superior to take any notice of his master. For this *seruus gloriosus* pose, compare Pseudolus at *Pseud.* 458 SI. *statum uide hominis, Callipho, quam basilicum.*

725 fateor: *me bonum uirum esse.*

726 lepide excuratus 'elegantly turned out'.

incessisti 'you have come marching in'.

excuratus incessisti raises a difficulty of scansion. Iambic shortening between two independent words without elision (*-tŭs inc-*) is contrary to accepted principles (Questa 31). On the other hand, there are surprisingly many parallels for this particular anomaly with this particular verb (O. Skutsch, *Prosodische und metrische Gesetze der Iambenkürzung* (1934) 14). The phenomenon has not been satisfactorily explained.

727–8 We must think of Olympio strutting about the stage, with Lysidamus trotting behind him, trying to get him to stand still. The whole of this part of the scene would give ample opportunity for homosexual suggestions and *doubles entendres* (cf. 452ff.).

727 fu fu: as in *Most.* 39 *fu, oboluisti alium* 'You smell of garlic.' It imitates the sound of somebody trying to blow something away.

  tuos sermo 'when you speak'.

728 quae res 'What is the matter?'

  haec res 'This is the matter', either just mimicking the other's words or with an impolite gesture.

  etiamne adstas 'Won't you stand still?' Cf. 737 *mane atque asta.* For *etiam* used colloquially in a question, meaning something like 'I ask you', cf. 977 *etiamne imus cubitum?*

  πράγματά μοι παρέχεις (*pragmata moi parecheis*) 'You are being a nuisance.' Greek found in Plautus is not taken from his model, but from contemporary speech at Rome, giving colloquial colour to the conversations. It is usually used by lower-class characters or slaves (G. P. Shipp, 'Greek in Plautus', *WS* 66 (1953) 105-12).

729b μέγα κακόν (*mega kakon*): Greek for *magnum malum.*

730 resistis 'stand still'.

731a Ὦ Ζεῦ (*O Zeu*) 'O Zeus!' The exclamation is *extra metrum.* There may be a pun here on the Greek ὄζειν 'to smell', as suggested by J. N. Hough in *TAPA* 71 (1940) 190 n. 8.

731b potin = *potisne* (*est*) = *potestne.*
  abeas: understand *ut.*

734ff Master and slave reverse their roles. Lysidamus needs Olympio's help so much that he fawns on him and calls him his master.

734 cuius: monosyllabic.

735-6 non sum ego liber? memento, memento: Lysidamus virtually promised Olympio his freedom in 474.

737 mane atque asta: cf. 727-8. Olympio is still prancing around.
  omitte 'Stop it!'

739 Olympisce mi 'darling Olympio'. Paratore's Italian translation is pleasing: 'Olimpionuccio mio'.

741 Olympio keeps up the show of disdain.

742 quam mox recreas me 'How soon are you going to restore me to life?'

743 For **mŏdō**, cf. 755, 758, *Pseud.* 689; the adverb is much more commonly scanned *mŏdŏ*.

744-5 hisce: nominative plural = *hi*; i.e. the cooks.
  deproperate: understand *cenam*.

746 facite: addressed to the cooks, following *ite* and *deproperate* in 744-5.
  cenam: for the accusative rather than the nominative, cf. 559 *meum uirum ueniat uelim*, 859.
  ebria 'rich', copious'; lit. 'drunk'.

748 Understand *cenare* twice in this line, depending on *uolo* and *nil moror*.
  nil moror 'I have no use for'; cf. 545.
  barbarico 'Roman'. This choice of word is striking evidence of the Roman submission to Greek culture; cf. *Trin.* 19 *Plautus uortit barbare* 'Plautus translated it into Latin.'
  bliteo 'plate of spinach', ablative of the neuter of the adjective *bliteus*, from *blitum*; it was considered a tasteless food (cf. *Truc.* 854).
  The cooks go into the house. Olympio turns to his master.

749 stasne etiam 'Why don't you go in?' Contrast 728 *etiamne adstas*.
  i sis 'you go' (*sis* = *si uis*.)
  ego hic habeo 'I'm staying here.' *habeo* can mean to live in a place (*Men.* 69 *qui Syracusis habet*); perhaps what we have here is an extension of that meaning.

750 quod morae siet 'to cause delay' (lit. 'may be for a delay', predicative dative).

751-8 This canticum also ends with a special and unusual feature (like the iambic monometers at the end of the Pardalisca-Lysidamus duet, 708-18), a regular sequence of *uersus Reiziani* and *cola Reiziana*.

751 The breaking of Ritschl's law (p. 219) in *īntŭs | hăbēre* is perhaps to be tolerated in a lyric iambic colon (Lindsay, *ELV* 90).

ait 'she says'. Lysidamus must assume that Olympio knows Pardalisca has been speaking to him.

qui…interimat 'with which to kill'.

752   scio: not 'I know', for he could not; but in effect 'Don't tell me.' This is fairly common; e.g. *Rud.* 998 *sunt alii puniceo corio, magni item; atque atri.* TR. *scio.*

sic sine habere 'Let her have it so.'

754   malas merces: a slang phrase, lit. 'bad goods', i.e. the women. Cf. 228 *mala res.*

758   uerum i modo 'all the same, come along', repeating *i modo mecum* of 755.

inibitur: impersonal passive; 'on t'accompagnera' (Ernout). Cf. 813 *exitur.*

ACT IV

Scene 1   759-779

Pardalisca reports to the audience what is going on inside the house: the cooks are delaying the preparation of the food, while the women dress up Chalinus as the bride.

Metre: senarii.

759-62 An elaborate pun on the two meanings of *ludus*, both of which could be represented as 'games' in English. The same joke is made at *Most.* 427-8 *ludos ego hodie uiuo praesenti hic seni | faciam; quod credo mortuo numquam fore.*

759   Nemeae, Olympiae: two of the four great athletic festivals of Greece (the others were at Delphi and the Isthmus of Corinth). Fraenkel (*EP* 7) pointed out that it is a regular feature of Plautine style to begin a speech with a striking and exotic comparison, often with something Greek; and that this feature should be ascribed to Plautus himself, and not to his various models. In other words, Plautus *adds* Greek allusions. Of this habit the present is a convincing example, for the play on *ludus* is evidently a Latin one.

Olympiae: the choice of allusion may have a connection with the name of the slave Olympio, as suggested by W. Forehand in *Arethusa* 6 (1973) 246.

761 ludificabiles: probably a made-up word. *ludos facere* is idiomatic for 'to make fun of'.

762 nostro: used by slaves to mean 'of our family'.
   nostro Olympioni uilico: this is the preferred word order; cf. Lindsay on *Capt.* 875 *tuom Stalagmum seruom.*

763 totis aedibus 'throughout the house', ablative of place.

765 'Why don't you get on with it? Why don't you produce the food if you are going to?' The weak use of *hodie*, and the indefinite *si quid datis*, are idiomatic in this sort of speech. For the former, and the whole line, cf. 831 *date ergo, daturae si umquam estis hodie uxorem.*

767 uilicus is autem: for the rhythm, and the otiose *is*, cf. 55 *filius is autem.*
   Olympio has a garland on his head for the celebration, and is dressed in white as the bridegroom; cf. 446 *candidatus.*

769 armigerum: cf. 55.

770 quem dent nuptum 'to give in marriage'; cf. 86.

771 nimium lepide 'very cleverly'.

772 huius: genitive depending on *nil*, and antecedent of *quod.*

773 nimis lepide: cf. 771.
   ei rei: antecedent of the *ne* clause.

774 aulas = *ollas* 'pots'.
   peruortunt 'they knock over'.

775 illarum oratu 'at the request of the women'.

778 ambestrices: from *ambestrix*, feminine noun from *ambesse* 'to eat up'.
   corbitam 'a ship-load' (*corbitae dicuntur naues onerariae* Festus p. 53 L.).

779 comesse: from *comedo.*
   The allegation of gluttony is part of the stock humour of comedy; matrons are fond of their food and drink.

Scene 2   780-797

Lysidamus comes out, having decided to do without dinner. He sends Pardalisca in again, and awaits Olympio.

Metre: senarii.

780   si sapitis 'if you take my advice'; cf. 838.

uos 'you women'.

tamen: the elliptical use of the word, 'You go ahead and have dinner (although I shall not be joining you)'; cf. 105 *praefeci ruri qui curet tamen.*

783   rus 'to the country'.

784   uolup: an adverb. *facite uostro animo uolup* = 'enjoy yourselves'.

786   tandem ut ueniamus luci 'So that we can get there while it is light, for heaven's sake.' *tandem* often has this impatient tone (Cic. Cat. 1.1 *quo usque tandem abutere, Catilina, patientia nostra?*).

luci: adverbial.

787   tamen: implying, 'although I shall not be here for dinner today'; cf. 780.

790   ipsa = *era* 'the mistress'. Pardalisca's reply is pert. She is not in fact going anywhere.

ueron 'Really?'

792   cunctas: for *cunctaris*, the verb being normally deponent.

793   sis = *si uis.*

794   quiduis 'anything'.

795   nullum: adverbial, 'not at all'; cf. *Mil.* 625 *nihil amas* 'you are not in love', and the common idiomatic use of *nullus* in phrases like *nullus uenit* 'he has not come at all'.

'The lover, even when he is hungry, does not want food'; cf. 725, 802 (*tibi amor pro cibost*).

796   lampade: torches were carried in the wedding procession.

797 A fine line to mark the entrance of Olympio, who comes in dressed as a bridegroom.

Scene 3   798–814

Olympio and Lysidamus wait impatiently outside the house for their bride.

Metre: trochaic septenarii, with the insertion at 800 and 808 of glyconics for the wedding refrain (*hўmēn, hўmēnāe(e) ō hўmēn*).

798 A flute player is addressed by a slave character also at Menander *Dysc.* 880 and Plautus *Stich.* 715 and 758ff. We are told by Livy that the *cantica* on the Roman stage were as a matter of course accompanied by a *tibicen* (Livy 7.2).

799 concelebra 'fill'.

plateam: the open space, or street, where the action is taking place.

hymenaeo meo 'with my wedding song'.

800 For the Greek refrain, repeated in 808, compare (in glyconic metre, as in Plautus)

Catullus 61.4 f.   *o Hymenaee Hymen*
                     o Hymen Hymenaee.

      and 117 f.   *Io Hymen Hymenaee io*
                     io Hymen Hymenaee.

Euripides, *Troades* 331 Ὑμήν, ὦ Ὑμέναι', Ὑμήν.
It probably originated as a ritual cry, with no specific meaning, *hymenaee* acting merely as a rhythmical variant or extension of *hymen*. The use of *hymenaeus* for the marriage song, already found in Homer (*Iliad* 18.493; cf. 799 above) and the belief in a god of marriage called Hymen were both secondary derivations from the cry itself. So P. Maas in *Philologus* 66 (1907) 590–6.

The first syllable of *hymen* is naturally short (although occasionally lengthened for metrical reasons by hexameter poets both Greek and Latin).

801 hau salubriter: a response to Lysidamus calling him *mea salus* ('my saviour').

802 nihili facio 'I don't care'; cf. 2 *facitis maxumi.*

804   nam quid...: cf. 630 *nam quid est quod haec huc timida* etc.
remeligines 'slowcoaches', a very rare word.

805   procedit: impersonal; 'progress is made'.

806   suffundam 'intone'.
qui: ablative of the indefinite pronoun, 'somehow'.

807   censeo 'I agree'.

808   Cf. 800.

809   dirrumpi: passive infinitive, 'to rupture myself'. This vulgar
expression is used by Cicero in his letters, e.g. *Ad fam.* 7.1.4 *dirupi me
paene in iudicio Galli Canini*; similarly *Capt.* 14 (the Prologue speaking)
ego me tua causa, ne erres, non rupturus sum.

810   illo morbo 'that complaint', i.e. sexual activity.
dirrumpi cupio 'I wish to exhaust myself (burst myself).'
dirrumpere has already been used in a (different) obscene sense in 326f.
non est copiae 'there isn't the opportunity'. Plautus uses both
copia est and *copiae est* (partitive genitive); Lindsay, *Syntax* 16.
In this sentence, the words *illo morbo* are to be taken with *non est
copiae*, but they have been attracted from the natural genitive into the
case of the immediately following relative *quo*; cf. *Curc.* 419 *istum quem
quaeris ego sum* (Lindsay, *Syntax* 6).

811   ne: The Greek νή or ναί, 'indeed'. It is always found in Latin
with a pronoun immediately following.
'If you were a horse, you would be untamable'; i.e. you behave like
a stallion. Cf. *Mil.* 112 *ad equas fuisti scitus admissarius* (translated by
Hammond, Mack and Moskalew 'You're a proper stallion for the
mares').

812   tenax 'grasping' (cf. *Capt.* 812 *tenaxne pater est eius?*), 'persistent'.
num me expertu's (= *expertus es*) **uspiam**: a passing joke.

813   di melius faciant 'God forbid!'
exitur: impersonal passive; cf. 758 *inibitur*.

814   iam oboluit Casinus procul: there is a double problem – the
sense of the words and the identity of the speaker.

The masculine *Casinus* is evidently a joke (compare the beggar Irus in *Odyssey* 18, so called because the suitors used to send him with messages (Iris); also 859 *nouom nuptum cum nouo marito*), and should not be emended away. It must be said by someone who is in the secret. *oboluit procul* means 'has been scented from a distance'; cf. *Amph.* 321 *olet homo quidam malo suo* 'I can smell somebody, the worse for him.'

So: 'the scent of the male Casina has preceded him', a comment on Lysidamus' last remark, and an explanation to the audience. Who should speak these words? As Leo says in a note, it must be either Pardalisca or Chalinus himself as he comes out. Of the two, we prefer Pardalisca, on the grounds that she seems to be stage-managing the wedding scene, and moreover she had already taken the spectators into her confidence at 685 and 759ff. (where she indeed explained this deception to them in 769–70).

Against this attribution, there is the difficulty that Pardalisca is not yet (according to the rubric in the manuscripts) on stage; and that the immediately following scene, which she begins, is in a completely different metre. There is however in this very play a parallel for a new character coming on stage and speaking a half-line at the end of one 'scene', and then being present for the following scene, which is in a different type of metre, namely at 959–60, where Chalinus comes out of the house with the words *heus! sta ilico amator*. (If another example is required, it may be found at *Capt.* 658.)

Our difficulty in accepting this is caused by uncertainty about what constitutes a scene; and by Plautus' *usual* practice that changes of metre coincide with the entrance of new characters. But already in this play we have found the scene divisions illogical at 279 and 720 (note on 719). Andrieu 89–206 has shown that the scene headings are post-Plautine, created by later editors from the internal evidence of the plays. In Plautus' own production there were neither acts nor scenes.

We may then imagine that the door opens; and before the wedding procession appears the skittish Pardalisca pops out and says these words to the spectators.

oboluit: there may be a reference to the aromatic spice cinnamon (*casia*) hidden in the name Casina, and perhaps alluded to elsewhere in the play (219n.).

Scene 4   815-854

The wedding procession comes on stage, including the matron Cleostrata who gives away the bride, the pert maid Pardalisca, and the slave Chalinus, dressed up for the part. This is a more lively and memorable comic scene even than that of the lot-taking (II 6) which gave its name to the Greek original of Plautus' play.

The question whether the details and ceremonial alluded to here are Roman or Greek is discussed by G. W. Williams in *J.R.S.* 48 (1958) 17–18. He points out that in Greece, after the wedding feast, the bride, accompanied by the bridegroom *and a close friend of the bridegroom*, rode to her new house in a wagon. In Rome, on the other hand, the bride was led to her new house by three young boys, accompanied by the wedding guests; the bridegroom did not go with her, but went on ahead. Moreover, the *hymenaeus*, or wedding hymn, was no part of Roman ritual. Thus the basic situation in our play is Greek, a fact which may have considerable bearing on the argument whether Plautus found the mock wedding in his original or added it himself (see Introduction, p. 36). Plautus has certainly, however, added Roman motifs to this Greek setting, as Williams points out (see notes to 815-16, 817ff., 819-20).

Metre: 815-46   *mutatis modis canticum*
          847-54   senarii

Metrical analysis
The general structure of the *canticum* is:

Monody (PA.)	815-24	mixed metre
Trio (OL., LY., CL.)	825-34	iambics and bacchiacs
Duet (LY., OL.)	835-46	mostly iambics, bacchiacs, cola Reiziana

815-16	$\underline{} - \cup\cup - \underline{}\cup\underline{}\underline{}\cup\underline{}\cup\cup\underline{}\cup$	gl + gl^ (Priapeus)
817	$- - \cup\cup - \cup - \cup\cup\cup - \cup -$	cr² + crᶜ
818	$- - - \cup - -$	ith
819-20	$\cup\cup - \cup\cup - - - \cup\cup - - - \cup\cup - - - \cup\cup -$	an⁸
821	$\cup\cup - \cup\cup - \cup\cup - \cup\cup -$	an⁴
822	$- - - \cup - \quad \underline{}\cup - - \cup\cup -$	ba²^ ith

823	− − − ∪ − | ⏓ ∪ − − ∪ ∪ −	ba²ᴬ ith
824	− ∪ − ∪ − −	ith
825	∪ ∪ − ∪ − − − ∪ − | ∪ ∪ − − − − − −	ia⁸ᴬ
826	∪ ∪ − ∪ ∪ − − − ∪ ∪ ∪ ⏓ ∪ ∪ ⏓ −	Vʳ
827	∪ ∪ − − | − − − ∪ − − ∪ − −	ba⁴
828	− − − ∪ − − ∪ − − ∪ ∪ −	ba⁴
829–30	∪ ∪ − ∪ − − − − − − − ∪ − − −	ia⁸ᴬ
831	∪ − − ∪ − − − − ∪ ∪ ∪ − − −	ba² ia⁴ᴬ
832	∪ − − ∪ − − ∪ − − ∪ − −	ba⁴
833	− − ∪ − ∪ − −	ia⁴ᴬ
834	∪ − − ∪ ∪ | − ∪ − ∪ − ∪	ba² + baᶜ

(*hiatus* and *brevis in longo* at caesura, as in 840)

835	− − − − − ̣− − ∪ − − ∪ − −	ba⁴
836	− − − ∪ ∪ − − − −	ia⁴ᴬ
837	∪ − − ∪ − − ∪ − − ∪ − −	ba⁴
838	∪ ∪ − ∪ − ∪ − −	ia⁴ᴬ
839	∪ − − ∪ − − ∪ − − ∪ − ∪ −	ba³ + ia²
		(cf. *Rud.* 205)
840	∪ − − ∪ ∪ | − ∪ − ∪ − −	ba² + baᶜ
		(see 834)
841	∪ ∪ − ∪ ∪ − ∪ ∪ − ∪ ∪ −	an⁴
842	∪ − − ∪ − − ∪ − ∪ ∪ ∪ − −	ba⁴
843–5	⏖ ⏓ ∪ ∪ ⏖ −	3 × cʳ
846	∪ ∪ − ∪ − ∪ − −	ia⁴ᴬ
847–54		ia⁶

815–16 limen: with *super*. The separation of the noun from the preposition is rare, giving perhaps a ritualistic flavour to the language.

'This little ceremony of warning the bride to cross the threshold with care, to prevent an ill-omened stumble...is part of the ritual of a Roman wedding, performed as the bride was about to cross the threshold of her new home, there to begin a new life' (Williams, *J.R.S.* 48 (1958) 16). Compare Catullus 61.159f. *transfer omine cum bono* \| *limen aureolos pedes.* It is of course strictly out of place here, where she is leaving her old home, not entering her new.

noua nupta: cf. Cat. 61.96, 106 *prodeas noua nupta.*

(The glyconic-pherecratean scansion of this line, proposed by

Lindsay but not accepted by other editors, adds to the comic effect
by making the canticum begin in the regular rhythm of *epithalamia*,
such as Catullus 61, quoted several times above; cf. the glyconic 800
(= 808).)

817ff.   sospes, superstes, pollentia: these are old-fashioned words
suited to the marriage ceremony; but of course Pardalisca's advice is a
parody of what would actually be said on such an occasion.

For *sospes* and *superstes* ('surviving', but carrying here also the sense
'superior'), cf. *As.* 16–17 *sicut tuom uis unicum gnatum tuae | superesse
uitae sospitem et superstitem* 'just as you wish your only son to survive
you, in health and strength'. This is the right wish to express for a son,
but comically tactless when desired for a new wife (Williams 18).
In the following two lines the advice that she should gain a superiority
over her husband is repeated five times.

819–20   potior pollentia, uincasque...uictrixque: examples of
Plautine word-play, but also on this occasion imitating the solemn
ritualistic language of Roman religious institutions (Williams 18).

822   despolies: the opposite of *uestire*. He is to clothe you, you are to
denude him. Compare 201 *subtrahat*.

823   diu 'by day'.

825   malo maxumo suo: understand *subdola erit* or *hoc faciet*.
  ilico: cf. 721n.
  tantillum 'ever so little'.
  peccassit = *peccauerit* (307n.).

826   tace: i.e. do not disturb the ceremony by interrupting (cf. 410).
  mala (nom. fem.) *malae* (dat. fem.) *male monstrat*; cf. *Poen.* 1216 *bonus
bonis bene feceris*.

828   id: antecedent of *ut*.
  quaerunt uolunt: two more or less synonymous words put
together without connection (*asyndeton bimembre*) are a natural feature
of early Latin: cf. *uelitis iubeatis*, the phrase used by magistrates when
they asked the *populus* for approval of a proposal (F. Leo, *Analecta
plautina* III (1906) 4).

829 It was O. Seyffert (Bursian's *Jahresbericht* 47 (1886) 12f.) who argued that this speech and that in 832 should be given to Cleostrata and not (as in the Palatine manuscripts) to Pardalisca. For Lysidamus' *iamne abscessit uxor* in 835 shows that his wife has been present, and to give her only the words *iam ualete* (834), as Lindsay does, seems too little. A more important argument is that it would be the responsibility of the *matrona* to hand over the bride to her new husband, so that the comedy is more effective if Cleostrata plays this part. This argument does not apply to the parody of the wedding advice in 815-24, which Williams wishes to give to Cleostrata also, because that almost sacrilegious composition is more suited to the humour of the slave.

832 **integrae:** i.e. the bride is a virgin.

833 **impercito** 'treat her gently'.

834 Cleostrata and Pardalisca re-enter the house.

835 **euax:** a strong cry of joy, like 'Hurrah!' (Hofmann 27).

837 For the diminutives, cf. 134ff.
  uerculum: in *Truc.* 353, the young man describes the girl as like spring – *uer uide:* | *ut tota floret, ut olet, ut nitide nitet.*

838 **malo cauebis:** cf. 411.
  si sapis: cf. 780.

840 **lampadem:** 796n.
  hanc tenebo: i.e. the supposed Casina.

842 **copiam** 'possession'.

843 **o corpusculum malacum:** accusative of exclamation.
  malacum: a Greek word, μαλακόν 'soft', equivalent to *molle*.

844 **quae res** 'What on earth?' (cf. 728).

845 **plantam:** as *planta* is properly the *sole* of the foot, it seems probable that this word is internal accusative with *institit* and refers to the supposed Casina's foot, 'She put down her foot (on mine) like an elephant'; so Ussing. Others have preferred to take *plantam* as Olympio's foot, and so the external object of *institit*, 'She stood on my foot.'

846   luca bos 'elephant', so called because it was in South Italy (Lucania) that the Romans first met elephants, in the war against Pyrrhus.

847–54   For a block of senarii in a canticum, one may compare *Truc.* 241–7.

848–9   A repetition of the comic sequence of 843–6; it is used again (with Lysidamus the victim this time) in 851–3.

848   papillam: accusative of exclamation again.

849   non cubito uerum ariete 'with a battering ram for an elbow'.

851   belle…bellum: a pun.

852   uah 'Ouch!'
   quid negotist: cf. 637–8.
   opsecro 'I ask you', a sort of exclamation.
   ut ualentula est 'What a strong little darling she is!', with the exclamatory use of *ut.*

853   exposiuit 'laid me out'.
   cubito…cubitum (supine of *cubare*): another pun.

854   belliatula: *belliata* is found at *Rud.* 463; cf. also *As.* 676 *i sane bella belle.*

The three enter Alcesimus' house. Beare 260 thinks that they would hardly go in by the front door, for fear of being seen, but would leave the stage by the side, so as to enter the house from the back. That is too logical. As this is a farce, they doubtless entered by the door on the stage.

ACT V

Scene 1   855–874

The three women, having dined well, now come out of the house to watch developments.

   (In this scene, from 866, begins a series of gaps in the text which disfigure the end of the play. There has already been damage in the Palatine manuscripts to the ends and beginnings alternately of passages of some eight lines' length at approximately twenty-line intervals, centring on 804, 823 and 847 (earlier lacunae in 744–51 and 766–71 may come from the same fault); but in these cases the text has been restored with the help of the Ambrosian palimpsest. From now on, A is rarely available, and the destruction in P, still of eight-line sections, gets worse. The lacunae centre on lines 868, 883, 905, 926, 947, 969 and 987, showing irrefutably that an ancestor of the P family, with approximately twenty lines to the page (A has nineteen, and we are evidently referring to a capital manuscript like A), had suffered increasing damage to the outside edge of five successive leaves. The last two lacunae (966–72 and 983–91) are total, with the best Palatine manuscript, B, leaving empty spaces of eight and nine lines respectively.)

Metrical analysis

855–8		$4 \times ba^4$
859		tr^8
860–3		$4 \times ba^4$
864	$\cup - - \cup -$	$ba^{2\wedge}$
865	$- \cup - - \cup - - \cup - \cup -$	$cr^2 + cr^c$
866	$- - - - \langle\cup -\rangle - - - \cup -$	$cr^2 + cr^c$
867	$\cup - - \cup - - \cup - - \cup -$	$ba^2 + ba^{2\wedge}$
868	$\cup \cup \underline{\prime} \cup \cup \cup \cup -$	cr
869	$\cup - - \cup -$	$ba^{2\wedge}$
870	$- \cup - - - - \quad - \cup - - \cup \cup -$	cr^2 ith
871–2	$\langle - \cup \cup - \rangle - \cup \cup - \quad \cup \cup - - \cup - \cup -$	$chor^2$ $tr^{4\wedge}$
873	$- \cup - - \cup - - \cup - \cup -$	$cr^2 + cr^c$
874	$- \cup \cup - \cup \cup -$	cr

(From 864 to 872 the division into lines is uncertain. The text and colometry given here result from a new consideration of the presentation in the P manuscripts, and the scanty remains of A; they are closer to Leo than to any other previous editor. In 866 and 871–2, additions have been made *exempli gratia*, to show how the lines may have been completed. Such letters as are visible in A agree with the presentation here, apart from line 870, where either the decipherers were deceived or A had a different text, perhaps containing one additional line.)

855   intus 'from inside' (cf. 351).

856   uisere: infinitive of purpose; cf. 688 *ludere*.
   huc in uiam: to be construed with *eximus*.

858   hoc quod relicuom est 'the rest of my life'. *hoc* is accusative
of duration of time.
   rĕlĭcŭom: quadrisyllabic, as always in older Latin.
   risuram: understand *me*.

859   Chalinum quid agat scire: *Chalinum* is the object of *scire*;
cf. 559 *meum uirum ueniat uelim*.
   nouom nuptum: the same joke as in 814 *Casinus*.

860–1   ullus poeta: Dramatic invention may be effectively alluded
to in comedy ('This is as good as a play'). Compare *Most.* 1149 *si
amicus Diphilo aut Philemoni es, | dicito is quo pacto tuos te seruos ludifi-
cauerit.*
   atque ut 'than how' = *quam*. The *ut* is redundant.
   fabre 'skilfully'; adverb.

863   Cf. 244.

864   illum: Alcesimus.

865–6   arbitrare: second person singular, addressed to Myrrhina.
   locum stupri 'a place for adultery'; cf. 82 *neque quicquam stupri*,
887 *inlecebram stupri*.

866–7   praesidem esse 'to be in charge', 'to take control';
cf. *Most.* 1096 *hic ego tibi praesidebo*.

867–8   qui…eum: she does not know which of the men will appear
first.
   hinc: pointing to the door of the house.

869–70   Cf. *Amph.* 198 *solens meo more fecero*.

870   omnia intus quid agant 'everything – what they are doing
inside'. The variation from plural *omnia* to singular *quid* is not
difficult.

871–2   Cleostrata tells her maid to stand behind her, and Myrrhina

points out that from that well defended position she can more confidently make fun of the man who comes out.

adstiteris (*adsisto*) 'take your place'; perfect subjunctive. Cf. Ter. *Ad.* 169 *hic propter hunc adsiste*.

pone = *post* 'behind'; cf. *Poen.* 611 *pone nos recede*.

audacius licet: if the second half of this line is iambic or catalectic trochaic, this ending breaks Luchs's law (p. 219), which may however be less stringent in the cola of cantica.

Scene 2   875-936

Olympio comes out of Alcesimus' house in a dishevelled state, and is made to report what has happened to him inside. It is one of the most comic, if most indecent, scenes in Plautus. Formally, this is the major and central part of the long canticum sequence which continues from 855 to 962, with metres (as can be seen below) of the most varied kind. It is much to be regretted that A is not available after 883, as the text of P is defective every twenty lines (855-74n.).

Metrical analysis

The general structure is:

A **875-93**   (Olympio starts his tale to the spectators, thinking that
                he is alone on the stage)
                anapaests and cretics
B **894-903** (Pardalisca intervenes and persuades him to continue)
                short cola, mostly anapaests and iambics
C **904-14**   (a surprising discovery)
                great variety of metre
D **915-21**   (the next stage; attempted seduction)
                mostly trochees and iambics
E **922-9**   (the climax of his efforts)
                probably anapaests
F **930-6**   (roughly handled, he has made his escape)
                iambics, followed by clausulae.

A

875-7		$3 \times \mathrm{an}^{8\mathrm{A}}$
878-82		$5 \times \mathrm{an}^{8}$
883	$- \cup - - \cup - - \cup - - \cup -$	cr^{4}

884	– ∪ – – ∪ – – ⟨∪ – – ∪ –⟩	cr⁴ (?)
885	– ∪ – – ∪ – – – – [	cr⁴ (?)
886	– – ∪ – ∪ – – ∪ ⏑ [	?
887	– ∪ ∪ – ∪ ∪ – ∪ ∪ – | ∪ ∪ ⏓ ∪ ∪ ⏓ –	gl cʳ
888a	– ∪ – ∪ ∪ ∪ –	cr²
b	∪ ∪ – ∪ ∪ ∪ –	crᶜ
889	– ∪ – – – –	ith
890-1	∪ ∪ – [ ] ∪ ∪ – ∪ ∪ – ∪ ∪ – ∪ ∪ –	an⁸
	∪ ∪ – ∪ ∪ ⏑	
892-3	∪ ∪ – ∪ ∪ – ∪ ∪ – ∪ ∪ ⏑ ∪ ∪ | – – –	an⁸
	∪ ∪ – ∪ ∪ –	

B

894	∪ ∪ – ∪ ∪ – – ∪ – | ∪ ∪ ⏑ ∪ ∪ ∪ ⏓ –	gl cʳ
895	∪ ∪ – ∪ ∪ ∪ – ∪ – – – ∪ ∪ –	gl an²
896a	∪ ⏓ – ⏓ –	cʳ
b	∪ ⏓ ∪ ∪ ∪ –	cʳ
c	∪ ∪ – ∪ ∪ ⏑	an²
d	∪ ∪ – ∪ ∪ –	an²
897	∪ ∪ – ∪ ⏑	ia²
898	∪ ∪ – ∪ ⏑	ia²
899	∪ ∪ – ∪ –	ia²
900	∪ ∪ – ∪	ia²ᴧ
901	∪ ∪ – –	ia²ᴧ
902a	– – – ∪ ∪ – – ∪ ∪ –	an⁴
b	∪ ∪ – ∪	ia²ᴧ
c	∪ ∪ – –	ia²ᴧ
903	– ⏑ ∪ – ∪ – – – ⏑ ∪ – ⏑ ∪ –	ba² cʳ

C

904	] – – – – – ∪ ∪ ∪ [	?
905	] ∪ – – – – [	?
906	– ∪ – – ∪ –	cr¹ cr¹
907	] – ∪ ∪ – – ∪ –	? + crᶜ
908a	] ∪ ⏓ – ∪ ∪ – | – ⏓ ∪ ∪ ⏓ –	ia⁴ᴧ cʳ
b		?
909	– ∪ ∪ – – – ∪ ∪ – – ⏑ ∪ – ⏑ ∪ –	ia⁴ᴧ cʳ
910	– – – ∪ – – ∪ ∪ – ∪ ∪ – – – – ∪ –	tr⁸ᴧ
911	– ∪ ∪ – ∪ – – – – – – ∪ – – ∪ ∪ –	tr⁸

912	∪ − − ∪ [ ] − ∪ − − ∪ ∪ −	ba²(?) ith
913	∪ ∪ − ∪ ∪ − ∪ ∪ ∪ − ∪ _ − ∪ ∪ − − −	tr⁴^ ia⁴^
914	∪ ∪ − ∪ ∪ − − ∪ −	tr⁴^
D		
915	− − − ∪ − − − −	tr⁴
916	∪ ∪ − − ∪ ∪ − −	ia²^ ia²^
917–18	∪ − − ∪ ∪ − − ∪ ∪ − ∪ ∪ − − − − −	ia⁸^
919	∪ ∪ − ∪ − − ∪ ∪ −	ia⁴^
920	∪ − − ∪ − − ∪ − − ∪ − −	ba⁴
921	− − − − ∪ ∪ ́− − − − − − − ∪ ∪ ∪ −	tr⁸^
E		
922	∪ ∪ − − − ∪ ∪ − − − ∪ ∪ − ∪ ∪ − ∪ ∪ − ∪	an⁸^
923	∪ ∪ − − − ∪ ∪ − − [	an?
924	− − − − [	an?
925	− ∪ ∪ ∪ ∪ [	?
926	− − ∪̲ [	?
927	− ∪ ∪ − − − [	an?
928	− ∪ − [	cr?
929	∪ ∪ ∪ ∪ − − ∪ ∪ ∪ − − − ∪ − −	Vʳ
F		
930–3		4 × ia⁸

    (**931 decídŏ, subsílĭt**: see note
    932 exĕ(o) hŏc: see note
    933 eòdem: synizesis)

934	∪ ∪ − − ∪ ∪ − ∪ − | − − ∪ ∪ − −	gl cʳ
935	− _ ∪ − ∪ ∪ ∪ ∪ − − − ∪ ∪ ∪ ∪ −	ia⁴^ cʳ
936	_ − ∪ ∪ − − ∪ − − ∪ − − ∪ ∪ −	gl ith

875 fugiam, lateam, celem: deliberative subjunctives.
  Notice the assonance, even rhyme, in this line and 877.

876 superauimus 'we have surpassed', 'excelled'; intransitive.

877 pudeo: in old Latin this personal use is found; later the verb is always impersonal, as in 878.
  inridiculo: predicative dative, 'we are both a laughing-stock'.

879 Olympio addresses the spectators directly, to make sure of their attention for the coming disclosures. It is common in both Greek and Roman comedy thus to break the dramatic illusion; Menander's characters frequently address the audience, and Plautus' slaves are forever telling the audience how clever they are. In fact, to maintain the dramatic illusion consistently is a relatively modern development. Ancient and Elizabethan audiences considered themselves more like participants in the drama than spectators (J. Hartwig, *Shakespeare's tragicomic vision* (1972) 3-33).

itero 'recount', not 'repeat'; i.e. he will tell on stage what happened off it.

operae pretium 'worth the trouble'.

880   auditu, iteratu: supines with *ridicula*.

quae ego intus turbaui 'the disturbances I caused inside'; *quae* is an 'internal accusative' with *turbaui*.

881   hanc: with a wave of the hand, 'over there' (35).

882   tenebrae: the darkness in the house adds some credibility to Olympio's story.

tamquam in puteo 'as if in a well'.

884-7   The general sense is clear, in spite of the gaps in the text. Olympio wished to take advantage of Casina before Lysidamus arrived. He had said earlier (323) that he would not give way to Jupiter himself, and Lysidamus is his Jupiter (331).

885   tardus: the text has been suspected. Lambinus offers the most convincing explanation, that Olympio's ardour cooled down because of his apprehension of the imminent arrival of his master (886); he attempts to kiss 'her' in 887, and in 890-1 he is 'now in a hurry'. *tardus* is used to mean 'slow in love' at Ter. *Eun.* 1079 *fatuos est, insulsus, tardus, stertit noctes et dies.*

886   identidem 'constantly'.

887   inlecebram stupri 'as an enticement to fornication'; cf. *Curc.* 56 *qui uolt cubare pandit saltum sauiis.*

eam sauium: separate objects of *posco. sauium = suauium.*

890-1   enim 'now indeed'.

892-3 surripere 'steal' (*subripio*).

forem obdo 'I shut the door'.

894–936 The pert and suggestive remarks to Olympio in the rest of this scene are best attributed to Pardalisca, as was observed by Schoell. Her participation here was in fact prepared in 867–9.

894 agedum: see note on 384 *mane dum*.

896–902 Plautus proceeds in successively shorter cola, from

$$c^r \; (\cup \underline{\cdot} \; \overline{\cup} \; \underline{\cup}\underline{\cup} \; -) \quad \text{to} \quad an^2 \; (\cup \cup \underline{\cdot} \cup \cup \underline{\cdot})$$
$$\text{to} \quad ia^2 \; (\cup \cup \underline{\cdot} \cup \underline{\cdot}) \quad \text{to} \quad ia^{2\wedge} \; (\cup \cup \underline{\cdot} \; -);$$

cf. 158–60, and (for the last two types of colon) 708–18.

896d satin morigera est: *morem gerere* ('obedience') was the correct behaviour of a wife. G. W. Williams points out that it is the direct opposite of the advice given by Pardalisca to the bride in 819–24 (*J.R.S.* 48 (1958) 19).

902 memorare: understand *te*. The text is uncertain; but the following indirect question, with the verb in the indicative, is perfectly Plautine.

903 flagitium est 'it is shameful'; cf. 937.
= (ii) *qui audiuerint cauebunt (ne idem) faciant.*

904 magnus est makes no sense. Leo's suggestion '*fortasse pudor*' hardly carries conviction. *magnum*, presumably referring to the same object as *maxumum* in 907, *grande* in 914, is more probable, in spite of the present tense of *est*.

perdis: as we might say, 'You're killing me.'

905 suptus (*subtus*) **porro:** the words do not make recognizable sense. *subtus* means 'below', 'underneath'; *porro* may possibly conceal the beginning of *porrigit*, as suggested by Leo.

906 babae: Greek βαβαί, a cry of surprise.

papae: Greek παπαῖ, exclamation of pain, fear or again surprise (Hofmann 24).

907 oh, erat maxumum: alluding to the size of the erect male organ, the subject of the repeated jokes in this section. Such low humour is fairly common in Aristophanes, in whose plays the male actors wore a leather phallus as part of their dress.

909   gladium: a clever echo of Pardalisca's warning that Casina had a sword (660, 692, 751).

ne habeat: the construction treats *quaero* as a verb of fearing or preventing, which under the circumstances it may reasonably be.

911   fui can have a long first vowel in Plautus; cf., in the same position in the line, *Capt.* 555 *quibus insputari saluti fūit atque is profuit.*

912   'It wasn't any kind of vegetable.'

913   nisi 'but this is certain'.

914   Dousa pointed out that *grandis* is a regular word for farm produce, 'well-grown'. Similarly *calamitas* in 913 is the technical word for blight on crops; so the vegetable imagery has continued.

916   ubi appello Casinam: *appellare est blanda oratione alterius pudicitiam adtemptare* (Ulpianus, quoted in *OLD* s.v. §4); so 'try to seduce'.

917–18   amabo 'please' (cf. 137). The word is used by women 84 times out of 91 in Plautus, invariably in Terence. Of the other seven instances in Plautus, six are by men addressing women (including our case, for Olympio is under that impression) and the final one (*Asin.* 707) is in a scene of horseplay between slave and master with evident homosexual suggestions. This limitation of speaker or addressee in early Latin contrasts with later practice, for both Cicero and Caelius use it quite freely in their letters (H. Blase, *Archiv f. lat. Lexikogr.* 9 (1896) 488–90).

   mea tu: cf. 646.

919–20   immerito meo 'undeservedly'.

921–8   The loss of the major part of these lines, at the climax of Olympio's indecent disclosures, naturally arouses the suspicion that the damage to the text was caused, perhaps by a monkish scribe, for reasons of morality. This would suit the losses in 879–86 and 902–8 also. However, as it is clear (855–74n.) that the ancestor of the Palatine manuscripts was affected for five successive leaves, the damage is more likely to have been accidental.

921   qui: ablative.

For this more or less delicate expression by Olympio, addressing the women, there is a close parallel in Varro (*R.R.* 2.4.10), where he calls the same part of the female body *natura qua feminae sunt.*

922   saltum: a fairly common metaphorical term for the *pudenda muliebria.*

altero: *altero saltu*; in other words, he proposes anal intercourse. Occasional references in ancient literature ascribe this alternative to the wedding night; cf. *Priapea* 3.7–8 *quod uirgo prima cupido dat nocte marito,* | *dum timet alterius uulnus inepta loci,* Seneca *Controv.* 1.2.22.

924   muttit: 'she' is still silent.

929   quasi saetis 'as if with bristles'.

compungit barba: here and in 909 Plautus seems to have chosen the colon Reizianum for the surprise 'punch-line': *arripio cápulum!* . . . *compúngit bárba!*

930–1   F. Skutsch (in *Rh.M.* 55 (1900) 283ff.) argued for a connection between our present scene and that described by Ovid in *Fasti* 2.331ff., where Faunus, attempting to assault Omphale, gets into bed with Hercules by mistake (Hercules having dressed up as the bride). The present situation is close to the end of Faunus' venture (*Fasti* 2.349–50): *cubito Tirynthius heros* | *reppulit: e summo decidit ille toro.*

930   in genua: he is kneeling on the bed (925 *surgo*).

astiti: from *adsisto* (cf. 872).

931   decídŏ, subsílit: scansion of a naturally cretic word as a dactyl by iambic shortening, frequent enough in anapaests, is occasionally found in the first foot of an iambic line or half-line. Questa 139 is of the opinion that the present balanced pair of examples aims at a particular sound effect.

praecipes: old form of *praeceps*. It is restored by conjecture here, but found in the manuscripts at *Rud.* 671 and in a fragment of the lost play *Commorientes.*

932   exé(o) hŏc: for this violent example of iambic shortening (producing a dactyl like *decído* and *subsílit* in the previous line), it is necessary that there should be elision between the two independent words; cf. 306n., Questa 57ff.

quo: we would expect *quem*. If this is attraction of the relative to the case of its antecedent, and it certainly looks like it, it is the only example in Plautus. Lindsay (*Syntax* 8) argues that we can avoid this by understanding *quo* (*me exeuntem*) *uides* – in which case *quo* is ablative of attendant circumstances like *ornatu*.

933 hoc eodem poculo...**biberet** 'that he should drink of this same cup', a metaphor familiar to us from the New Testament (Matthew 26.39), 'Father, if it be possible, let this cup pass from me.'
   biberet: the historic sequence of tenses (in spite of *exeo*) is to be explained by the fact that this was his intention at the time when he decided to leave the house.

935 *manum adire alicui est* '*fallere*', '*decipere*' (Bentley); in other words, 'to trick'. This strange phrase is found five times in Plautus (the others are *Aul.* 378, *Pers.* 796, *Poen.* 457, 462). It is clearly metaphorical, but its origin remains uncertain, in spite of many attempts to explain it (B. Brotherton, *The vocabulary of intrigue in Roman comedy* (1926) 91–3).

Scene 3 937–62
Lysidamus follows Olympio out of the house.

Metrical analysis

This is the last section of lyric metre in the play. As if to show his final mastery, Plautus has used the difficult glyconics as the basis of his composition. The general structure is:

A **937–42** glyconics with cretic clausula
B **943–50** anapaests, trochees, cretics
C **951–62** glyconics, interspersed with cretic cola and cola Reiziana

A

937	– ∪ ∪ – ∪ ∪ – ∪ ∪ –	gl (da⁴ᴬ)
938	– ∪ ∪ – ⏝ – ∪ ∪ –	gl (da⁴ᴬ)
939	– ∪ ∪ – – – ∪ ∪ –	gl (da⁴ᴬ)
940	– ∪ ∪ – ∪ ∪ – ∪ ∪ –	gl (da⁴ᴬ)
941	– ∪ ∪ ∪ – – ∪ ∪	gl (tr⁴ᴬ)
942	– ∪ – ∪ – – ∪ – ∪ –	cr⁶ cr⁶

B

943	] ∪ ∪ ∪ ∪ – – – ∪ ∪ ∪ ∪ –	? an⁴ᴬ
944	] ∪ ∪ ∪ – – – ∪ ∪ – ∪ ∪ ⌣ –	? an⁴ᴬ
945	] – – ∪ – – – ∪ –	tr⁸ᴬ (?)
946	] – – – – – ∪ –	tr³ᴬ (?)
947	] – ∪ –	cr⁴ (?)
948	] – ∪ –	cr⁴ (?)
949	] – ∪ – – – ∪ –	tr⁸ᴬ (?)
950	– ∪ – – ∪ – – ∪ – – ∪ –	cr⁴

C

951	∪ ∪ ∪ – ∪ ∪ – ∪ ∪ –	gl
952	– ∪ – – –	cr²ᴬ
953	– – ∪ ∪ – ∪ ∪ ∪ ∪ – ∪ – ∪ ∪ – ∪ ∪ –	gl gl
954	– ∪ – ∪ ∪ –	cr²ᴬ
955	– ∪ – – – ∪∪ –	gl
956	– ∪ – ∪ ∪ –	cr²ᴬ
957	– – – ∪ ∪ ⌣ ∪ – – ∪ – ∪ ∪ – ∪ ∪ –	gl gl
958	– ⌣ ∪ ∪ ∪ ∪ –	cʳ
959	– ∪ – ∪ ∪ – ∪ ∪ –	gl
960	– – ∪ ∪ – –	cʳ
961	– ∪ – ∪ ∪ – ∪ –	gl
962	– – ∪ ∪ – –	cʳ

937 **ārdĕŏ**: Aeolic verses have the same freedom of iambic shortening as anapaests.

flagitio 'disgrace' (903).

938 **agam**: deliberative subjunctive, 'What I am to do.'
meis rebus 'in my present circumstances'; ablative.

939 **ut** 'how'.

940 **contra** 'in the face'.

942 **occidi** = *perii*.

943 **faucibus teneor** 'I am held by the throat', half throttled, unable to get away.

945 **expalliatus**: a made-up word. He has in fact lost both staff and cloak (975).

948–50   He thinks the only thing he can do is to go and submit to the justified anger of his wife.

950   sufferamque ei meum tergum: as if she will beat him for his misdemeanours. Here and in the next few lines, Lysidamus behaves more like a slave expecting punishment than a free man.

951–2   The thought of enrolling a substitute at a critical moment occurs also to the slave Tranio in *Most.* 354–5 *ecquis homo est qui facere argenti cupiat aliquantum lucri | qui hodie sese excruciari meam uicem possit pati?*

953–4   The last resort of a slave, to run away from home, become a *fugitiuos* (397).

955–6   Another way of saying he will be beaten.

957   nugas dicere istaec licet 'You can describe all that as nonsense', referring to his wild ideas of getting hold of a substitute or running away. The texts of A and P, almost the same, make neither sense nor metre. The transposition suggested here, coupled with a small change in the ending of the pronoun, produces good sense (cf. 333 *nugae sunt istae magnae*), and a line which scans as two glyconics, balancing 953.
     tamen: with *inuitus* (63n.).

959–60   hac: adverb, 'in this direction'.
     hac dabo: *me* should be understood, and possibly supplied (it could have fallen out between *prŏtinam* and *et*), as *dare* is not elsewhere intransitive. For the phrase itself, cf. *Curc.* 363 *ostium ubi conspexi, exinde me ilico protinam dedi.*
     sta ilico, amator: obviously spoken by Chalinus, as he follows Lysidamus out of the house. The half line spoken by a character coming on to the stage right at the end of a scene, followed by a change of metre for the new scene, where the new character is the first speaker, is exactly parallel to 814, and has caused nearly as much difficulty. Editors, with the exception of Leo, Lindsay and Paratore, have felt that the words must be given to somebody known to be on stage, Olympio or Cleostrata.
     sta ilico: from the corruption of the Palatine manuscripts (*stalicio*, 'corrected' to *Stalino* by Z), there came the belief that this was the

name of the *senex*, which does not otherwise appear in the text of the play. Consequently, Stalicio is given as his name in the scene heading at 217 in B, Stalino there and elsewhere in the other manuscripts; and Stalino he is called in all printed editions of the *Casina* until in the nineteenth century Lysidamus was read in the scene headings of the Ambrosian palimpsest. (This corruption also affected the rare word *tittibilicio* in 347.)

ilico = *in loco* 'where you are'; cf. 721n.

961–2 quasi non audiam: subjunctive because it is an imaginary condition.

Scene 4 963–1018

The farce is brought to an end, Lysidamus shamed, but finally forgiven.

Metre: trochaic septenarii.

963 úbi tu és: with hiatus of a monosyllable in the unaccented half of the foot, not to be described as prosodic hiatus, but more like that in *cum hác cum ístac* (612).

mores Massilienses: the people of Marseilles had a reputation for effeminacy (Μασσαλιῶται…ἀσχημονοῦσι γυναικοπαθοῦντες Athen., *Deipn.* 12.523c).

965 sis = *si uis*.

There is some advantage in assigning *periisti hercle* to one of the two *matronae* (see app. crit.); but it is not essential.

966–72 We are fortunate that A is almost wholly legible at this point, and so can supplement the lacuna in P.

966 aequom arbitrum 'an arbitrator', who can help to settle a dispute, i.e. (as suggested by Studemund) the club (in reality Lysidamus' own staff) mentioned in 967 and 971. The same word is used for a weapon in *Truc.* 629 *ego tecum, bellator, arbitrum aequom ceperim*. One may compare the slang term 'equalizer' for a gun, favoured at one time by thriller writers.

extra considium 'outside the courtroom'. The word *considium* was unknown in Latin until it was read here in the palimpsest. If correct, it evidently derives from *con-sedeo* (cf. *praesidium*); there remains however the possibility that it is simply a mistake in A for *consilium*.

967   fusti: 975 and 1009, taken together, show that Chalinus is in
fact holding Lysidamus' own staff (*scipio*); this is no doubt what he is
using as a *fustis*.

defloccabit: Nonius (p. 12 L.) *defloccare est adterere: tractum a
uestibus sine flocco. Plautus Casina: perii! flocco habebit iam illic homo
lumbos meos.* The corruption in the quotation itself does not spoil the
value of the grammarian's evidence. The verb is found also in *Epid.*
616 (*duo defloccati senes*, meaning 'fleeced'). As Nonius says, it comes
from rubbing the 'nap' off cloth.

968   lumbifragium: found also at *Amph.* 454. Plautus liked such
compounds.

Lysidamus tries to leave the scene in the other direction, but finds
himself facing his wife.

969   Her greeting is formal: 'A very good day to you, Casanova!'

970   inter sacrum saxumque 'between the sacrificial victim and
the knife', for *saxum* is the ancient flint knife used by the priest (Livy
1.24.9 *id ubi dixit porcum saxo silice percussit,* 21.45.8 *secundum pre-
cationem caput pecudis saxo elisit*). The proverb occurs in the same words
at *Capt.* 617 *nunc ego inter sacrum saxumque sto nec quid faciam scio.* It
obviously gains apparent significance from the similarity of the
sounds of the words (assonance; cf. 'might is right'). For the effect,
compare English 'between the devil and the deep sea'.

nūnc ĕg(o) ĭntĕr: iambic shortening between unconnected words,
but with elision between them, as in 306 *spēcŭl(a) ĭn sŏrtĭtust mihi.*

971   hac lupi, hac canes: another proverb. He is a hunted creature
between the wolves and the dogs. Horace *Sat.* 2.2.64 *hac urget lupus,
hac canis, aiunt.* His wife is the *canis* (320 *cum cane aetatem exigis*).

lupina scaeua: *scaeua* as a feminine noun means an omen,
usually a bad one (S. B. Gulick in *H.S.C.P.* 7 (1896) 244f.; the verb
obscaeuare is found at *Asin.* 266). *lupina scaeua* would be the howling of a
wolf, *canina scaeua* the barking of a dog.

972–3   Apparently this means that he will change the old proverb
(*hac lupi hac canes*) by deliberately going to meet one of the two
menacing alternatives.

974   dismarite 'bigamist' (twice married). The word is a hybrid from Greek δίς (twice) and Latin *maritus*. Its attestation here is unsure (see app. crit.); and it is not found elsewhere. Equally unique is the word *bimaritus* with the same meaning, found only in Cic. *Pro Planc.* 30. Both were doubtless independently invented for their particular occasions.

975 scipione: a stick or staff was an identifying feature of the *senex* in comedy.

pallium is in the accusative because it has been attracted into the relative clause, into agreement with *quod* (cf. 810). The manuscripts (both A and P) read *scipionem* in the accusative as well, but this is not possible (F. Leo, *Analecta plautina* I (1896) 13); it must therefore be an early corruption.

976 moechissat: this is how the Romans adapted Greek verbs in -ιζω, although in fact μοιχίζω is not found.

This line is best given to Myrrhina, who may with propriety join Cleostrata in ridiculing Lysidamus. It would be less proper for Pardalisca to speak in this scene.

977 imus cubitum: cf. 853 *cubitum ergo ire uolt*. For the tense, cf. 405 *ferio*.

i in malam crucem: 93.

979–80 In 186 B.C., as a result of a tremendous scandal at Rome, the Senate banned the worship of the god Bacchus (Livy 39.8–18; *senatus consultum de Bacchanalibus CIL* I² 581, X 504). Naudet seems to have been the first to suggest that the reference in these lines is to that banning of Bacchic revels; he has been followed by Ritschl and others. If so – and the two lines lose all point unless there is some topical allusion – then this is strong evidence for the date of the Latin play. And, as Plautus died in 184 B.C., it supports the other indications, particularly the abnormally high proportion of lyric metre, which suggest that this is one of the last, if not the very last, of the surviving plays.

979 Bacchae hercle uxor: Lysidamus is desperately trying to invent a reason for having lost his cloak. The implication of the word *Bacchae* is shown by Livy's description (reference in the last note) to be one of sexual irregularity and violence (cf. *Aul.* 408, *Amph.* 703,

Merc. 469, the last of which refers to their tearing of Pentheus to pieces; W. T. MacCary, 'The Bacchae in Plautus' *Casina*', *Hermes* 103 (1975) 459–63.

981   Lysidamus' two halting utterances in this line show that he is totally at a loss; cf. 366–8.

982   nam: explaining *times* in her previous speech.

983   CL. *eti*]**am me rogas** seems very probable, especially in view of 997 *rogitas etiam.* Apart from this, 983–90 are beyond conjecture. Even the occasional letters deciphered in A are for the most part quite unreliable.

988   Casinust: if correct, this is a repetition of the joke in 814.

991   This line must, as Schoell saw, be the end of a speech by Olympio, joining in the vituperation of his former associate.
   famosum 'infamous'.

994–5   tŭi amoris: prosodic hiatus (p. 216).
   LY. ego istuc feci?: a disingenuous question.
   OL. immo Hector Ilius: as if in a modern play we were to get the backchat – A. Did I do that? B. No, it was Julius Caesar.

996   oppresset: an abbreviated form of the pluperfect subjunctive *oppressisset.* There is doubt about the text. Indeed the reference to Hector of Troy was only established (by Palmer) as recently as 1888. But, in the atmosphere of recrimination and vituperation, the following sequence does not seem ineffective:
   LY. (*wonderingly*) Did I do that?
   OL. No, it was Hector of Troy.
   LY. He'd have knocked you down for a start. (*Turning to the two women*) Did I really do what you say?
   Whether *oppresset* has a more obscene meaning (like 362 *comprimere*) may well be suspected.
   dicta quae uos dicitis: simply 'what you say'.

998   monebo 'I will remind you.'
   qui: ablative of the indefinite pronoun, 'in any way'; to be taken with *minus*.

999   potius uobis credam 'I'd rather believe you', *quod uos dicitis* 'with respect to what *you* say' (than have you remind me indoors of what I have done).

1000   sĕd ŭxor: here the accented syllable of the noun is certainly shortened by iambic shortening; cf. 304n.

A. Klotz argued (*Würzb. Jahrb.* 2 (1947) 352–3) that the hiatus after *uiro* is permitted at this position in the line; cf. *Bacch.* 530 *reddidi patrí omne aurum.*

1001–2   amasso, occepso, amasso: equivalents of future perfects (*amauero* etc.); see note on *decolassit* 307. So also *faxit* 1016.
    occepso 'begin'.

1002   ne ut eam amasso: this must mean something like 'let alone make love to her' (as it is translated by Nixon), and *ne* must stand for *nedum.* Even then, it is difficult to see how *ne ut* could possibly be followed by what is in effect a future indicative tense. Leo suggested that the formulation of the phrase may have antique legal overtones.

It is best to make this limiting clause qualify the second half of this line, not the second half of 1001. 'If ever after this I either make love to Casina, or just begin to do so, if I ever – not to speak of making love – do from now on anything of the sort...'

1003   pendentem: cf. 390n.

1004   As the line is transmitted, there is hiatus after *censeo* (at the *locus Jacobsohnianus*, cf. p. 217), and either a diaeresis after *ueniam* (with rhythmically uncomfortable *hánc dandám* to follow), or more probably a diaeresis after *hanc* and a second hiatus after *faciam.*

1005   prospero 'I grant'.

**1006   The joke breaks the dramatic illusion; cf. *Merc.* 1007 *eadem breuior fabula* | *erit, Pseud.* 388.

1008   nemo quisquam: the second word is redundant; the same combination is found at *Persa* 648, *Pseud.* 809.
    The sense is *nemo habet lepidiorem uxorem quam ego hanc habeo.*

1010–11   The final joke from the pretended bride.

1011   dŭŏbus: synizesis.

solet: understand *fieri*.

1012ff.   The epilogue explains what there has not been time for in the play, that Euthynicus, the son of the house, will return (see 64–5) and marry Casina, who will be discovered to be the neighbour's daughter (see 41ff.). This motif, typical of New Comedy plots, is abruptly attached at the end of the *Casina*, as though by force of convention, for it is irrelevant to the play as we have it. How large a part the recognition scene played in the play of Diphilus is a matter for conjecture.

There is disagreement about the speaker of the epilogue. Unless we imagine a separate *cantor*, or a leader of the group of actors, nobody is more suitable than Chalinus, who is already speaking (cf. 1014 *nostro erili filio*).

1013   huius…ex proxumo: Alcesimus (cf. 687).

1014   nostro erili filio 'our young master'.

1015   meritis: rather awkward next to the ablative *manibus*; but this must be a dative, and refer to the actors.

meritis meritam: the former word is active in sense, the latter passive – 'deserving, deserved'.

1016–18   A crude appeal to the low taste of the Roman audience, parallel to the lines at the end of the prologue (84–6).

1016   faxit = *fecerit* (307n.).

quod: *scortum* is of course neuter.

1018   pro 'in place of'.

supponetur: *supponi dicuntur quae non desideramus* (Donatus *ad* Ter. *Eun.* 911).

hircus: he-goats are notorious for their offensive smell (550).

nautea: Nonius (p. 12 L.): *nautea est aqua de coriis* (i.e. from tanning leather; Festus also (pp. 164–5 L.) gives a connection with tanning) *uel, quod est uerius, aqua de sentina* (i.e. bilge water); in either case, it would make the scent of the he-goat even more unpleasant.

APPENDIX 1

THE SCANSION OF PLAUTINE VERSE

The latest and most complete description of Plautine metre is that of Questa. In English, the best is still perhaps Section III (pp. 56–102) of the Introduction to Lindsay's *Captivi*, useful material will be found in J. Halporn, M. Ostwald and T. Rosenmeyer, *The meters of Greek and Latin poetry* (1963) and D. S. Raven, *Latin metre* (1965).

The information that follows falls under three headings:

I Prosody (the metrical value of individual words);

II Special features of the placing of the words in the lines;

III The schemes of the metres themselves.

I. PROSODY

1 Long and short syllables; definition of 'syllable'

The scansion of all classical Latin verse is based on the *length* of the syllables in the words (i.e. the time taken to pronounce them), and upon a somewhat arbitrary assumption that there are two kinds of syllable only, called 'long' and 'short', and that the 'long' is exactly equal to two 'shorts'.

Syllables end either with a vowel or with a consonant, and are described respectively as 'open' or 'closed'. The general rules which decide this are that:

(i) A single consonant between vowels within a word belongs to the following syllable; e.g. the first two syllables of *fa-ci-tis* are open.

(ii) Of two or more successive consonants within a word, at least the first belongs to the preceding syllable; e.g. the first (as well as the second) syllable of *pes-tis* is closed (*x* and *z* are double consonants, and are therefore shared (*k-s*, *d-s*) within a word; *h* is disregarded).

(iii) As an exception to (ii), the particular collocation of consonants called 'mute and liquid' (in practice *br*, *cr*, *gr*, *pr*, *tr*, *cl*, *pl*, *tl*) may, within the same word, be treated as belonging wholly to the following syllable; e.g. the first syllable (as well as the second) of *pa-tre* is open.

This is in fact the invariable rule in Plautus, except where the two
consonants evidently belong to different parts of a compound word
(e.g. *ab-ripio*).

All syllables containing a long vowel or diphthong are **long**; so are
closed syllables containing a short vowel, if they are followed by a
syllable beginning with a consonant. **Short** are open syllables containing a short vowel; and closed syllables containing a short vowel, if
they are followed by a syllable beginning with a vowel. Thus, *fĭdēm
quī fācĭtīs māxŭmī* (2), *lūdūs dătŭs ēst ārgēntārĭīs* (25). Note that, by these
rules, a short open final syllable remains short before any number of
consonants at the beginning of the following word; and that in the
particular circumstances of 'mute and liquid' (see (iii) above), the
preceding syllable is short if it contains a short vowel: *cum pătre* (36),
impĕtret (56), *perĕgre* (62).

This *quantitative* nature of ancient scansion is difficult for us to
appreciate, and we tend to read Latin verse as if it were English
(which depends largely on stress accent, not on length of syllables).
We pronounce the two following lines in the same way

> Téll me nót in moúrnful númbers, 'Lífe is bút an émpty dréam'
> án marĭtum séru(om) aetátem déger(e) ét gnatós tuós (291).

This is a legitimate way of indicating the metre, but we should not
imagine that we are pronouncing the second as the ancients did. (All
the same, length of syllables was not the only criterion in Plautine
metre; on the role of word accent, see below.)

2 **Word accent** (Allen 83–8)

It is certain that Latin, in contrast to Greek, had a stress accent. As to
the syllable on which it fell, the great majority of words obeyed the
'rule of the penultimate', whereby, if the penultimate syllable was
long, it received the accent; if it was short, the accent went back to the
antepenultimate. Thus (from line 1) *saluĕre*, but *iŭbeo*; *spectatŏres*, but
ŏptumos (the symbol ᵛ is here used to show the accented syllable, to
distinguish it from the metrical ictus, whose sign is ´, section **14**).
The resulting accentuation is not difficult for us, because it is how we
should tend to pronounce the words in any case, if they were English.

The exceptions to the 'rule of the penultimate' are three:

   (i) Words of four syllables beginning with three shorts (∪ ∪ ∪ ⊻, e.g. *fămiliă*) regularly retained an original word accent on their first syllable – *fămilia*.

(ii) Some words which had lost a final *e* had in consequence an accent on their last syllable, e.g. *istŭc, illĭc*.

(iii) Certain words were enclitic, e.g. *-que, -ue*, weak personal pronouns, probably parts of the verb 'to be'; these attached themselves to the previous word, and the accent was based on the word group thus formed, e.g. *patérque, uoluptắs mea* (not *uolŭptas mĕa*). There were also 'proclitic' words, which attached themselves closely to what followed; the most obvious examples are prepositions – *in illísce*, not *ĭn illĭsce*.

The word accent was not the primary determinant in establishing the relationship of the word to the verse; that was the function of the length of the syllables. Accent however did have a certain effect, as will be seen in sections **8** (Iambic shortening) and **14** (Ictus and accent).

3 Vowel length (Questa 9–11)

Many vowels in final closed syllables were long in early Latin, but short later. The commonest example is the third person singular of those tenses of the verb in which the second person singular has a long vowel, e.g. *amāt* (49), *monēt, audīt, amabāt*, etc., but *regit, amabit*; the third person of the perfect indicative also seems to be long, *adiīt* (696); secondly, most final syllables in *-ar, -er, -or, -al* were still long; thirdly, certain syllables ending in *-s* are long in Plautus, e.g. *ēs* (615), *impōs* (629), *sospēs* (817), *superstēs* (818).

4 Loss of final *e* and *s* (Questa 14–21)

In certain common words, mostly disyllables, final short *e* may have no metrical value even before a consonant; thus *nemp', ill', ess'*; e.g. 599 (senarius)

> quin tú suspéndis té? nemp' túte díxerás.

This feature, called syncope, was convincingly argued by F. Skutsch in *Plautinisches und Romanisches* (1892). It is common with *ille* (witness the modern *il* in French and Italian) and invariable in Plautus and Terence with *nempe*, which always scans as a single long, whether it is followed by a vowel or a consonant. In 230 and 231 it provides an alternative scansion, by *ess'* and *mitt'*.

s following a short vowel at the end of a word may count or not as the poet wishes. *omnibus modis* may scan $- \cup - \cup -$ or $- \cup \cup \cup -$. In the latter case the affected word is sometimes (but not in this edition) printed with an apostrophe – *omnitu'*. Where, as often, the word is iambic in shape, it is not possible to tell for certain whether the final *s* has been dropped or iambic shortening (**8** below) has taken place *mĕŭs* 137, *mǎgĭs* 224, *bŏnŭs* 238).

5 Prodelision (Questa 23–5)

est and *es* lose their vowel when they coalesce into one word with a word that precedes them; thus we find *decretumst* 94, *negotist* 97, *lustratū's* (for *lustratus es*) 245, *commentust* (for *commentus est*) 241.

6 Synizesis (Questa 79–85)

Two contiguous vowels may coalesce into a single long syllable, *eāndem* 61, *deōsculer* 136, *deāēque* 279, *cuĩus* 282, *Cleōstrata* 393. It is often not possible to tell for certain, in the case of an iambic word, whether there is synizesis or iambic shortening (**8** below), e.g. *ēā* 18, *ēām* 48, *tūām* 103, *mēā* 304.

7 Enclisis (*Kürzung durch Tonanschluß*, fully discussed by Vollmer; Questa 71–8)

For reasons which are not clear, some long syllables are shortened in scansion when joined into one word with *quidem* or *quis*, e.g. *siquidem* 327, 409, 474, *tūquidem* 208–9, *ĕcquis* 165–6.

8 Iambic shortening (Questa 31–70)

An iambic word or word-group, or the iambic beginning of a longer word or group, may have the second syllable shortened. This phenomenon may be found in any type of metre, although it is rare in cretics and bacchiacs. The situation is always that a short syllable (called the *brevis brevians*) appears to cause the shortening of a following long syllable. There are three common varieties:

   (i) iambic words: $\cup -$ becomes $\cup \cup$. Thus *sĕnĕx* 35, *ăbĭ* 103; this is very common;

   (ii) cases of *ille* and *iste* (and more rarely *ipse*) preceded by a monosyllable: it is as if the first syllable of these words is weak, and takes what opportunities it can to be shortened. $\cup \mid - \cup$ becomes $\cup \mid \cup \cup$. Thus in *illisc(e)* 36, *sib(i) istanc* 53, *ăd illam* 79;

(iii) longer words or groups: a long syllable preceding the accented syllable of the word or word-group, and itself preceded by a short syllable, may be shortened; typically ∪ – ⌣ ⌣ becomes ∪ ∪ ⌣ ⌣. Thus *quī ŭtŭntur* (?) 5, *uŏlŭptăs mea* 136, 453.

In every case the two shorts produced by the operation of iambic shortening must act as the resolution of a single long; they cannot form parts of separate elements in the line. Also, the syllable which is shortened may not in normal circumstances be the accented syllable of the word.

Iambic shortening, which is extremely common, is handled in this edition as follows: for the first few examples, it is pointed out in the notes; thereafter, only unusual and difficult cases are commented on; the rest are indicated with the help of an ictus mark (′) in the text (for ictus, see **14**). Thus *scies hóc* (115) indicates *sciĕs hóc*; *úbi illi* (255) indicates *ŭb(i) illi*.

Exceptional situations

Cases of iambic shortening not exactly covered by (i), (ii) and (iii) above: 103, 217, 306, 726, 932, 970

Shortening of an accented syllable: 227, 240, 1000

Cretic words shortened to dactyls in iambic or trochaic verse: 159, 229, 931

Greater licence in anapaests: 165–7 (metrical note), 237

II. THE PLACING OF WORDS IN THE LINE

9 Elision

Any open syllable, or syllable ending in *m*, at the end of a word loses its metrical value before a vowel, or syllable beginning with *h*, at the beginning of the next. In fact, total loss probably did not take place; it was rather a slurring of the two syllables. In the examples of scansion given in this Appendix, elision is shown by brackets round the affected letters: e.g.

257 *pótius qu(am) illi séruo néquam dés, armíger(o)*

atqu(e) ímprobó.

10 Hiatus

This describes situations where, in spite of the conditions mentioned in **9**, elision does not take place. The text of Plautus is full of examples of hiatus, which scholars used to attempt to remove by emendation; but in fact many are not susceptible of removal. Leaving aside 'prosodic hiatus' (**11** below), we may identify certain circumstances in which hiatus is recognized as 'legitimate':

   (i)   at a change of speaker: 214, 321, 488

   (ii) before or after an interjection: 536, 800

  (iii) at a pause in speech: 2, 245

  (iv) at a break in the metre, such as between two cola making up a line, at the diaeresis of a long verse, or at the caesura of a senarius (for diaeresis and caesura, see **17**): 41, 49, 73, 79, 150, 190, etc.

Even when these categories are allowed, however, there still remain other cases which are firmly embedded in the text, but have no generally accepted justification: 7, 47, 48, 59, 126, 564, 612, 963, 1000. Others are less certain, or ambiguous: 162, 259, 271, 287.

In this edition, hiatus is indicated by the placing of an ictus mark (′) in the text (for ictus, see **14**), except where the phenomenon is commented on in the notes. Thus *aetatem út* (47), indicates hiatus between the two words. In the metrical analyses of the cantica hiatus is shown by a vertical line (e.g. 150).

11 Prosodic hiatus

A long monosyllable, or a monosyllable ending in *m*, in hiatus may be scanned as short, becoming the first of two shorts of a resolved long: *quī ĕrat* 66, *quŏm ămo* 225, *tū ăgis* 229. It may then even act as the *brevis brevians* (**8**) to shorten the following syllable if unaccented and long: *sī ĕfféxis* 708, *quī ūtúntur* (?) 5.

Iambic disyllables may also stand in prosodic hiatus, scanning as two shorts: *sibĭ uterque* 50, *uirŭm amori* 58, *tŭĭ amoris* 994–5. Less certain cases are 215, 271, 496, 725.

12 Brevis in longo (often less correctly termed *syllaba anceps*)

This denotes a short syllable appearing where the metre requires a long. It may be found under the same conditions as those of 'legitimate hiatus' in **10** above; e.g. (at the diaeresis of an anapaestic line)

646-7   *ere mí* – : : *quid uís, mea t(u) áncillá* ? : : *nimiúm*
                                          saeuís. : : *numeró dicís.*

So also 134 (at the *locus Jacobsohnianus* (**13**)), 416 (at change of
speaker), 834, 840 (both at the caesura of a bacchiac line).

13 The loci Jacobsohniani

H. Jacobsohn, in a famous dissertation (*Quaestiones Plautinae*, 1904),
showed that hiatus and/or *brevis in longo* are commonly found
   (i) at the end of the fourth foot of the senarius and at the equivalent place in the trochaic septenarius. The two stock examples are
   (hiatus) | *quindecím habeo minas* (*Pseud.* 346)
   (*brevis in longo*) | *fingeré fallaciam* (*As.* 250)
For examples in this play, see 134, 140, 550;
   (ii) at the end of the initial cretic of a trochaic septenarius, e.g.
   (*brevis in longo*) *ceterá quae uolumus uti* | (*As.* 199)
   (hiatus) *cui hominí hodie peculi* | (*Cas.* 258)
The most plausible explanation of this phenomenon is that of
H. Drexler, who points out that the essential feature of these two *loci*
is that they come at the end of cretic sections, and argues for a strong
pressure in iambic and trochaic verse towards the cretic accentuation
(and thus scansion) of dactylic words (cf. *Einführung* 42).

   Associated with position (i) is a further complication – that of the
apparently 'aufgelöste drittletzte Hebung' (divided long element
three from the end of the line). A large number of lines, both senarii
and septenarii, show a word break as in *dicĕrĕ uŏlŭï femur* (*Mil.* 27).
Luchs's law and Ritschl's law combined (section **15**) will lead us to
the conclusion that such an ending is to be scanned with an anapaest,
not an iambus, in the penultimate foot, and *brevis in longo* at the *loc.*
           $-\lor\lor|\ \lor\lor-|\lor\ -\ |$
Jac.: *dicere uolui femur* (these are the foot divisions in the senarius;
they differ in the septenarius, but the principle is the same). Examples
in our play are 134 *mi animulé, mi Olympio*, 427 *mortuós equidem tamen*,
470 *deperit. habeo uiros.* (See Drexler *Lizenzen* 59–71, Questa 155.)

14 Ictus and accent

   (i) **Ictus.** In every metrical foot, at least one syllable receives the
ictus, i.e. the *beat* of the rhythm, also called by the ambiguous Greek
word *arsis* or the German *Hebung*. This may be indicated by a sign (')
8   M P C

in the text; if the long syllable on which the ictus should fall is resolved into two shorts, the mark is placed on the former of the two. Some older editions indicate the ictus in every foot, others in alternate feet; it is commoner now to use the ictus sign only to show something (such as hiatus or the operation of iambic shortening) which might initially escape the notice of a modern reader. This is the practice followed in this edition.

(ii) **Coincidence of ictus and accent** (section 2). It was long ago observed by Bentley that in Plautine verse, particularly in iambic and trochaic lines, there is a tendency for the words to be so placed in the line that their word accent coincides with the metrical ictus. For example, in line 1 (senarius)

saluere iubeo spéctatores optumós

the accent of each word coincides with the ictus of one of the iambic feet. This suggests – what would in any case be probable in itself – that it was part of the aim of the comic poet to achieve the pronunciations of spoken speech within the rhythms of the verse. Thus, a word like *spectatores* will be so placed in the line that the ictus falls on the first and third syllables, and not on the second and fourth (which, if one scans by length of syllables only, would be equally possible).

This phenomenon has been hotly disputed, and there are scholars who deny any influence of the word accent on the position of words in the line; and others, including Professor Questa, who deny the existence of ictus. Such scepticism, however, is unconvincing, as the very fact of rhythm (Latin *numerus*) necessarily carries with it some idea of a repeated beat. From observation we can surely say that there is a tendency towards coincidence of word accent with this metrical ictus. It seems therefore legitimate to use this tendency as evidence to help to decide the metre in cases of doubt, even in cantica; cf. 73, 162, 214n.

The tendency towards coincidence does not apply to anapaestic verse, which in other respects also enjoys greater freedom than the other metres. (For an explanation, see Lindsay, *Captivi* 76–7, *ELV* 296–8.)

15 Laws governing word divisions primarily in iambic and trochaic verses

(i) **Luchs's law**: If an iambic line or half line (or a catalectic trochaic line) ends with an iambic word, the preceding 'foot' may not be formed by an iambic word or the iambic end of a longer word (Questa 188–94). See 60, 287, 395, 611; the rule appears to be broken in 871–2.

(ii) **Hermann's law**: The two shorts of a resolved long or anceps should not be the final syllables of a trisyllabic or longer word (Questa 129–35). This rule is broken in 229, 242.

(iii) **Ritschl's law**: There should not be word division between the two shorts of a resolved long or anceps unless the former of the two is a monosyllabic (or elided disyllabic) word (Questa 125–9). This rule is broken in 238, 239, 242.

N.B. The laws of Hermann and Ritschl (which may be summarized as 'rules against a broken anapaest') do not apply in the first foot of a line or half line (cf. 55, 306, 456); nor if the words go very closely together, e.g. *inter eos* 561; nor do they apply in anapaestic verses, or cola Reiziana, or in Aeolic metres.

III. METRICAL SCHEMES

16 General description

Plautine metres, ultimately derived from those of Greek drama, but modified to suit the Latin language, show extraordinary variety. In this our poet differs from the dramatists of Greek New Comedy, whose plays, although they occasionally used other metres, were predominantly (as we may judge from Menander) in the metre closest to ordinary speech, the iambic trimeter, the equivalent of the Plautine senarius.

Plautus' plays are more like musical comedies; and in them it is usual to distinguish three classes of metrical composition:

(i) **Spoken**: senarii (ia^6).

(ii) **Sung** (cantica):

(a) **'Recitative'**: i.e. close to spoken speech, but with a musical accompaniment. This term describes any continuous sequence of long lines (septenarii or octonarii) in iambic, trochaic or anapaestic rhythms ($ia^{8\wedge}$, ia^8, $tr^{8\wedge}$, tr^8, $an^{8\wedge}$, an^8).

(b) **True songs**. This includes all the rest: shorter iambic, trochaic
or anapaestic units, bacchiacs, cretics, Aeolic metres, and combinations of these. The songs may show a continuous use of the same
metrical form, but more commonly they have a mixture of several or
many (*mutatis modis cantica*). Within such mixed songs may also be
found the types of line which, when in continuous sequence, make up
classes (i) and (ii) (*a*) above.

In what follows, only metres which are found in the *Casina* are
included. This in fact excludes very little, because the *Casina* has
greater metrical variety than any other Plautine play. The descriptions are of the basic structure of the lines; special features and
technical variations are explained in notes following the metrical
analyses in the Commentary, or in the Commentary itself at the
individual lines, references only being provided here.

17 Some definitions   *may appear as*
   Elements   ∪ short   ∪
                 − long   − or ∪ ∪
                 × anceps   ∪ or − or ∪ ∪
                 ⌒ indifferens   ∪ or −
    (in anapaests)   ⌣⌣ biceps   ∪ ∪ or −

The final element in every metre is *indifferens*.

Note. A closed final syllable at the end of a line is shown as long in
the examples that follow, even if the vowel that it contains is short
(cf. General Note 3 on p. 118).

The symbol ^ means that a line is 'catalectic', i.e. short by one
syllable.

Caesura and diaeresis: These terms are used for regular breaks
between words in the metrical schemes: caesura when the break falls
internally in a foot (as in ia⁶), diaeresis when it falls between feet (as is
normal in the longer lines).

18 Iambics (iambus = ∪ ⊥)
Any foot which appears in a scheme as ⦂ × − ⦂ may take any of the
six following forms
                 ∪ −   iambus
                 ∪ ∪ ∪   tribrach

– –	spondee
– ∪ ∪	dactyl
∪ ∪ –	anapaest
∪ ∪ ∪ ∪	proceleusmatic

The final foot, which appears in the schemes as ⦙ ∪ ⌒ |, may be either ∪ – iambus or ∪ ∪ pyrrhic.

Senarius = ia⁶

$$⦙ \times \underset{\cdot}{\llcorner} ⦙ \times \underset{\cdot}{\llcorner} ⦙ \times \mid \underset{\cdot}{\llcorner} ⦙ \times \underset{\cdot}{\llcorner} ⦙ \times \underset{\cdot}{\llcorner} ⦙ ∪ \acute{⌒} \mid$$

There is a regular caesura after the fifth element, less commonly after the seventh element (example in line 90).

89-94

non mihi licere meam rem me sol(um) ut uolo,

loqu(i) atque cogitare sine ted arbitro?

quid tu, malum, me sequere? :: quia certum (e)st mihi

quas(i) umbra, quoquo t(u) ibis, te semper sequi;

quin edepol etiam s(i) in crucem uis pergere,

sequi decretumst.

(**89** *meām*: either iambic shortening or synizesis

91 *cērtūm (e)st*: prodelision; also, although differently presented, *decretumst* 94)

Technicalities in senarii

Dactylic word in first foot: 55, 767
Line without caesura: 424, 510
Locus Jacobsohnianus: 134, 140 (?), 427, 470
Luchs's law: 60, 611
Molossus in third and fourth feet: 447
Trochaic word beginning the line: 456, 566

Iambic octonarius = ia⁸

$$⦙ \times \underset{\cdot}{\llcorner} ⦙ \times \underset{\cdot}{\llcorner} ⦙ \times \underset{\cdot}{\llcorner} ⦙ \genfrac{}{}{0pt}{}{∪\acute{⌒}}{\times-} ⦙ \times \underset{\cdot}{\llcorner} ⦙ \times \underset{\cdot}{\llcorner} ⦙ \times \underset{\cdot}{\llcorner} ⦙ ∪ \acute{⌒} \mid$$

As in the other long metres, there is usually diaeresis at the half-way point; the permitted scansion of the fourth foot differs according to whether this diaeresis is present or not.

For an English equivalent (*mutatis mutandis*) to the iambic octonarius, one may cite

> Eternal Father strong to save, whose arm doth bind the
>
> > restless wave.

637–40 face uent(um), amabo, pallio. ∷ time(o) hoc negoti quid

> > > > siet,

nis(i) haec meraclo s(e) uspiam percussit flore Liberi.

Technicalities

Cretic word scanned as a dactyl, filling a foot: 229, 931

ia^8 without central diaeresis: 251

Iambic septenarius = ia^{8A}

$$: \times \underline{\bot} : \times \underline{\bot} : \times \underline{\bot} : \overset{\cup \acute{\cap}}{\underset{\times - :}{}} \times \underline{\bot} : \times \underline{\bot} : \times \underline{\bot} : \cap |$$

The position about the central diaeresis is the same as in the octonarius. For an English 'equivalent' –

> The King of Love my shepherd is. His goodness faileth never.

829–30 ag(e), Olympio, quando uis uxor(em), accip(e) hanc ab

> > > > nobis.

917–18 amabo, mea t(u) uxorcula, cur uirum tuom sic me spernis?

> (**829–30** No central diaeresis
>
> **917–18** *brevis in longo* at the diaeresis (*syllaba indifferens*)
>
> > **uirŭm:** iambic shortening
>
> > **tŭŏm:** either iambic shortening or synizesis)

Shorter iambic cola found in the cantica

ia^4 (iambic dimeter)

$$: \times \underline{\bot} : \times \underline{\bot} : \times \underline{\bot} : \cup \acute{\cap} |$$

⏐– – ⏐∪ – ⏐– –⏐ ∪ –⏐
170   iussin colum ferri mihi?

⏐– – ∪ ∪ ⏐∪ –⏐   ⏐– ‿∪⏐∪ –   ⏐
198   nos sumus. :: ita (e)st. und(e) ea tibi (e)st?

ia⁴ᴧ (catalectic iambic dimeter)

⏐× ⊥⏐× ⊥⏐× ⊥⏐⌒ ⏐

⏐– –⏐∪ – ⏐ ∪ –⏐   ⏐
833   impercito. :: futurum (e)st.

⏐– –⏐ – ∪ ∪⏐– –⏐– ⏐
836   nunc pol dem(um) ego sum liber.

ia² (iambic monometer)

⏐× ⊥⏐∪ ⌒ ⏐

⏐‿ –⏐∪– ⏐
715-17   eo nunciam

⏐∪ ∪ – ⏐∪– ⏐
      nisi quippiam

⏐∪ ∪ –∪ –⏐
      remorare me

ia²ᴧ (catalectic iambic monometer)

⏐× ⊥⏐⌒ ⏐

⏐– ∪ ∪–⏐
236b   oh peri i!

⏐∪ ∪ ––⏐
718   ab(i) et cura.

19 Trochaics (trochee = ⊥ ∪)

Any foot which appears in a scheme as ⏐– ×⏐ may take any of the six following forms

– ∪	trochee
∪ ∪ ∪	tribrach
– –	spondee
∪ ∪ –	anapaest
– ∪ ∪	dactyl
∪ ∪ ∪ ∪	proceleusmatic

Trochaic septenarius = **tr⁸ᴧ** (the commonest metre in Plautus, commoner even than ia⁶)

⏐⊥ ×⏐⊥ ×⏐⊥ ×⏐⊥ ⌒⏐⊥ ×⏐⊥ ×⏐⊥ ∪⏐⌒ ⏐

There is regular diaeresis after the eighth element. The equivalent metre is common in English, e.g.

Tell me not in mournful numbers, 'Life is but an empty dream'.

252-5 sed quid a i s? iam domuist(i) ani mum, poti us ut quod

uir uel it

fi er(i) id fac ias qu(am) aduorsere contra? : : qua de re? : :

rogas?

super anc illa Cas in(a), ut detur nuptum nostro uil ico,

seruo frug(i) atqu(e) ub(i) illi bene sit lign(o), aqua

cal ida, ci bo.

Technicalities in trochaic septenarii

Caesura after seventh element, instead of diaeresis: 406, 408
Hermann's law: 264
Loci Jacobsohniani: 258, 550, 1004
Luchs's law: 287, 395
No central diaeresis or caesura: 399
Ritschl's law: 306, 543, 561

Trochaic octonarius = tr⁸

There is regular diaeresis after the eighth element (244 may be an exception). The English 'equivalent' is the metre of Longfellow's *Hiawatha*

By the shores of Gitche Gumee, by the shining Big-Sea-Water.

245-6 und(e) is, nihili? ubi fu isti? ubi lustratu's? ubi bi bisti?

mades mecastor: uide palliol(um) ut rugat. : : di m(e) et

t(e) infel i cent.

Shorter trochaic cola found in the cantica
tr⁴ (trochaic dimeter)

$$: \perp \times : \perp \times : \perp \times : \perp \cap \,|$$

: ∪∪ – :   ∪ ∪ – : ⎯⎯ – : – – |
734-6 erus sum. :: quis erus? :: cuius tu seruo's.

: – ∪ ∪   : – ⌣⌣ :   –   ∪ ∪: – – |
      seruos eg(o)? :: ac meus. :: non s(um) ego liber?

tr⁴ᴬ (catalectic trochaic dimeter)

$$: \perp \times : \perp \times : \perp \cup : \acute{\frown} \,|$$

: – ∪: – ⌣⌣ : – ∪:∪|
195-7 uilico suo se dare

: ∪ ∪ ∪: ∪   ∪ – : – ∪: –|
      sed ipsus e(am) amat. :: obsecro

: ∪ ∪   – : – ∪ ∪: – ∪:∪|
      tace. :: n(am) hic nunc licet dicere.

ith (ithyphallic) = **tr³**

$$: \perp \times : \perp \times : \perp \cap \,|$$

: ∪ ∪ ∪: – ∪:– –|
147b senex sibi parari.

: –   – : –   ∪: – –|
      semper sis superstes.

tr² (trochaic monometer)

$$: \perp \times : \perp \cap \,|$$

: ∪ ∪   ∪: – –|
730a-b ut eg(o) opinor

: ∪ ∪ ∪: – – |
      nisi resistis.

Technicalities in trochaics (apart from septenarii)

Cretic word scanning as a dactyl by iambic shortening: 159
Hermann's law: 242
Ritschl's law: 239

20 Anapaests (anapaest = ∪ ∪ ⊥)

Any foot which appears in a scheme as $: \underset{\smile\smile}{\frown} - :$ may take any of the
four following forms

ᴗ ᴗ –	anapaest
– –	spondee
– ᴗ ᴗ	dactyl
ᴗ ᴗ ᴗ ᴗ	proceleusmatic

anapaestic octonarius = an⁸

$$: \underset{\smile\smile}{} \overset{\prime}{} : \underset{\smile\smile}{} \overset{\prime}{} : \underset{\smile\smile}{} \overset{\prime}{} : \underset{\smile\smile}{} \acute{\frown} \,|\, \underset{\smile\smile}{} \overset{\prime}{} : \underset{\smile\smile}{} \overset{\prime}{} : \underset{\smile\smile}{} \overset{\prime}{} : \underset{\smile\smile}{} \acute{\frown} \,|$$

There is regular diaeresis after the eighth element. The English 'equivalent' is

> The Assyrian came down like a wolf on the fold; and his
> cohorts were gleaming in purple and gold.

222-4 neque salsum neque suau(e) esse potest quicqu(am) ub(i)

amor non admiscetur:

fel quod amarumst, id mel faciet, homin(em) ex tristi

lepid(um) et lenem.

hanc ego de me coniecturam domi facio magis qu(am) ex

auditis.

anapaestic septenarius = an⁸ᴧ

$$: \underset{\smile\smile}{} \overset{\prime}{} : \underset{\smile\smile}{} \overset{\prime}{} : \underset{\smile\smile}{} \overset{\prime}{} : \underset{\smile\smile}{} \acute{\frown} \,|\, \underset{\smile\smile}{} \overset{\prime}{} : \underset{\smile\smile}{} \overset{\prime}{} : \underset{\smile\smile}{} \overset{\prime}{} : \frown \,|$$

There is regular diaeresis after the eighth element. The English 'equivalent' is

> Which is something between a large bathing-machine and a
> very small second class carriage.

875-7 neque quo fugiam nequ(e) ubi lateam nequ(e) hoc dedecus

quo modo celem

scio, tant(um) erus atqu(e) ego flagitio superauimus

nuptiis nostris

:◡◡ — : ◡ ◡ (o) —:   ◡◡ — : ◡ ◡ (o) — | ◡
ita nunc pude(o) atqu(e) ita nunc paue(o) atqu(e) it(a)

◡ —:◡ ◡ —: ◡ ◡ — :—|
inridiculo sumus ambo.

Shorter anapaestic cola found in the cantica

an⁴ (anapaestic dimeter)

:◡◡ ≟ :◡◡ ≟ :◡◡ ≟ :◡◡ ⌃ |

:◡   ◡ ◡◡: —   —: — ◡◡ : —— — |
167   eg(o) hic ero, uir s(i) aut quispiam quaeret.

:—   ◡ ◡ : — ◡◡: — ◡ ◡   : —— — |
179   sed quid est quod tuo nunc anim(o) aeg. est?

an⁴ᴬ (catalectic anapaestic dimeter)

:◡◡ ≟ :◡◡ ≟ :◡◡ ≟ :⌃ |

: —   ◡ ◡ :— —:—   —: — |
741-3 quid m(i) opust seruo tam nequam?

: —   — : —   — :◡ ◡—: —|
quid nunc? quam mox recreas me?

:— ◡ ◡:— —:— — — :◡|
cena modo si sit cocta.

an³

:◡◡ ≟ :◡◡ ≟ :◡◡ ⌃ |

(Doubtful)

:— ◡   ◡:— —:◡ ◡ —|
634   ne cad(am) amabo, tene me.

an² (anapaestic monometer)

:◡◡ ≟ :◡◡ ⌃ |

: ◡ ◡ ◡ —:◡◡ ◡|
896c-d quid agit Casina?

:◡◡   —:◡ ◡ — |
satin morigera (e)st?

an²ᴬ (catalectic anapaestic monometer)

:◡◡ ≟ :⌃ |

: ◡◡ —: —|
732a-b nisi me uis

:◡ ◡   ◡ ◡:—|
uomer(e) hodie

Technicalities in anapaests

Free use of iambic shortening: 165-7, 217

Proceleusmatic word with the ictus on the third syllable: 165-6, 217, 723

21 colon Reizianum = c^r

$$× \underline{} × \underline{} \frown$$

This colon reasonably follows the anapaests, because it has clear affinities with that rhythm (Questa 245). On the other hand, the first and third elements are occasionally short, so that the scheme is $× - × - \frown$ and not $\underset{\smile\smile}{} - \underset{\smile\smile}{} - \frown$. With this scheme, c^r is not formally different from ba^c (see below among the bacchiacs); but (i) ba^c is associated exclusively with other bacchiac cola, (ii) c^r allows much greater licence, showing a predilection for disyllabic *ancipitia*, free use of iambic shortening, and disregard for the rules against broken anapaests (the laws of Hermann and Ritschl, p. 219).

752-4   sciŏ. síc sĭn(e) hăbḗrĕ;
            nūgắs ăgŭnt; nóuī
            ĕg(o) illắs mălăs mércēs.

22 Bacchiacs (bacchius = $\smile \underline{} \underline{}$)

bacchiac tetrameter = ba^4

$$\underset{}{\overset{\underline{}\acute{\frown}|\,×}{}}$$
$$\vdots × \underline{} \underline{} \vdots × \frown| - \vdots × \underline{} \underline{} \vdots × \underline{} \acute{\frown}|$$
$$- -\vdots\smile|$$

There is normally either a diaeresis after the sixth element, or a caesura after the fifth or the seventh.

697-700   nem(o) audet prop(e) acceder(e).::: exoret.:: orat;

            negat poner(e) alio mod(o) ullo profecto,

            nisi se sciat uilico non dat(um) iri.

            atqu(e) ingratiis, quia non uolt, nubet hodie.

Shorter bacchiac cola

ba³ (bacchiac trimeter)

$$\vdots \times \_\_ \vdots \times \_\_ \vdots \times \_ \acute{\wedge} \mid$$

$$\vdots \ \cup \ - \qquad - \qquad \vdots \ \cup \ - \qquad - \vdots \cup\cup \ \cup \acute{\cup}\mid$$
659 quid erg(o)?::ah – :: quid est?:: interemere

ba² (bacchiac dimeter)

$$\vdots \times \_\_ \vdots \times \_ \acute{\wedge} \mid$$

$$\vdots \ \cup \quad -\ - \vdots \qquad \cup \quad -\ -\mid$$
656 dar(e) uxor(em), e(a) intus

$$\vdots - \quad - \quad -\vdots\cup \ - \quad -\mid$$
662 insectatur omnis

ba²ᴬ (catalectic bacchiac dimeter)

$$\vdots \times \_\_ \vdots \cup \acute{\wedge} \mid$$

$$\vdots \ - \qquad - \quad -\vdots\cup \ - \mid$$
183a–b nec qu(a) in plura sunt

$$\vdots \ \cup \ - \qquad \cup \ \cup\vdots \ \cup -\mid$$
mihi qu(ae) ego uelim

baᶜ (bacchiac colon = syncopated bacchiac dimeter)

$$\vdots \times \_ \vdots \times \_ \acute{\wedge} \mid$$

$$\vdots\cup\cup \quad -\vdots \cup \quad -\ -\mid$$
659 ait uelle uitam

$$\vdots \ \cup \ -\vdots \cup \ - \quad -\mid$$
662 domi per aedis

Technicalities in bacchiacs

Avoidance of iambic shortening: 149

Note. Half the lines in the long canticum 621–718 are bacchiac.

1. The commonest variant on ba⁴ is ba²+baᶜ (i.e. a syncopated tetrameter); ba³+baᶜ (a syncopated pentameter) occurs at 654 and 659.

2. Lines composed of catalectic dimeter followed by syncopated dimeter (ba²ᴬ+baᶜ) occur at 663, 691, 703.

3. *brevis in longo* is found at the caesura after the fifth element in 674, 693, 696.

23 Cretics (cretic = $\_\cup\_$)

cretic tetrameter = cr⁴

$$\vdots \_\times\_\vdots \_\times \overset{\acute{\wedge}}{\_}\vdots \_\times\_\vdots \_\cup \acute{\wedge}\mid$$

There is usually diaeresis at the halfway point.

: _   ᴗ _ : _ ᴗ _ | _ ᴗ _:_   ᴗ _ |
189–92 uir m(e) habet pessumis despicatam modis,

: _   ᴗ _:_   ᴗ́ |_ ᴗ _ :   _ ᴗ_ |
nec mihi ius meum optinend(i) optio (e)st.

: _ ᴗ _   :_ᴗ _| __ᴗ _ : _   ᴗ_|
mira sunt, uera si praedicas, nam uiri

:_   ᴗ   _ : ᴗᴗᴗ _|_ ᴗ _ :   __   ᴗ_ |
ius su(om) ad mulieres optiner(e) haud queunt.

Shorter cretic cola

cr³ (cretic trimeter)

: ⏓ × ⏓ : ⏓ × ⏓ : ⏓ ᴗ ᴧ́ |

:ᴗ ᴗ   ᴗ _:_   ᴗ __:_ ᴗ_|
151 anim(i) amorisque causa sui

cr² (cretic dimeter)

: ⏓ × ⏓ : ⏓ ⏑̆ ᴧ́ |

:   _   ᴗ_ :_ ᴗ _|
147 prandium iusserat

:ᴗ   ᴗ   ᴗ _ : ᴗ   ᴗ ᴗ_|
149 tac(e) atqu(e) abi; neque paro

cr²ᴧ (catalectic cretic dimeter)

: ⏓ × ⏓ : ⏓ ᴧ |

:_   ᴗ_ : ᴗᴗ_|
216 nunc uale. : : ualeas.

:_   ᴗ_: _   _|
952 fungier pro me

crᶜ (cretic colon = syncopated cretic dimeter)

: ⏓ × : ⏓ ⁽ᴗᴗ⁾ ᴧ́ |

:   _ ᴗ:__ ᴗ_|
750 quod morae siet

:ᴗ   ᴗ _ : ᴗᴗ ᴗ _|
888b nequ(e) enim dare sibi

Technicalities in cretics

Avoidance of iambic shortening: 149

24 Aeolic metres

choriambic tetrameter = chor⁴ (choriamb = $\underline{} \cup \cup \underline{}$)

$$\vdots \underline{} \cup \cup \underline{} \vdots \underline{} \cup \cup \underline{} \mid \underline{} \cup \cup \underline{} \vdots \underline{} \cup \cup \acute{\frown} \mid$$

$$\vdots {-} \cup \cup \quad {-} \vdots {-} \quad \cup \cup {-} \mid \quad {-} \, \backsim\backsim \, {-} \vdots {-} \cup \cup \, {-}\mid$$

629 eripit(e) isti gladi um, quae suist impos animi.

choriambic dimeter = chor²

$$\vdots \underline{} \cup \cup \underline{} \vdots \underline{} \cup \cup \acute{\frown} \mid$$

$$\vdots {-} \quad \cup \qquad \cup {-} \vdots {-} \quad \cup \qquad \cup {-} \mid$$

203 tu quid(em) aduorsum tu(am) amic(am)

glyconic = gl

$$\underline{} \times \underline{} \, \overline{\cup\cup} \, \underline{} \, \breve{\cup} \, \acute{\frown}$$

This metre, as Questa 255 says, is probably of wider occurrence than has yet been realized. It is a more varied rhythm than the Greek glyconic, and is to be recognized (and distinguished from tr⁴ᴬ in cases where the penultimate element is short) by a mixture of trochaic and dactylic 'feet', free use of iambic shortening, and disregard for the rules against broken anapaests (the laws of Hermann and Ritschl, p. 219). Because of a predilection for disyllabic elements in the unstressed positions, it may take a form which could also be called a catalectic dactylic tetrameter ($-\cup\cup-\cup\cup-\cup\cup-$), as in 937–40. Adding further to the variety, there are lines in which the *longa* are resolved (e.g. 951, 953).

937–8   māxŭm(o) ĕg(o) ārdĕŏ flāgītĭō
nēc quĭd ăgām mēis rēbŭs scĭō.

951   sĕd ĕcquĭs ēst qu(i) hŏmŏ mūnŭs uĕlīt

955   nām sălūs nūllā (e)st scăpŭlīs

In 800 and 808 there appears a glyconic with a short initial syllable in close imitation of Greek, for this is the Greek marriage refrain

Hўmēn, Hўmĕnāe(e) ō Hўmēn

Adoneus

$$\underline{} \cup \cup \underline{} \frown$$

(Doubtful)

645   quāe m(e) hăbŭistī

25 Composite lines

Many combinations of cola are possible, as will be seen from the
metrical analyses. Normally the cola are of the same, or evidently
compatible, metres; from time to time, however, more violent
combinations appear, such as those (if correctly identified) of trochees
and anapaests in 630–4.

The following is a universally accepted composite unit (found in a
long continuous sequence at *Aul.* 415–45):

V^r (versus Reizianus) $=$ ia^4 c^r

$$\vdots\times\,\_\,\vdots\times\,\_\,\vdots\times\,\_\,\vdots\cup\acute{\cap}\,|\qquad \times\,\_\,\times\,\_\,\cap$$

$$\vdots\,\_\qquad\,\_\vdots\cup\,\_\vdots\,\_\,\_\,\vdots\cup\,\_\,|\,\_\,\_\,\_\,\cup\cup\quad\acute{\cup}\cup\_$$

755-6 quin t(u) i modo mecum domum. :: at pol malum metuo.

$$\vdots\_\,\_\vdots\cup\cup\quad\_\vdots\cup\cup\_\vdots\cup\_|\qquad\cup\,\_\,\_\,\cup\cup\,\_\,\_$$

i tu modo, perspicito prius   quid intus agatur.

The following are isolated lines identified with a known Greek
combination:

Diphileus ($=$ da$^{3\wedge}$– da$^{3\wedge}$)

$$\_\cup\cup\_\cup\cup\_\,-\,\_\cup\cup\_\cup\cup\acute{\cap}$$

644 iām tīb(i) īstūc cĕrĕbrūm dīspērcŭtĭ(am) ēxcĕtră tū.

Priapeus ($=$ glyconic $+$ pherecratean, gl $+$ gl$^\wedge$)

$$\_\times\_\,\overline{\cup\cup}\,\_\,\overset{\smallfrown}{\cup\cup}\,\acute{\cap}\_\times\_\,\overline{\cup\cup}\,\_\,\cap$$

(Doubtful)

815-16 sēnsim sŭpĕr āttōllĕ līmĕn pĕdĕs nŏuă nūptă.

APPENDIX 2

THE TEXT

Our text of Plautus derives from two editions of late antiquity,[1] represented for us on the one hand by the single capital manuscript A, the Ambrosian palimpsest, of about the fourth century A.D., on the other by all our minuscule manuscripts, of which the earliest is B (the *codex vetus*) of the tenth century; these latter are given the collective name of the Palatine recension, because B (and also C, the *codex decurtatus*) reposed at one time in the library of the Elector Palatine at Heidelberg.

A was rediscovered in the Ambrosian library at Milan in 1815. It is a palimpsest – i.e. the original text (Plautus) had been erased so that the parchment could be re-used. It once contained all twenty-one of the so-called Varronian[2] plays of Plautus; much however had been lost, and much that survived was illegible. It is available for about half of the *Casina*.[3] The Palatine recension contained the same twenty-one plays; among the older extant manuscripts, the *Casina* is found in B, V, E and J. B is the best, showing a text closest to that of their common ancestor, a minuscule manuscript of Carolingian times, to which W. M. Lindsay gave the name P. Moreover, B, as well as offering the most accurate text, was corrected at an early stage from an even better source; these corrections (B[2]) often provide the right reading as against all other manuscripts of the Palatine family.

V and E are collaterals; their agreement is of approximately equal

---

[1] For the earlier history of the plays, and the relationship between A and P, see Leo, *PF* 48–62 and G. Pasquali, *Storia della tradizione e critica del testo*[2] (1952) 331–54.

[2] Marcus Terentius Varro, late in the first century B.C., identified twenty-one plays as genuine out of the great number ascribed to Plautus at that time (Gellius, 3.3.3). These are the plays which have survived.

[3] The readings of A in the *Casina* are to be found in W. Studemund's *Codicis rescripti Ambrosiani apographum* (1889), with some additional evidence on pp. xv and xvi of the Preface to F. Schoell's edition of the *Mostellaria* (1893).

value to the readings of B, but more subject to surface error. J (the *codex Britannicus*) is an enigma. Lindsay considered that it represented a 'doctored' text of the branch of the tradition from which we have V and E, i.e. a text full of corrections by a medieval scholar, from a collateral of which descended the mass of Renaissance manuscripts, called *Itali* or *recentiores*. It is quite true that the readings of J often coincide with V and E against B; and often with the Renaissance manuscripts against B, V and E. On the other hand, there are occasions when J agrees with B against VE, and not a few when J agrees with B², or even A, against the whole of the rest of the tradition. If every case of this sort is the result of conjectural emendation by the unknown scholar or scribe of the manuscript from which J was copied, he was singularly successful in his corrections. A final judgement on J has not yet been made. The manuscript has suffered damage at the edges, so that it is not always legible.

Finally, there was a now lost manuscript used by the sixteenth-century French scholar Adrien de Tournebu (Turnebus), from which some excellent readings are known.[1] It was of the Palatine recension, but not closely related to our other manuscripts.

Manuscript readings are given most fully in the large Teubner edition of the *Casina* (1890) by F. Schoell, a pupil of F. Ritschl, the great nineteenth-century Plautine scholar. The collations, however, which Schoell used for V and J are known to have been less accurate than those for B and E. A re-examination of photographs or microfilms of all four of these manuscripts has corrected or improved the information in the apparatus criticus in this edition in about twenty places;[2] none of these affects the reading in the text except at line 895.

In addition to the direct evidence of the Ambrosian palimpsest and the Palatine manuscripts, we have many quotations in ancient grammarians, particularly Nonius Marcellus (fourth century A.D.), but also Varro, Festus, Priscian and others. The text of these quotations sometimes agrees with A, sometimes with P, sometimes with neither.

The modern presentation of the play, and the numeration of the

---

[1] See e.g. *Cas.* 639–40.
[2] At lines 51, 126, 184–5, 279, 280, 281, 283–4, 311, 350, 488, 500, 572, 604, 757a, 837, 864, 882, 895, 1017. Also errors that have found their way into the *apparatus* of the most recent editions (those of Ernout and Paratore) have been corrected at lines 60, 210–11, 248, 349.

lines, derive from Schoell. Important editions since his time are those of three outstanding Latin scholars, F. Leo, W. M. Lindsay and A. Ernout. The text printed here is indebted to all three of these; new conjectures, mostly to fill known gaps, are offered in a few places.[1] The punctuation has been altered from time to time (it is closest to Ernout), as has the colometry (line division) of the cantica, in obedience to metrical considerations.

It is accepted that the line divisions in A are reliable, and go back to a period in the ancient world when the obscure metres of Plautine song were still understood; and that the older Palatine manuscripts show essentially the same picture, although even in B much has been changed through the metrical ignorance of scribes and their wish to economize on space.[2] On the whole we have followed the manuscript tradition, except in such a case as 708-12, where the metrical form can more effectively be shown by printing the short cola on separate lines.

Attribution of speakers causes intermittent difficulty. No names or other indications are visible in A, although if there was a change of speaker *within* a line, we can tell that the palimpsest once contained an indication, because there is a vacant space. In the Palatine manuscripts, attributions are sometimes confused, especially in the long scene II 6 where there are four speakers present, sometimes missing altogether. Modern scholars, working on foundations laid particularly by Camerarius and Acidalius, have progressively improved the presentation in this respect.

[1] At lines 866, 871-2, 917-18, 922, 957.
[2] On the common origin of the colometry of A and P, see now C. Questa, 'L'antichissima edizione dei *cantica* di Plauto', *R.F.I.C.* 102 (1974) 58-79, 172-88.

BIBLIOGRAPHY

This list consists for the most part of works cited in the Introduction, Commentary and Appendices by the name of editor or author alone.

1. EDITIONS, COMMENTARIES, TRANSLATIONS, ETC.

Lambinus, D. 1576. Text of Plautus, with commentary in Latin.

Gulielmius, J. *Plautinarum quaestionum commentarius.* 1583. Discussion of selected passages.

Acidalius, V. *In Plautum divinationes et interpretationes.* 1607. Discussion of selected passages.

Guyet, F. 1658. Critical text of Plautus.

Bothe, F. H. Vol. ii, 2nd ed. 1822. Critical text of Plautus.

Naudet, J. Vol. i. 1830. Text of Plautus, with commentary in Latin.

Loman, J. B. *Adnotationes criticae in Casinam.* 1850. Discussion of selected passages.

Ussing, I. L. Vol. iii Pt 1. 1887. Critical text of Plautus, with commentary in Latin.

Schoell, F. 1890. Critical text of *Casina*, with full information of manuscript readings and an 'appendix critica'.

Goetz, G. and Schoell, F. 1892 (G–S¹), 1904 (G–S²). Critical text (Teubner).

Leo, F. Vol. i. 1895. Critical text of Plautus.

Lindsay, W. M. Vol. i, 2nd ed. 1910. Critical text (Oxford Classical Series).

Nixon, P. Vol. ii. 1917. Text, with English translation (Loeb).

Ernout, A. Vol. ii. 1933. Critical text, with French translation (Budé).

Duckworth, G. E. *The complete Roman drama.* 1942. English translation.

Paratore, E. 1959. Critical text of *Casina*, with Italian translation.

Casson, L. *Six plays of Plautus.* 1963. English translation.

2. ANCIENT GRAMMARIANS

Charisius: *Flavii Sosipatri Charisii artis grammaticae libri V*, ed. K. Barwick, rev. F. Kühnert. 1964.

Festus: *Sexti Pompei Festi De verborum significatu quae supersunt cum Pauli epitome*, ed. W. M. Lindsay. 1913 (repr. 1965).

Fulgentius: *Fabii Planciadis Fulgentii opera*, ed. R. Helm. 1898 (repr. 1970).

GLK: Grammatici latini, ed. H. Keil; 8 vols. 1855–80 (repr. 1961). Vols. II and III contain the *Institutiones grammaticae* and other works of Priscian.

Nonius: *Nonii Marcelli De compendiosa doctrina*, ed. W. M. Lindsay. 1903 (repr. 1964).

Varro: *M. Terenti Varronis De lingua latina*, ed. G. Goetz and F. Schoell. 1910 (repr. 1964).

3. GENERAL

Allen, W. S. *Vox latina*. 1965.

Andrieu, J. *Le dialogue antique*. 1954.

Beare, W. *The Roman stage*. 3rd ed. 1968.

Drexler, H. *Einführung in die römische Metrik*. 1967.
  Die Iambenkürzung (IK). 1969.
  '*Lizenzen*' *am Versanfang bei Plautus*. 1965.
  'Prokeleusmatische Wörter bei Plautus', *B.P.E.C.* 12 (1964) 3–31.

Duckworth, G. E. *The nature of Roman comedy*. 1952.

Ernout, A. and Meillet, A. *Dictionnaire étymologique de la langue latine*. 2nd ed. 1951.

Ernout, A. and Thomas, F. *Syntaxe latine*. 2nd ed. 1953.

Fraenkel, E. *Elementi plautini in Plauto (EP)*. Italian translation by F. Munari, with *Addenda*, of *Plautinisches im Plautus* (1922). 1960.
  Iktus und Akzent im lateinischen Sprechvers (IuA). 1928.

Friedrich, W. *Euripides und Diphilos*. 1953.

Frye, N. *Anatomy of criticism*. 1957.

Gomme, A. W. and Sandbach, F. H. *Menander: a commentary*. 1973.

Haffter, H. *Untersuchungen zur altlateinischen Dichtersprache*. 1934.

Happ, H. 'Die lateinische Umgangssprache und die Kunstsprache des Plautus', *Glotta* 45 (1967) 60–104.

Harrison, A. R. W. *The law of Athens*. 1968.

Hofmann, J. B. *Lateinische Umgangssprache*. 3rd ed. 1951.

Jachmann, G. *Plautinisches und Attisches*. 1931.

Kühner, R. and Stegmann, C. *Ausführliche Grammatik der lateinischen Sprache*. 4th ed. rev. A. Thierfelder. 2 vols. 1962.

Leo, F. *Plautinische Forschungen (PF)*. 2nd ed. 1912.

Lewis, C. T. and Short, C. (LS). *A Latin dictionary*. 1879.

Lindsay, W. M. *The Captivi of Plautus*. 1900.

　Early Latin Verse (ELV). 1922.

　Syntax of Plautus. 1907 (repr. 1936).

Lodge, G. *Lexicon plautinum*. 1924–33 (repr. 1962).

Luck, G. *Über einige Interjektionen der lateinischen Umgangssprache*. 1964.

MacCary, W. T. 'The comic tradition and comic structure in Diphilos' *Kleroumenoi*', *Hermes* 101 (1973) 194–208.

　'The significance of a comic pattern in Plautus and Beaumarchais', *Modern Language Notes* 88 (1973) 1262–87.

Maurach, G. *Untersuchungen zum Aufbau plautinischer Lieder*. 1963.

Otto, A. *Die Sprichwörter und sprichwörtlichen Redensarten der Römer*. 1890 (repr. 1962).

Oxford Latin dictionary (OLD). 1968– (in progress).

Palmer, L. R. *The Latin language*. 1954.

Questa, C. *Introduzione alla metrica di Plauto*. 1967.

Segal, E. *Roman laughter*. 1968.

Skutsch, F. *Kleine Schriften*. 1914.

Taladoire, B.-A. *Essai sur le comique de Plaute*. 1956.

Vollmer, F. *Kürzung durch Tonanschluß im alten Latein*. 1917.

Watson, A. *The law of persons in the later Roman republic*. 1967.

Webster, T. B. L. *Studies in later Greek comedy*. 2nd ed. 1970.

INDEXES

(*Numbers in square brackets refer to to pages of the Introduction or Appendices; other numbers refer to lines of the play.*)

1. *Latin words*

-*so* 307
-*ssere* 271
st 148

tamen (elliptical) 63, 105, 780, 787, 957

temperi 412
tragula 297

uocare, uociuos 29, 527

2. General

ablative
  of the degree of difference 359
  of price 538
accusative
  adverbial 106, 127, 460, 582
  exclamatory 843, 848
act and scene divisions [34]
Aristophanes [3, 15]
Atellan farce [10, 11, 36]
attraction
  of the antecedent 810, 975
  of the relative, 261, 932

brevis brevians [214]
brevis in longo [216–17]

Caecilius [12], 18
caesura [220]
catalectic [220]
cook humour 720

diaeresis [220]
Diphilus [1, 8–9, 16–17, 34–8], 32

enclisis [214]
enclitics [213], 384
Euripides [4–5, 35]
exposing of babies [7], 41

figures of speech *see* language
future imperative 296

genitive
  defining 82, 97, 620, 637–8
  of description 152
  partitive 15, 70, 120, 810
  of value 2, 98, 119, 802
Greek idioms 198, 490, 509, 559

Greek words 226, 728–31a, 811

Hermann's law [219]
hiatus [216]

iambic shortening [214]
ictus [217]
imagery [27–34]
  animal 239, 476, 535, 550, 811, 1018
  food and sex 153–4, 219, 725, 795, 801–2
  Jupiter and Juno 230, 323, 331–7, 406–8
  military 50, 344, 352, 357, 417–18
impersonal passive 149, 186, 522, 758, 813
indicative in indirect questions 246, 591, 902
infinitive
  exclamatory 89
  future indeclinable 671
  of purpose 688, 856
ius primae noctis [38]

language, figures of speech, etc. [23–7]
  alliteration 87, 282, 819–20
  anacoluthon 39–41
  assonance 108, 204, 223, 245, 690, 875, 970
  asyndeton 329–30, 828
  diminutives 1c8, 134, 739, 837
  figura etymologica 217, 516, 970
  interjections 38
  made-up words 26, 945, 976
  parataxis 484
  personification of abstract nouns 128, 225

1792756R0016

Printed in Great Britain
by Amazon.co.uk, Ltd.,
Marston Gate.